Beginning Rust

Get Started with Rust 2021 Edition

Second Edition

Carlo Milanesi

Apress®

Beginning Rust: Get Started with Rust 2021 Edition

Carlo Milanesi
Bergamo, Italy

ISBN-13 (pbk): 978-1-4842-7207-7   ISBN-13 (electronic): 978-1-4842-7208-4
https://doi.org/10.1007/978-1-4842-7208-4

Managing Director, Apress Media LLC: Welmoed Spahr
Acquisitions Editor: Steve Anglin
Development Editor: James Markham
Coordinating Editor: Mark Powers
Copy Editor: Mike Read

Cover designed by eStudioCalamar

Cover image by Sajad Nori on Unsplash (www.unsplash.com)

Distributed to the book trade worldwide by Apress Media, LLC, 1 New York Plaza, New York, NY 10004, U.S.A. Phone 1-800-SPRINGER, fax (201) 348-4505, e-mail orders-ny@springer-sbm.com, or visit www.springeronline.com. Apress Media, LLC is a California LLC and the sole member (owner) is Springer Science + Business Media Finance Inc (SSBM Finance Inc). SSBM Finance Inc is a **Delaware** corporation.

For information on translations, please e-mail booktranslations@springernature.com; for reprint, paperback, or audio rights, please e-mail bookpermissions@springernature.com.

Apress titles may be purchased in bulk for academic, corporate, or promotional use. eBook versions and licenses are also available for most titles. For more information, reference our Print and eBook Bulk Sales web page at www.apress.com/bulk-sales.

Any source code or other supplementary material referenced by the author in this book is available to readers on GitHub (github.com/apress/beginning-rust-2e). For more detailed information, please visit www.apress.com/source-code.

Printed on acid-free paper

This book is dedicated to my mother and to my father's memory.
I owe them my interest in learning and explaining things.

Table of Contents

About the Author

Carlo Milanesi is a professional software developer, expert in C++, graphics programming, and GUI design. He graduated from the State University of Milan and has worked in the financial and CAD/CAM software industries. He enjoys designing, writing, and testing software. He also loves teaching and acting.

He authored the book *Creative Projects for Rust Programmers*, and developed the Rust library `https://github.com/carlomilanesi/rs-measures`.

About the Technical Reviewer

Satej Kumar Sahu works in the role of Senior Enterprise Architect at Honeywell. He is passionate about technology, people, and nature. He believes that through technology and conscientious decision making, each of us has the power to make this world a better place. In his free time, he can be found reading books, playing basketball, and having fun with friends and family.

Preface

Welcome to *Beginning Rust*. This book teaches beginners how to program with the exciting Rust programming language in an easy, step-by-step manner. It is a fully revised version of the 2018 book, with several additions, expanded clarifications for the most hard-to-master concepts, and removal of redundant sections. It utilizes the 2021 edition of the Rust language, developed by the Rust Team community.

What You Need to Know

Only a basic knowledge of programming is required. Rust is mainly targeted for systems programming tasks, a sector currently dominated by the C and C++ languages. So, to ease the transition from such languages, the text contains many comparisons with C and C++, and even code examples in those languages. Yet, this book can also be enjoyed by people who are only familiar with other programming languages, like Java or C#.

Knowledge of command-line environments is assumed, like a Linux shell, macOS Terminal, or Windows Command Prompt, because all the examples contained in this book need to be compiled and run in such environments.

How to Read This Book

It is strongly recommended you read the book from beginning to end, without skipping chapters, because every chapter assumes that the reader understands what was explained in previous chapters.

The text presents a lot of code examples, which should be read thoroughly, and possibly compiled and run on your own computer. You can type them, or use the freely available downloaded code.

Where to Find the Source Code

All of the examples used in this book can be accessed on GitHub at `github.com/apress/beginning-rust-2e`.

What This Book Does Not Cover

Please note that this book does not cover everything needed to develop professional programs using Rust. It just teaches the concepts of the language, including the most difficult ones. For writing professional software, you will need to download and learn some third-party frameworks and libraries. There are quite a few of them which are of good-to-outstanding quality and freely available.

CHAPTER 1

Getting Started

In this chapter, you will learn:

- How to write and run your first program in the Rust language

- How to print text and numbers on the terminal

- How to write comments in your code

How to Start

The smallest valid Rust program is this:

```
fn main(){}
```

Of course, it does nothing. It just defines an empty function named "main." By "function" we mean a set of instructions that does something, and that has been given a name.

`fn` is shorthand for "function," while `main` is the name of this function. The round parentheses contain the function's possible arguments; in this case, there are no arguments. To close, the braces contain the possible statements that comprise the body of the function; in this case there are no statements.

When a program written in Rust is run, its `main` function is executed. If there is no `main` function, then it isn't a complete program; it may be a library, though. Any Rust library may contain several entry points; instead, any Rust program has just one entry point, and its name must be `main`.

To run this program, first you must install the Rust toolset. The official Rust toolset can be downloaded for free from the website `www.rust-lang.org`. Linux, Windows, and macOS platforms are supported. For each platform, there are three versions: *stable*, *beta*, and *nightly*. The stable version is recommended; it is the oldest, but also the most tested one and the one less likely to change. All of these program versions should be used from the command line of a console. After installation, to check which version is installed,

© Carlo Milanesi 2022
C. Milanesi, *Beginning Rust*, https://doi.org/10.1007/978-1-4842-7208-4_1

type at a command line (with uppercase V): `rustc -V`. The code in this book has been checked using version 1.56.0, but probably later versions will be OK too.

When you have a working installation, you can perform the following actions:

- Create or choose a folder where your Rust exercises will be stored and, using any text editor, create in that folder a file named `main.rs`, having as contents the example program shown at the beginning of this chapter.

- At a command line, in that folder, type: `rustc main.rs`. The prompt should be printed almost immediately, after having created a file named `main` (in a Windows environment, it will be named `main.exe`). Actually, the `rustc` command has correctly compiled the specified file. That is, it has read it, it has generated the corresponding machine code, and it has stored this machine code in a file in the same folder.

- At the command line, if in a Windows environment, type: `main`

  For other operating systems, type:

  `./main`

  You just run the program generated before. The prompt should be printed immediately, as this program does nothing.

Hello, World!

Let's see how to print some text on the terminal. Change the program of the previous section to the following one:

```
fn main() {
    print!("Hello, world!");
}
```

If such code is compiled and run as before, it will print: `Hello, world!`.

2

Notice that the newly added line contains eight syntax items, aka *tokens*. Let's examine them:

- `print`: It is the name of a macro defined in the Rust standard library.

- `!`: This character specifies that the preceding name indicates a macro. Without such a symbol, `print` would instead indicate a function. There is no such function in the Rust standard library, so you would get a compilation error. A macro is a thing similar to a function—it's some Rust code, having a name. By using this name, you ask to insert such code at this point. The main difference between a function call and a macro invocation is that a function call executes at runtime the code of the function definition, which is located in another part of the program, so the control of execution is transferred elsewhere, while a macro invocation asks the compiler to replace the macro invocation with the body of the macro definition.

- `(`: It starts the list of arguments of the macro.

- `"`: It starts the literal string.

- `Hello, world!`: It is the content of the literal string.

- `"`: It ends the literal string.

- `)`: It ends the list of the arguments of the macro.

- `;`: It ends the statement.

Let's examine the meaning of the *literal string* phrase. The word *string* means *finite sequence of characters, possibly including spaces and punctuation*. The word *literal* means *specified directly in source code*. Therefore a *literal string* is a *finite sequence of characters (possibly including spaces and punctuation) specified directly in source code*. A nonliteral string, instead, is a variable whose value at runtime is a string. Such a string could be read from a file, or typed by the user, or copied from a literal string, as we will see when string variables are explained.

The `print` macro simply inserts into the program some code that prints on the terminal the text that it has received as an argument.

Rust always distinguishes between uppercase and lowercase letters—it's *case sensitive*. For all characters that are outside literal strings and comments, if you replace an uppercase letter with a lowercase one or conversely, typically you get a compilation error, or anyway a program with a different behavior. Instead, making such changes inside literal strings always allows a successful compilation, but it's likely the behavior of the program will be different.

For example:

```
fn Main() {}
```

If you compile this program, you get the compilation error `main function not found`, as no `main` function (with a lowercase `m`) is defined in the program.

From now on, except when specified, we will assume the example code will be inside the braces of the `main` function, so the braces and the text preceding them will be omitted.

Printing Combinations of Literal Strings

Instead of using a single literal string, you can print several of them, even in a single statement, in this way:

```
print!("{}, {}!", "Hello", "world");
```

This statement, put inside the braces of the `main` function, will print again: `Hello, world!`.

In this case, the `print` macro receives three arguments, separated by commas. All three arguments are literal strings. The first string, though, contains two pairs of braces (`{}`). They are placeholders, indicating the positions in which to insert the other two strings.

So, the macro scans the arguments after the first one, and for each of them it looks inside the first argument for a pair of braces and replaces that pair of braces with the current argument.

This resembles the following C language statement:

```
printf("%s, %s!", "Hello", "world");
```

But there is an important difference. If you try to compile:

```
print!("{}, !", "Hello", "world");
```

you get the compilation error `argument never used`, as the first argument contains just *one* placeholder, but after the first argument, there are *two* other arguments to print. So, there is one argument that doesn't have any corresponding placeholder.

And if you try to compile:

```
print!("{}, {}!", "Hello");
```

you get a compilation error too, as the first argument contains *two* placeholders, but after the first argument there is only *one* argument to print. So, there is a placeholder that doesn't have any corresponding argument.

Instead, the corresponding statements in C language usually raise just a warning, and then they generate a compiled program that will misbehave.

Printing Several Lines of Text

So far, we wrote programs that print only one line, but a single statement can print several lines. It is done in this way:

```
print!("First line\nSecond line\nThird line\n");
```

This will print:

```
First line
Second line
Third line
```

The sequence of characters \n (where n stands for *new line*) is transformed by the compiler into the character sequence that represents the line terminator for the currently used operating system.

Actually, it is very common to go to a new line exactly once for every printing statement. You can do this by adding the two characters \n at the end of the line; you can also use another macro of the standard library, `println`, whose name is to be read "print line." It's used in this way:

```
println!("text of the line");
```

This statement is equivalent to:

```
print!("text of the line\n");
```

Printing Integer Numbers

If you want to print My number: 140, you can type:

```
print!("My number: 140");
```

or, using a placeholder and an additional argument:

```
print!("My number: {}", "140");
```

or, removing the quotes around the second argument:

```
print!("My number: {}", 140);
```

In the last statement, the second argument is not a literal string, but it is a *literal integer number*, or, for short, a *literal integer*.

The integers are another data type, with respect to strings.

The print macro is also able to use integer numbers to replace the corresponding placeholder inside its first argument.

In fact, the compiler interprets the string 140 contained in the source code as a number expressed in decimal format. It generates the equivalent number in binary format, and then it saves that binary number into the executable program.

At run time, the program takes that binary number; it transforms it into the string "140", using the decimal notation; then it replaces the placeholder with that string, therefore generating the string to print; and finally it sends the string to the terminal.

This procedure explains, for example, why if the following program is written:

```
print!("My number: {}", 000140);
```

the compiler generates exactly the same executable program generated before. Actually, when the source string 000140 is converted to the binary format, the leading zeros are ignored.

The argument types may be mixed too. This statement:

```
print!("{}: {}", "My number", 140);
```

will print the same line as before. Here the first placeholder corresponds to a literal string, while the second one corresponds to a literal integer.

Comments

As any other programming language, Rust allows comments embedded in code:
The following code:

```
// This program
// prints a number.
print!("{}", 34); // thirty-four
/* print!("{}", 80);
*/
```

will print 34.

The first two lines start with a pair of slashes (//). Such a pair of characters indicates the start of a *line comment*, which is a comment ending at the end of the line. To write a comment on several lines, the pair of slashes must be repeated at every line of the comment, as in the second line of the preceding program.

Rust programmers use to leave a space character just after the double slash, to improve readability.

As it appears in the third line, a line comment may start after a statement, usually separated by at least one space character.

There is another kind of comment, exemplified in the fourth and fifth lines. Such a comment starts with the character pair /* and ends with the pair */; it may extend on several lines, so it is named *multi-line comment*.

Rust programmers usually avoid the multi-line comment in production code, using only single line comments, and use multi-line comments only to temporarily exclude some code from compilation. This is because single-line comments have some advantages: when extracting source lines using a search tool, or when comparing different versions of a code base, it is immediately clear which lines are comments and which are not.

Rust comments look identical to modern C language comments. In fact, there is an important difference between Rust comments and C comments: Rust comments may be nested, and they must be nested correctly. In this way, you can first exclude some portions of a source file from compilation, and then exclude a larger portion that contains the smaller portions.

Here is a valid comment:

```
/* This is /* a valid*/
comment, even /* if /* it contains
comments*/ inside */itself.   */
```

And here is some code that generates the compilation error: `unterminated block comment`.

```
/* This /* instead is not allowed in Rust,
while in C is tolerated (but it may generate a warning).*/
```

CHAPTER 2

Doing Arithmetic and Writing More Code

In this chapter, you will learn:

- How to compute an arithmetic operation between integer numbers or between floating-point numbers

- How to write a program containing several statements

- How to print strings in several lines

Adding Integer Numbers

Let's see how to compute the sum of two integer numbers, for example, 80 and 34.

Put the following line as the only contents within the braces of the `main` function:

```
print!("The sum is {}", 80 + 34);
```

The execution will print: `The sum is 114`.

The second argument of the `print` macro is the expression `80 + 34`.

The compiler does not store into the executable file such numbers as they appear in source code, using the decimal format. The compiler may convert the two numbers into binary format, and then it may store into the executable file such binary numbers and the addition machine language instruction. At runtime, the two binary numbers are added, obtaining the number 114 in binary format.

But, as this expression contains only constant values, the compiler probably optimizes the addition operation by directly evaluating that expression, obtaining the integer number 114; then it stores that number, in binary format, into the executable file.

© Carlo Milanesi 2022
C. Milanesi, *Beginning Rust*, https://doi.org/10.1007/978-1-4842-7208-4_2

In both cases, at runtime, the resulting binary number is converted to the three-character string "114" in decimal format, and then the placeholder {} of the literal string is replaced by the generated string. Finally, of course, the resulting string is printed to the console.

Notice that the string The sum is 114 has been generated by the program; it is not present in source code, so it is still a string, but not a literal string.

Similarly, the two-character sequence 80 represents an integer number directly in the source code, and so it is called a *literal integer*. The same holds for the two characters 34. Instead, the integer number 114 is not a literal integer, as it does not appear in source code.

You can also write:

```
print!("{} + {} = {}", 34, 80, 80 + 34);
```

whose execution will print 34 + 80 = 114.

In such a case, the second argument of the macro will be put where there is the first placeholder, the third argument where there is the second placeholder, and the fourth argument where there is the third placeholder.

You can specify hundreds of arguments for the print macro, as long as the arguments after the first one are as many as the placeholders {} inside the first argument.

Other Operations Between Integer Numbers

All the integer arithmetic operators of C language can be used. For example, in this statement:

```
print!("{}", (23 - 6) % 5 + 20 * 30 / (3 + 4));
```

This will print 87.

Let's see why.

Such a formula is evaluated by the Rust compiler exactly as the C compiler would.

First, the operations in parentheses, 23 - 6 and 3 + 4, are evaluated, obtaining, respectively, 17 and 7.

At this point, our expression has become 17 % 5 + 20 * 30 / 7.

Then, the multiplication and division operations are evaluated, as they have precedence over addition and subtraction. Operations of the same precedence are evaluated in order from left to right.

17 % 5 is the *remainder of the integer division* operation. The remainder of the operation 17 / 5 is 2. The expression 20 * 30 is evaluated before the following division, as it is at its left. Its result is 600.

At this point, our expression has become 2 + 600 / 7.

Then, the *integer division with truncation* 600 / 7 is performed, and so our expression becomes 2 + 85.

Finally, the sum is evaluated, the result is formatted in decimal notation, the placeholder is replaced by the formatted number, and the resulting string is printed.

These arithmetic operations are always performed on integer binary numbers, obtaining integer binary numbers, and the result is converted to decimal format only when it is used to replace the placeholder of the print macro.

The Rust compiler is highly optimizing, so it tries to evaluate directly at compile time the expressions that it is possible to evaluate using the information available in source code. Our expression is made only of literal integers, and so the whole expression will be evaluated already at compile time, storing into the executable program only the result to print. Though, conceptually, usually you can think that all the computations are performed at runtime.

Floating-Point Arithmetic

Let's see how to compute the sum between two numbers with fractional parts. For example, let's add 80.3 and 34.9.

Replace the statement with this:

```
print!("The sum is {}", 80.3 + 34.8);
```

It will print The sum is 115.1.

Now, in the second number only, replace the character 8 with a 9, obtaining:

```
print!("The sum is {}", 80.3 + 34.9);
```

It will print The sum is 115.19999999999999.

This will surprise those who would expect 115.2 as the result.

This phenomenon also happens in many other programming languages; it is due to the fact that Rust, like most programming languages, performs computations involving noninteger numbers using the *floating-point* format. But here we won't treat this format any more.

All the arithmetic operators available for integer numbers are also available for floating-point numbers. For example, in this statement:

```
print!("{}", (23. - 6.) % 5. + 20. * 30. / (3. + 4.));
```

It will print 87.71428571428571.

Let's see why.

By putting a dot after a literal number, it is transformed into a literal floating-point number. Some programming languages require a digit after the dot, but not Rust. The precedence rules are the same as those for integer arithmetic. Division has a different result, though.

Let's see how the evaluation of the expression is performed.

The evaluation of 23. - 6. and of 3. + 4. is similar to that of integer numbers.

By evaluating 17. % 5., 2. is obtained, similarly to integer numbers. Such an operator does not exist in C language for floating-point numbers. It corresponds to the expression fmod(17., 5.) of the C standard library.

By evaluating 20. * 30., 600. is obtained, similarly to integer numbers.

The expression 600. / 7. performs a floating-point number division. The theoretical result of such division is a number that cannot be exactly represented either in binary notation or in decimal notation. Internally, a binary-format approximate representation is generated; if you ask Rust to convert such a binary number into a decimal format, you would get the approximate representation 85.71428571428571.

Finally, the value 2. is added to such a binary number, obtaining another value that cannot be exactly represented, which is printed in the way shown earlier.

Notice that, differing from C language, in Rust you cannot simply mix integer numbers and floating-point numbers. The following statement generates a compilation error:

```
print!("{}", 2.7 + 1);
```

A way to make it valid is to add a dot after the integer literal, making it a floating-point literal:

```
print!("{}", 2.7 + 1.);
```

However, this one is a syntax-only limitation, not an operative one; anyway, machine code cannot sum an integer number and a floating-point number without first converting one of the two operands to the type of the other operand. When a C compiler encounters the expression `2.7 + 1`, it implicitly emits the machine language instruction to convert the integer number 1 to a floating-point number; or better, being that 1 is a constant, it is converted to a floating-point number at compile time. In Rust, such conversions must be explicit.

At last, a note about the "%" operator. This is often improperly named *modulo operator*. Well, it should be better named *remainder operator*, because the mathematical *modulo operator* has a different behavior for negative numbers.

The remainder operator, when applied to integer numbers, behaves in Rust exactly like the "%" operator in C language, and when applied to floating-point numbers it behaves exactly like the "fmod" function of the C standard library. Here is an example with negative numbers, both integers and floating-point:

```
print!("{} {}", -12 % 10, -1.2 % 1.);
```

This will print `-2  -0.19999999999999996`.

Sequences of Statements

As the body of the main function, write these three lines:

```
print!("{} + ", 80);
print!("{} =", 34);
print!(" {}", 80 + 34);
```

This will print `80 + 34 = 114`.

The program now contains three statements, each of them terminated by the ";" character. Such statements are executed in order of appearance.

If the body of the main function would become

```
  print!("{} + ",80);print!("{} = ",34);
          print  !  (  "{}"  ,
     80      + 34 )  ;
```

its result wouldn't change. Actually, additional white spaces (blanks, tabs, and line breaks) are ignored.

However, Rust programmers have the following habits that are recommended:

- Indent lines by four spaces inside functions.

- Avoid adding several consecutive spaces inside statements.

- Avoid exceeding 80 columns, possibly splitting long statements into several lines.

Breaking Literal Strings

As said before, to avoid code lines that are too long, you can break them at any point between syntax symbols, like in C language, though the syntax to break a literal string is different. This code is illegal:

```
println!("{}", "This"
    "is not allowed");
```

Actually, in Rust you cannot simply juxtapose literal strings, like in C. However, you can start a literal string in one line, and end it a few lines below. For example, this is a valid program (notice that this program and the others in this section explicitly specify the main function):

```
fn main() {
    println!("{}", "These
        are
        three lines");
}
```

This is what is printed:

```
These
        are
        three lines
```

As you can see, the literal string contains all the characters that in the source file are between the start and the end of the string, including newline characters and line leading spaces.

Maybe this is what you want, but you may need instead a single resulting line. In such case, you can write this:

```
fn main() {
    println!("{}", "This \
        is \
        just one line");
}
```

It will print:

```
This is just one line
```

By adding a backslash character ("\") inside a literal string, just before the end of a line, the resulting string will contain neither that end-of-line character nor the following spaces; therefore, the leading spaces of the next line are omitted. Given that we wanted at least one space before each break, we inserted such spaces just before the backslashes.

Finally, if we want to generate a single literal string containing several resulting lines, but with no leading white space, we can write this:

```
fn main() {
    println!("{}", "These
are
three lines");
}
```

or this:

```
fn main() {
println!("{}", "These\n\
    are\n\
    three lines");
}
```

Both will print:

```
These
are
three lines
```

The first solution has the drawback of being disrespectful of indentation conventions, and therefore usually the second solution is preferable. In such a solution, at the end of the lines there is the sequence \n, which is codified as a newline sequence, and then another backslash to exclude from the string the source code newline and the following spaces.

CHAPTER 3

Naming Objects

In this chapter, you will learn:

- The concepts of "value," "object," and "variable"

- The concept of "mutability" of variables

- The difference between initialization and reassignment

- How to avoid warnings for unused variables

- The concept of "Boolean expression"

- Which type of checks are performed by the compiler for assignments

- How some operators can perform both an arithmetic operation and an assignment

- How to invoke functions defined in the Rust standard library

Associating Names to Values

So far, we have seen three kinds of values: strings, integer numbers, and floating-point numbers.

But values should not be confused with objects or variables. So, let's define what the words "value," "object," and "variable" actually mean in this book.

The word "value" indicates a representation of an abstract, mathematical concept. For example, when you say "the value 12" you mean the mathematical concept of the number 12. In mathematics, there is just *one* number 12 in the world. Even true or "Hello" are values, so they conceptually exist in one single instance in the universe, because they are concepts.

But *values* may be stored in the memory of a computer. You can store the number 12 or the string "Hello" in several memory locations. So, you can have two distinct memory locations that both contain the 12 value.

© Carlo Milanesi 2022
C. Milanesi, *Beginning Rust*, https://doi.org/10.1007/978-1-4842-7208-4_3

The portion of memory that contains a value is named "object." Two distinct objects, located in different positions of memory, are said to be *equal* if they contain the same value. Instead, two values are said to be *equal* if and only if they are not distinct, that is, they are actually the same value.

When Rust source code is compiled and run, the running executable program (i.e., the *process*) contains only machine instructions and objects. Such objects have a memory location and a value, but they do not have names. Though, in source code, you may want to associate names to objects, to reference them later. For example, you can write, as the body of the main function:

```
let number = 12;
let other_number = 53;
print!("{}", number + other_number);
```

This will print 65.

The word let, as the already seen word fn, is a keyword reserved by the language. That means that it is a word that cannot be used for other purposes.

The first statement introduces in the program an object containing the value 12 and associates the name number to such object. The second statement introduces another object and associates it to another name. The third statement accesses these two objects by using the names previously defined.

The first statement has the following effects:

- It reserves an object (i.e., an area of memory) large enough to contain an integer number.

- It stores the value 12 in such object, in binary format.

- It associates the name number to such object, so that such name can be used in later points of the source code to indicate such object.

Therefore, such a statement means "a memory space shall be reserved to initially contain the value 12, and from now on, every time we use the word number, we will mean such memory space." So, such a statement declares both an object and a name of that object. A synonym of "name of object" is *identifier*.

Identifier-object pairs are called *variables*. So, that statement is a declaration of a variable.

But it is more than a declaration. A simple declaration of a variable just reserves space for an object, and associates an identifier to such object. The value of the object remains undefined. Instead, this statement also assigns the initial value of such object. Assigning the initial value of an object is called *initializing* that object. So, we say that this statement *declares and initializes a variable.*

The operation of reserving a memory area for an object is named *allocation* of that object. Conversely, the removal of an object, causing its memory area to become available for allocating other objects, is named *deallocation* of that object. So we can say that this statement allocates an object, associates it to an identifier, and initializes that object, giving a value to it. Equivalently, we can say that this statement declares a variable (composed by an identifier-object pair), and initializes such variable.

These concepts are the same as those of C language.

The second statement is similar to the first one.

After having declared and initialized a variable, you can use the name of such variable inside expressions, and the evaluation of such variable gives the value stored in its object. Actually, the preceding third statement appears to compute the sum between the names of two variables, with the effect of adding the current values of such variables.

If any of the first two statements were omitted, the third statement would generate a compilation error, as it would use an undeclared variable, which is forbidden.

In the second statement of the following code:

```
let number = 12;
print!("{} {}", number, 47);
```

two numbers are printed, 12 and 47, but 12 is printed because it is the current value of a *variable*, while 47 is printed because it is the immutable value of a *literal*.

Mutable Variables

After having appropriately declared a variable, you can modify its value in another kind of statement, named "assignment":

```
let mut number = 12;
print!("{}", number);
number = 53;
print!(" {}", number);
```

This will print 12 53.

The first statement declares the variable number and initializes it to the value 12. The second statement prints the value of such variable. The third statement assigns the value 53 to the same variable. The fourth statement prints the new value of the variable.

That assignment does not allocate objects. It just modifies the value of an already allocated object.

You probably noticed that the first statement contains the word mut; it is a keyword of Rust, and it is an abbreviation of *mutable*. Actually, it is needed to declare a variable whose value can be changed.

In fact, the conventional name *variable* is somewhat improper, as it also applies to identifier-object pairs that actually do not allow change to their value, and therefore they are actually *constant*, not *variable*. Someone proposed to use the alternative name *binding*, but the name *variable* is so entrenched in so many languages that its meaning is almost universal. So, in this text, we'll always use the word *variable*, even to refer to something that cannot mutate. Also the error messages of the Rust compiler use the word *variable*.

So, the word *variable* is used both for name-object associations that allow use of that name to change the value of that object, and for name-object associations that do not allow use of that name to change the value of that object. To distinguish these two cases, the variables of the first kind are named *mutable variables*, while the second ones are named *immutable variables*.

The simple keyword "let" declares an immutable variable, whereas the sequence "let mut" is required to declare a mutable variable.

In the previous section, we declared two immutable variables, and actually the values of those variables were never modified after their initialization.

Instead, in the last program shown previously, given that we wanted to modify the value of the variable, we declared it as mutable. Otherwise, in the third statement, we would have gotten a compilation error with this message: cannot assign twice to immutable variable `number`.

In C language, a program equivalent to the first Rust program in the previous section is this:

```
#include <stdio.h>
int main() {
    int const number = 12;
```

```
    int const other_number = 53;
    printf("%d", number + other_number);
    return 0;
}
```

while a program equivalent to the Rust program in this section is this:

```
#include <stdio.h>
int main() {
    int number = 12;
    printf("%d", number);
    number = 53;
    printf(" %d", number);
    return 0;
}
```

Notice that when a Rust declaration *does not contain* the mut keyword, the corresponding C declaration *contains* the const keyword; conversely, when a Rust declaration *contains* the mut keyword, the corresponding C declaration *does not contain* the const keyword.

In other words, in C language the simplest declaration form defines a mutable variable, and you must add the const keyword to obtain immutability, while in Rust the simplest declaration form defines an immutable variable, and you must add the mut keyword to obtain mutability.

Not Mutated Mutable Variables

As we said before, if, after initialization, you try to assign a new value to an immutable variable, you get a compilation error. On the other hand, it is not an error to declare a variable as mutable and then never assign new values to it. However, the compiler notices the inadequacy of such a situation, and it reports it as a warning. The code

```
let mut number = 12;
println!("{}", number);
```

could generate the following compilation message (that could change according to the version of the compiler and the compilation options):

```
warning: variable does not need to be mutable
 --> main.rs:2:9
  |
2 |       let mut number = 12;
  |           ----^^^^^^
  |           |
  |           help: remove this `mut`
  |
  = note: `#[warn(unused_mut)]` on by default
```

The second line of the warning message indicates the portion of source code that caused the warning. It is the file main.rs, starting from column 9 of row 2. The next six lines of the message show such a line of code, underlying the relevant portion of code and suggesting a correction.

The last line indicates that there is a compilation directive that can be set to enable or disable this specific kind of warning reports. As the warning indicates, the compiler's default behavior is to print warnings when some mutable variables are never changed.

Uninitialized Variables

So far, each time we declared a variable, we also initialized it in the same statement. Conversely, we are also allowed to declare a variable without initializing it in the same statement, and to initialize that variable in a subsequent statement, like in the following program:

```
let number;
number = 12;
print!("{}", number);
```

It will print 12.

Then what does the following code do?

```
let number;
print!("{}", number);
```

It generates a compilation error. The compiler notices that in the second line the variable number is evaluated without being assigned any value, so the second statement would have undefined behavior.

Instead, the following code is valid:

```
let number1;
let number2 = 22;
number1 = number2;
print!("{}", number1);
```

This program will print 22. Such a value first is used to initialize the variable number2 in the second statement. In the third statement, the value of the variable number2 is used to initialize the variable number1.

The following code, instead, will generate another compilation error:

```
let number1;
print!("{}", number1);
number1 = 12;
```

The error message is: borrow of possibly-uninitialized variable: `number1`, meaning that the second line uses (*borrows*) a variable the may be not yet initialized.

Actually, in this case the variable number1 is initialized in the third statement, but it is evaluated already in the second statement, when its value has not been defined yet.

The first assignment of a value to a variable is named *initialization* of such variable, whether it happens in the declaration statement itself or in a subsequent statement. Instead, further assignments are named *reassignments*.

Therefore, the rule is that every variable, mutable or immutable, must have one initialization before encountering statements that try to evaluate such variable. Immutable variables cannot have reassignments. If a mutable variable has no reassignments, the compiler can emit a warning.

The Leading Underscore

Sometimes though, it happens to declare a variable, assign a value to it, and never use such a variable again. Of course, all this has a well-defined behavior; but what is the usefulness of initializing a variable, yet never use its value? The compiler rightly suspects it is a programming error, and reports it as a warning. If you compile this code:

```
let number = 12;
```

you get the following warning:

```
warning: unused variable: `number`
 --> main.rs:2:9
  |
2 | let number = 12;
  |     ^^^^^^ help: if this is intentional, prefix it with an underscore:
  `_number`
  |
  = note: `#[warn(unused_variables)]` on by default
```

If such a warning is annoying, a way to silence it is by following the advice contained in the warning message:

```
let _number = 12;
```

This code generates no warnings. The underscore character ("_") is allowed in any part of an identifier, but if it is the first character, it has the effect of silencing this kind of warning. Therefore, by convention, you put a leading underscore to an identifier whenever you are not going to evaluate such variable after it has gotten a value.

The following statement also generates no errors or warnings:

```
let _ = 12;
```

This statement, though, has another meaning. A single underscore character is not a valid identifier, but it is a placeholder that indicates that you don't want to specify any name. It is a *don't-care* symbol, that in this situation creates a throwaway variable.

The difference appears when you try to evaluate that symbol. The following program is valid:

```
let _number = 12;
print!("{}", _number);
```

but the following one is not:

```
let _ = 12;
print!("{}", _);
```

It generates a compilation error containing the message: in expressions, `_` can only be used on the left-hand side of an assignment.

Therefore, an isolated underscore is not a valid expression; instead, it is a placeholder of some syntax symbol that you don't want to specify. Of course, it is not allowed in any point of the code. We already saw that it is allowed to specify a throwaway variable, but it is not allowed in an expression to be evaluated, because such a symbol has no value.

Boolean Values

To represent truth values, the keywords true and false are used. Such keywords are expressions having a non-numeric type, named *Boolean*.

Write this code:

```
let truth = true;
let falsity = false;
print!("{} {}", truth, falsity);
```

This will print true false.

Boolean values, in addition to being generated by evaluating the keywords true and false, are generated by relational expressions. For example:

```
let truth = 5 > 2;
let falsity = -12.3 >= 10.;
print!("{} {} {}", truth, falsity, -50 < 6);
```

This will print true false true.

In the preceding code, the expression 5 > 2, which should be read as "five is greater than two," is arithmetically true, so it initializes the truth variable with the true Boolean value.

A similar operation is performed in the second line, where two floating-point numbers are compared with the *greater-or-equal* operator.

Finally, in the third line the *less-than* operator is used directly in the expression that is the fourth argument of the invocation of the print macro.

The relational operators available are the following ones:

- ==: is equal to

- !=: is different from

- <: is less than

- <=: is less than or equal to

- >: is greater than

- >=: is greater than or equal to

As you can see, Rust relational operators are the same ones used in C language.

Each of them is applicable to two integer numbers, or to two floating-point numbers, or even to values of other types like strings. For example:

```rust
print!("{} {} {}", "abc" < "abcd", "ab" < "ac", "A" < "a");
```

This will print true true true.

However, the two values to be compared must be of the same type. For example, the expression 3.14 > 3 is invalid.

When comparing strings, the "<" operator, instead of being thought of as "is less than," should be thought of as "precedes" and the ">" operator should be thought of as "follows". The sort criterion is that of language dictionaries, also known as *lexicographical*.

Such a criterion is the following one. You start by comparing the first characters of the two strings, and then you proceed to compare characters in the same positions of the two strings until one of the following situations happens:

- If both strings have no more characters, they are equal.

- If one string has no more characters, while the other has more characters, the shorter string precedes the longer one.

- If both strings have more characters, and the next corresponding characters are different, the string having the character preceding the other character in the alphabet precedes the other string.

In the first comparison in the example, after having processed the first three characters of both strings, the first string ends, while the second one proceeds, so the first string precedes the second string in the order.

In the second comparison, the second character is different, and the "b" letter precedes the "c" letter, so the whole string "ab" precedes the string "ac."

In the third comparison, an uppercase "A" is compared with a lowercase "a." Uppercase letters are defined to precede lowercase letters, so also in this case the first string precedes the second one.

Boolean Expressions

Boolean values can be combined with the so-called *logical connectives*: Here are all the possible combinations of them:

```
let truth = true;
let falsity = false;
println!("{} {}", ! truth, ! falsity);
println!("{} {} {} {}", falsity && falsity, falsity && truth,
    truth && falsity, truth && truth);
println!("{} {} {} {}", falsity || falsity, falsity || truth,
    truth || falsity, truth || truth);
```

This will print:

```
false true
false false false true
false true true true
```

Those who know C language will find nothing new.

The operator "!", read "not," produces a true value for a false argument and a false value for a true argument.

The operator "&&", read "logical-and," produces a true value if both its arguments are true and a false value in the other cases.

The operator "||", read "logical-or," produces a false value if both its arguments are false, and a true value in the other cases.

Logical connectives do not have the same precedence:

```
print!("{}", true || true && ! true);
```

This will print: `true`.

The operator `"!"` has top precedence, and it transforms the first expression into `true || true && false`; then the `"&&"` operator has a higher precedence than the `"||"` operator, so it is evaluated next, and it transforms that expression into `true || false`. Finally, the `"||"` operator is evaluated, and it transforms that expression into `true`.

If you'd like a different evaluation order, you can use parentheses:

```
print!("{}", (true || true) && ! true);
```

This will print: `false`.

In this case, the evaluation transforms the expression first to `true && false` and then to `false`.

Type Consistency in Assignments

This program:

```
let mut n = 1;
print!("{}", n);
n = 2;
print!(" {}", n);
n = 3;
print!(" {}", n);
```

will print: `1 2 3`.

But if we change the fifth line to

```
n = 3.14;
```

the compiler will report the error: `mismatched types`, with the further message: `expected integer, found floating-point number`, referring to the literal `3.14`. Actually, the first line creates a variable that, being initialized using an integer number, is of type *integer number*; the third line assigns to such variable a value that is still of type *integer number*; but the fifth line would assign to such variable a floating-point number value. This is not allowed, as only values of type *integer number* can be assigned to a variable of type *integer number*.

In general, in Rust every variable and every expression have a type defined at compile time.

For example, all of the following three expressions are of type *integer number*: `12`, `12 - 3`, `12 - (7 % 5)`. But the following three expressions are of type *floating-point number*: `12.`, `12. - 3.`, `12. - (7. % 5.)`. The expression `"hello"` is of *string* type, and the expressions `false` and `4 > 3` are of *Boolean* type.

Type Inference

The type of a variable can be deduced, or, as it is commonly said, *inferred*, from the type of the expression used to initialize such variable. A program containing only the line:

```
let number;
```

is illegal, because the compiler cannot assign a datatype to such a variable. The error message is: `type annotations needed`, meaning that the type of that variable must be specified.

Once the compiler understands which is the type of a variable, all the assignments to such a variable must use expressions of such type.

In addition, notice this:

```
let number1 = 12;
let _number2 = number1;
```

Here, the literal integer number `12` is of type *integer number*, so the `number1` variable is also of type *integer number*. Therefore, the initialization expression appearing in the second line at the right of the `=` sign is of that type. Finally, the variable `_number2` is also of the same type, as it is initialized by such expression.

Going back to the previous example, where we attempted to use the number `3.14`, there are several ways to solve the problem of type mismatch. One way is to write:

```
let mut n = 1.;
print!("{}", n);
n = 2.;
print!(" {}", n);
n = 3.14;
print!(" {}", n);
```

It will print: `1  2  3.14`.

In this code, there are only floating-point numbers, and therefore there is no type error.

Change of Type and of Mutability

There is also the following way to make valid the previous code:

```
let mut n = 1;
print!("{}", n);
n = 2;
print!(" {}", n);
let n = 3.14;
print!(" {}", n);
```

In this case, the first statement declares the variable n of type *mutable integer number* and initializes it; the third statement changes the value of such variable. Then, the fifth statement *redeclares* the variable n, and initializes it using an expression of type *floating-point number*; therefore, the variable itself must be of that type.

In most programming languages, it is not allowed to redeclare a variable. However, Rust allows it. Notice that redeclarations do not overwrite existing variables, they simply create new variables.

Of course, after such a declaration, the previously existing variable is no longer accessible. It hasn't been destroyed, though. We say that the old variable has been *shadowed* by the new variable.

Notice that this last declaration creates a variable of another type and also of different mutability. That is, while the variable declared in the first statement was mutable, the one declared in the fifth statement is not. Therefore, for example, the following code generates, at the last statement, the compilation error: `cannot assign twice to immutable variable `_n``:

```
let mut _n = 1;
_n = 2;
let _n = 3.14;
_n = 5.9;
```

As a redeclaration introduces a new variable that shadows the first one, such variable can be of any type:

```
let x = 120; print!("{} ", x);
let x = "abcd"; print!("{} ", x);
```

```
let mut x = true; print!("{} ", x);
x = false; print!("{}", x);
```

This will print: `120 abcd true false`.

Compound Assignment Operators

In Rust, often there is the need to write code like this:

```
let mut a = 12;
a = a + 1;
a = a - 4;
a = a * 7;
a = a / 6;
print!("{}", a);
```

This will print 10. Similarly to C language, such expressions may be abbreviated in this way:

```
let mut a = 12;
a += 1;
a -= 4;
a *= 7;
a /= 6;
print!("{}", a);
```

Actually, those aren't only abbreviations; they are different operators, though usually their behavior is just to perform an arithmetic operation followed by an assignment. That is, for example, the operator += is equivalent first to perform an addition and then to assign the resulting sum.

Using the Functions of the Standard Library

As any programming language, even Rust can do little using only the built-in features of the language, and most of the available features are delegated to external libraries.

In addition to using third-party libraries, every Rust installation provides an official library, the so-called *standard library*. Differing from C language, which requires using the #include directive to include in the source code the needed file of the standard library, Rust, by default, includes its whole standard library. So the application code can immediately use the features of the standard library, with no need to include external modules:

```
print!("{} {}", str::len("abcde"), "abcde".len());
```

This will print 5 5.

Here a function, or routine, is invoked or called. Its name is len, an abbreviation of *length*, and it is part of the standard library. It returns the number of bytes contained in the string passed as an argument. Notice that the number of bytes in a string is not always the same value as the number of characters of that string.

To invoke many functions in Rust, including the len function, there are two possible syntax forms, and the preceding example shows both of them.

The first syntax form shown has a procedural style, while the second one has an object-oriented style.

In the first form, the name of the module containing the function is specified first. In this case it is str; that is the module of the standard library that defines the string manipulation functions. Then the name of the function is specified, separated by a couple of colon characters (::). Then possible arguments are specified, enclosed in parentheses.

In the second form, the expression begins with the first argument; then there is the name of the function, separated by a dot; and finally, there are the possible other arguments, enclosed in parentheses.

The parentheses are always required, even if there are no arguments, like in C language.

The second form is more compact, so when it is available, it is recommended.

CHAPTER 4

Controlling Execution Flow

In this chapter, you will learn:

- How to use if statements to execute different statements based on a Boolean condition

- How to use if expressions to generate different values based on a Boolean condition

- How to use while statements to repeat some statements as long as a Boolean condition holds

- How to use for statements to repeat some statements for a definite number of times

- What is the scope of validity of variables

Conditional Statements (`if`)

The main usage of Boolean values, introduced in the previous chapter, is in making decisions about how to let the execution of the program proceed. Suppose you want to print a word, but only if a given number is positive:

```
let n = 4;
if n > 0 { print!("positive"); }
```

This will print `positive`.

The second line contains an `if` statement, similar to that of many other languages. In such a statement, the Boolean expression following the `if` keyword is evaluated. Such an expression is referred to as the *condition*. Only when the outcome of evaluating the condition is `true` will the statements enclosed in the following braces be executed.

© Carlo Milanesi 2022
C. Milanesi, *Beginning Rust*, https://doi.org/10.1007/978-1-4842-7208-4_4

The braces can enclose zero or more statements. Therefore, they resemble the body of the `main` function. In general, a sequence of statements enclosed in braces is named **block**.

This syntax differs from that of other languages, like C, for the following reasons:

- The condition must be of Boolean type. Therefore, the following syntax is not allowed: `if 4 { print!("four"); }`.

- It is not required to enclose the condition between parentheses, and usually it is not done. In fact, the compiler reports a warning if you do so.

- After the condition, a block (of statements) is required. Therefore, the following syntax is not allowed: `if 4 > 0 print!("four");` neither is the following one: `if (4 > 0) print!("four");`.

If you want to do something even in case the condition is evaluated to `false`, you can introduce the alternative case, preceded by the `else` keyword:

```
let n = 0;
if n > 0 {
    print!("number is");
    print!(" positive");
}
else {
    print!("not positive");
}
```

This will print `not positive`.

As you can see, because the whole `if` statement is very long, it has been split into seven lines, and the statements enclosed in blocks have been indented by four columns, to make the blocks evident.

If there are more than two cases, of course, you can insert `if` statements inside blocks in this way:

```
let n = 4;
if n > 1000 {
    print!("big");
}
```

```
else {
    if n > 0 {
        print!("small");
    }
    else {
        if n < 0 {
            print!("negative");
    }
        else {
            print!("neither positive nor negative");
        }
    }
}
```

It will print small, as the condition in the second line is false and the condition in the sixth line is true.

However, the following equivalent syntax is allowed, to make it more readable:

```
let n = 4;
if n > 1000 {
    print!("big");
}
else if n > 0 {
    print!("small");
}
else if n < 0 {
    print!("negative");
}
else {
    print!("neither positive nor negative");
}
```

Notice that after any else keyword, you must put a block or another if statement.

Conditional Expressions

Instead of writing the previous code, you could write the following equivalent code:

```
let n = 4;
print!("{}",
    if n > 1000 {
        "big"
    }
    else if n > 0 {
        "small"
    }
    else if n < 0 {
        "negative"
    }
    else {
        "neither positive nor negative"
    }
);
```

Here, a *conditional expression* is used, similar to the C-language ternary operator "?:". The corresponding code in C language is:

```
#include <stdio.h>
int main(int argc, char **argv) {
    int n = 4;
    printf("%s",
        n > 1000 ?
            "big" :
        n > 0 ?
            "small" :
        n < 0 ?
            "negative" :
            "neither positive nor negative");
}
```

The last Rust program, instead of containing four invocations of the "print" macro, contains just one invocation, having two arguments. The first argument is just the format string for the second argument, and the second argument is an expression extending over 12 lines. Such expression uses, as in the previous example, the `if` and `else` keywords, but instead of containing statements in the blocks, it contains simple literal strings.

The evaluation of such a composite expression proceeds in a way that is similar to that of the `if-else` statement in the previous example, with the following difference. After it has been determined which block should be executed, while in the previous example the statements enclosed in the block were *executed*, in the last example the expression enclosed in the block is *evaluated*, and the value obtained from such evaluation is considered as the value of the whole "if-else" expression. Afterward, such value will be used by the macro to be printed.

To understand all this, it is required to know the difference between *statements* and *expressions* in programming languages.

A statement is a piece of code that specifies a command to be *executed*. Such execution usually changes the state of some objects or the state of the external world. Usually, a statement does not have the purpose of returning a value or having a value.

An expression is a piece of code that specifies a value that can be obtained by *evaluating* such piece of code. Such execution usually does not change the state of any object or the state of the external world. The purpose of an expression is just to return a value, that is, to have a value.

In C language, "if" constructs are just statements, and "?:" constructs are just expressions. Instead, in Rust, "if" statements can be used both as statements and as expressions, as we have just seen. What characterizes them as expressions is the fact that all their blocks end without a semicolon. In such a case, the expressions contained in the blocks give the value of the composite `if` expression.

Though, consider this expression:

```
let val = if cond { "abc" };
```

What is the type of `val`, in case the `cond` condition is false? It wouldn't be defined, so this expression is forbidden, generating the message error: `` `if` `` may be missing an `else` clause.

And now, consider this expression:

```
let val = if cond { "abc" } else { 12 };
```

What can be inferred as the type of val? The first block has a string as its value, while the second block has an integer number, so the compiler wouldn't be able to determine a type for the val variable, and it generates the error message: `if` and `else` have incompatible types.

In general, in order to have a unique type for a conditional expression, it is required that the expression have at least one else branch and that all its blocks end with expressions of the same type.

So, it is allowed to write the statements

```
let _a = if true { "abc" } else { "xy" };
let _b = if true { 3456 } else { 12 };
let _c = if true { 56.9 } else { 12. };
```

because, in the first statement we have only strings, in the second one only integer numbers, and in the third one only floating-point numbers. So _a is a string, _b is an integer number, and _c is a floating-point number.

Conditional Loops (`while`)

Let's suppose you want to print the integer numbers from 1 to 10, including 1 and 10, squared. You can do that with the statements

```
let mut n = 1;
while n <= 10 {
    print!("{} ", n * n);
    n += 1;
}
```

That will print: 1 4 9 16 25 36 49 64 81 100 .

Here, the while keyword is used, similarly to C language. The Boolean condition following it is evaluated, and, if its value is true, the ensuing block is executed. The while statement differs from the if statement because, after having executed the block, it repeats the evaluation of the condition, and possibly re-executes the block, until the condition is evaluated to false or until the block is exited for some other reason.

This syntax differs from other languages, like C, for the same aspects already seen about the syntax of if statements.

In our example, the mutable variable n is declared, as an integer number, and it is initialized to 1. Such value represents the number of which you want to print the square.

The while statement checks whether such value is less or equal to the 10 value and, as it is so, the block is executed. Inside the block, the value of n is incremented. After the execution of the block, the Boolean condition is evaluated again. After ten iterations, the value of n is 11; at this point the condition of the loop is no longer satisfied, so the execution of the while statement ends.

While in C language there is also the do … while-statement, there is no such statement in Rust. Instead, the same **break** and **continue** statements of C language also exist in Rust. Their purpose is, respectively, to exit prematurely from the whole loop, and to exit prematurely from the sole current iteration of the loop.

For example, if for each integer number from 1 to 50 that wouldn't be divisible by 3, we would like to print its square, as long as such square is not larger than 400, we could write:

```
let mut n = 0;
while n < 50 {
    n += 1;
    if n % 3 != 0 {
        if n * n <= 400 {
            print!("{} ", n * n);
        }
    }
}
```

or, using continue and break, we can write the equivalent code:

```
let mut n = 0;
while n < 50 {
    n += 1;
    if n % 3 == 0 { continue; }
    if n * n > 400 { break; }
    print!("{} ", n * n);
}
```

Both programs will print: 1 4 16 25 49 64 100 121 169 196 256 289 361 400.

These two versions have the same first three lines.

In the first version, if the remainder of n divided by three is different from zero, that is, the number *is not* divisible by three, the iteration goes on. In the second version of the program, if the number *is* divisible by three, the `continue` statement is executed, so the current iteration is immediately ended and the next iteration is reached.

Notice that, to let the next iteration process the next number, it is needed to increment such number. Therefore, such increment is put at the beginning of the iteration.

The usage of the `continue` keyword allows us to improve readability, because it reduces by one the nesting level of blocks.

In addition, the first version of the program checks whether the square of n is larger than 400, and the value is printed only if the limit is not exceeded. The second version takes into account the fact that, given that the number is steadily incremented, once its square exceeds 400 it will exceed it in every following iteration. Therefore, as soon as the square of n exceeds 400, the `break` statement is executed, with the effect of immediately getting out of the whole loop.

The usage of the `break` keyword allows us to improve readability too, similarly to the `continue` keyword. It also allows us to improve speed, as it avoids several useless iterations.

Infinite Loops (loop)

It happens to execute so-called infinite loops, meaning loops in which the execution flow exits from them only by executing the `break` statement or the `return` statement, or when the program is forcefully terminated. For example, to print all the squares less than 200, we can write

```
let mut n = 1;
while true {
    let n2 = n * n;
    if n2 >= 200 { break; }
    print!("{} ", n2);
    n += 1;
}
```

That will print: 1 4 9 16 25 36 49 64 81 100 121 144 169 196 .

The compiler will, though, suggest to denote infinite loops with `**loop** { ... }`. The compiler advises to replace the while true clause with the more expressive loop keyword, so obtaining the equivalent program:

```
let mut n = 1;
loop {
    let nn = n * n;
    if nn >= 200 { break; }
    print!("{} ", nn);
    n += 1;
}
```

Counting Loops (for)

What about the famous for loop of the C language (and many others languages)?

Even in Rust there is the for keyword, and also in Rust it is used to iterate a definite number of times, but its use in Rust is very different from that in C language.

Here is a program that solves the problem of printing the integer numbers from 1 to 10, including 1 and 10, squared:

```
for n in 1..11 {
    print!("{} ", n * n);
}
```

It will print: 1 4 9 16 25 36 49 64 81 100 .

After the open brace, the syntax of the for statement is the same as that of the while statement, meaning that the break and continue statements are allowed. However, the first part of the statement is very different.

Just after the "**for**" keyword, there is the name of the n iteration variable, that will be created in such way.

Then, there is the "**in**" keyword, followed by two integer numeric expressions, separated by the symbol "**..**".

The construct composed of two numeric expressions separated by the double dots symbol represents a *range*, that is, a sequence of consecutive numbers. In particular it is a *right-exclusive range expression*, meaning that the first number of the expression is part of the sequence, but the second number is not part of it.

For example, the expression 3 .. 7 represents the sequence 3, 4, 5, and 6, excluding the number 7.

The pair of dots is a Rust operator, named *right-exclusive range operator*.

So, the preceding program simply executes the body of the for statement once for each item in that range.

To execute this loop means to assign to the n variable the value 1, which is the first value of the specified range; then to execute the block, with such value for the n variable; then to increment by one the value of n; then to execute the block another time with such value for n; and so on. When the value of n reaches 11, which is the second value of the range expression, the block is *not* executed and the for statement ends. Therefore, while the first limit is *included* in the sequence of used values, the second one is *excluded*.

As the second limit is excluded from the loop, to iterate from 1 to 10 you must write 1..11.

The Rust language also has another operator, ..=, named *right-inclusive range operator*. For example, the range expression 3 ..= 7 represents the sequence 3, 4, 5, 6, and 7.

Using that operator, the previous program could be rewritten as the equivalent program:

```
for n in 1..=10 {
    print!("{} ", n * n);
}
```

Notice that now the upper limit is 10 instead of 11, because it is included in the range.

As mentioned, the iteration variable, automatically incremented at any iteration, is declared by the for statement. Because it is declared just for that statement, it is destroyed when the for statement ends. If there were already a variable having the same name, such a pre-existing variable would be shadowed (i.e., ignored) for the whole for statement, and it would become valid again after the loop, as shown by this code:

```
let index = 8;
for index in 0..4 { print!("{} ", index); }
print!(":{}", index);
```

This will print: 0 1 2 3 :8.

Notice that the upper and lower limit specified in the for statement may be arbitrary expressions. However, both such expressions are evaluated *before* the beginning of the loop. The program

```
let mut limit = 4;
for n in 1..limit + 2 {
    limit -= 1;
    print!("{} {}, ", limit, n);
}
print!("{}", limit);
```

will print 3 1, 2 2, 1 3, 0 4, -1 5, -1. Let's see why.

First, the limit variable is created, and it is initialized to the 4 value.

Then, the range that represents the extremes of the loop is evaluated. The initial extreme, included, is 1, while the final extreme, excluded, is 6. The addition operator has precedence over the range operator, so first the expression limit + 2 is evaluated to 6 and then the range 1..6 is evaluated.

Therefore, the block is executed five times; the first one with n=1, the second time with n=2, and so on. Each time the block is executed, the value of limit is decremented by one, therefore passing from 4 to -1 at the end of the loop. However, this does not affect the number of iterations that will be executed, because such iterations depend on the precalculated range.

This is different from the following C language program:

```
#include <stdio.h>
int main() {
    int limit = 4;
    for (int n = 1; n < limit + 2; n++) {
        limit -= 1;
        printf("%d ", n);
    }
    printf(":%d ", limit);
}
```

This will print 1 2 3 :1, because, as limit is decremented the loop condition n < limit + 2 is no longer satisfied after the third iteration, because the value of n is 4 and the value of limit is 1.

Variables Scopes

We have already seen many statements using blocks: the main function, the if statement/expression, the while statement, the loop statement, and the for statement.

In such cases, using blocks is required by the syntax of the statements used, though you can also use blocks everywhere you want to enclose some statements. For example:

```
print!("1");
{
    print!("2");
    print!("3");
    {
        print!("4");
        {
            print!("5");
            { { } };
            print!("6");
        }
    }
    print!("7");
}
```

This will print 1234567. Of course, braces must be correctly paired.

Indents and other spaces are optional, and they do not change the generated executable; their purpose is just to make the source code more readable.

But what's the purpose of all those braces? In the preceding example, they are useless, but if you compile the following code:

```
{ let n = 10; }
print!("{} ", n);
```

you get the error: cannot find value `n` in this scope at the second line, like if the n variable hadn't ever been declared. It happens so, because each variable ceases to exist at the end of the block in which it has been declared.

The block where a variable has been declared is called the *scope* of that variable.

So, in our example, the scope of n ends at the end of the same line in which it begins.

Scopes can be more complex than this. Consider this code:

```
{
    let n = 10;
    {
        let m = 4;
        {
            print!("{} ", n);
        }
        print!("{}", n + m);
    } // End of the scope of `m`
} // End of the scope of `n`
```

It will print 10 14. We have three nested blocks.

The n variable is declared in the outer block, so its scope lasts for nine lines, from where it is declared, to the end of the code snippet. It can be used also inside inner blocks, because blocks do not shadow variables declared in outer blocks.

Instead, the m variable is declared in the second-level block, so its scope lasts only for six lines, from the fourth to the ninth line.

Now let's examine this code:

```
{
    let n = 10;
    {
        let n = 4;
        print!("{} ", n);
    } // End of the scope of the second `n`
    print!("{}", n);
} // End of the scope of the first `n`
```

It will print 4 10.

We already said that it is allowed to define a variable having the same name of a variable already existing, and that in such case this last variable is *shadowed* and not *overwritten* by the new declaration.

Here, first, a variable named n is declared, and it is initialized with the value 10. Then another variable having the same name is declared, and it is initialized with the value 4. Then, the value of a variable with such name is printed. As the second variable shadows the first one, it's the value of the second variable that is used, so 4 is printed. Then, the second variable gets out of its scope and therefore it is destroyed, so the first variable becomes visible again. So, the second print statement uses the value of the first variable, which hasn't been destroyed yet.

Therefore, we saw that pairs of braces may be inserted to purposely limit the scope of a variable.

But variable visibility rules hold also for the blocks of `if`, `while`, and `for` statements. Therefore the following code

```
let mut _i = 1;
if true { let _i = 2; }
print!("{} ", _i);
while _i > 0 { _i -= 1; let _i = 5; }
print!("{} ", _i);
```

will print 1 0.

Actually, it is true that in the second line the statement `let _i = 2;` is executed, but the effect of that statement is to create a new variable and to destroy it in the same line. So, in the third line, the value of the first _i-named variable is printed.

In the last-but-one line, as _i was initially greater than zero, the body of the `while` statement is executed the first time. Inside that body, the value of _i is decremented to zero, and then another variable having the same name _i is created and immediately destroyed. Given that now the original _i is zero, the `while` statement ends, and finally the value of the first (and only remaining) variable is printed.

You should think that any variable declaration *creates* an object, and that such an object is *destroyed* when the scope where such variable has been declared ends.

And each time you use a variable name, except for declaring it, the variable actually referred to is the latest declared variable having that name and not yet destroyed.

Using metaphorical language, the creation of an object can be considered its birth, and the destruction of an object can be considered its death. So, we can say that each use of a variable name refers to the *youngest live variable* having that name.

CHAPTER 5

Using Data Sequences

In this chapter, you will learn:

- How to define sequences of objects of the same type, having fixed length (arrays) or variable length (vectors)
- How to specify the initial contents of arrays or vectors, by listing the items or by specifying one item and its repeat count
- How to read or write the value of single items of arrays or vectors
- How to add items to a vector or to remove items from a vector
- How to create arrays with several dimensions
- How to create empty arrays or vectors
- How to print or copy whole arrays or vectors
- How to specify whether the compiler should deny, allow with a warning, or silently allow possible programming errors
- What is a panic, and why it may be generated when accessing an array or a vector

Arrays

So far, we have seen how to store in a variable a string, a number, or a Boolean. But if you want to store several strings into a single variable, you can write this:

```
let x = ["English", "This", "sentence", "a", "in", "is"];
print!("{} {} {} {} {} {}",
    x[1], x[5], x[3], x[2], x[4], x[0]);
```

47

© Carlo Milanesi 2022
C. Milanesi, *Beginning Rust*, https://doi.org/10.1007/978-1-4842-7208-4_5

That will print: `This is a sentence in English.`

The first statement declares the x variable as an immutable object made of an array of six objects, specified in the statement itself. Each of such objects is of string type. Such a compound kind of object is indeed named *array*.

The second statement contains six expressions, each of them making a read access to a different element of x. Such accesses specify the item to be accessed by means of a positional index, or *subscript*, put between brackets. Notice that indexes always start from zero, and so, as the array has six elements, the index of the last item is 5. This behavior is similar to that of C language arrays.

To determine how many elements there are in an array, you can do this:

```
let a = [true, false];
let b = [1, 2, 3, 4, 5];
print!("{}, {}.", a.len(), b.len());
```

It will print: `2, 5`.

The a variable is an array of two Booleans, while the b variable is an array of five integer numbers.

The third statement invokes on the objects a and b the `len` function of the standard library, to get the number of the objects contained in the array. Both the syntax and semantics of these invocations are similar to those of the expression `"abc".len()`, used to get the length in bytes of a string.

Notice that in the examples, every array contains elements of the same type; only strings, only Booleans, or only integer numbers.

If you try to write

```
let x = ["This", 4];
```

or

```
let x = [4, 5.];
```

you get a `mismatched types` compilation error, indicating the array cannot contain objects of different types.

It is possible to create arrays of any types of items, as long as in every array all the items are of the same type.

It is so, because there is not a single type *array*. The concept of *array* is that of a *generic* type, which is parameterized by its items type, and also by the number of its items. So, in the first example of the chapter, the variable x is of type "array of 5 strings"; instead, in the second example, a is of type "array of 2 Booleans," and b is of type "array of 5 integer numbers."

In the following program, every line but the first one will generate a compilation error:

```
let mut x = ["a"]; // array of strings
x[0] = 3;
x[-1] = "b";
x[0.] = "b";
x[false] = "b";
x["0"] = "b";
```

The second statement is wrong because it tries to assign an integer number to an item of an array of strings. So the compiler emits a `mismatched types` error message.

The other statements are wrong because the compiler expects any index used to access an array to be a non-negative integer number, and the expressions used in such statements are not.

The following one is a different case:

```
let x = ["a"]; // array of strings
let _y = x[1];
```

It has a valid syntax, but nevertheless it is wrong, because the second statement tries to access the second element of an array having only one element.

The compiler error message is: `this operation will panic at runtime`. It means that this statement would generate a runtime error when executed. The compiler message also contains the explanation: `index out of bounds: the length is 1 but the index is 1`.

Rust Attributes

The Rust compiler is somewhat flexible about the strictness of analysis in the Rust language. For some possible error conditions, like not using a variable after its last assignment, the compiler allows the developer to specify three possible behavior of compilation:

- *Deny*: The compiler emits an error message, and it does not generate the executable code.

- *Warn*: The compiler emits a warning message, but it does generate the executable code.

- *Allow*: The compiler does not emit any message, and it does generate the executable code.

To specify such behaviors, the developer must write into the code specific statements, named *attributes*.

Here is an example:

```
#[deny(unused_variables)]
let x = 1;
#[warn(unused_variables)]
let y = 2;
#[allow(unused_variables)]
let z = 3;
```

When compiling this code, the following error is emitted:

```
error: unused variable: `x`
```

Then the following warning is emitted:

```
warning: unused variable: `y`
```

And then no executable code is generated, because there is at least one error.

The last statement does not generate any output.

This code contains three attributes. Any attribute usually is on a line by itself. It begins with a "#" character followed by an expression in brackets. It applies to the statement immediately following it.

In the cases shown, the expressions are the word deny or warn or allow, followed by an identifier in parentheses. The identifier must be a known compiler option. If this case it is unused_variables; that means that this attribute specifies how the compiler must handle the case that the value of the variable declared in the following statement is not used after the last assignment.

If a compiler option is not specified by an attribute, it has a default value anyway. The default value of the unused_variables option is warn. It is for this reason that if you don't use the value of a variable after its last assignment, the generated warning is followed by the following line:

```
note: `#[warn(unused_variables)]` on by default
```

Instead of specifying an attribute just before any declaration, it is possible to declare it before a function definition, in the following way:

```
#[allow(unused_variables)]
fn main() {
    let x = 1;
    let y = 2;
}
```

This whole program does not generate any warnings, because the attribute in the first line applies to the whole main function, and therefore to both the x and y variables.

Another compiler option regards runtime errors.

Panicking

Accessing an array with a too large index has notoriously undefined behavior in C language. Instead, the Rust language has the goal of avoiding any undefined behaviors.

To avoid such an undefined behavior, the compiler inserts into the generated executable code some statements to check whether any access to arrays use a proper index, that is, an index less than the length of the array. In case an out-of-bounds index is actually used, such checking statements generate an abort operation for the current thread, that, by default, causes the immediate termination of the thread itself. If the process has just one thread, such thread termination causes the termination of the whole process.

In Rust jargon, such an abort operation is named *panic*, and the action of aborting the current thread is named *panicking*.

In general, the compiler cannot detect out-of-bound indexing errors, because array indices may have variable values; though, consider the following code, already cited before:

```
let x = ["a"];
let _y = x[1];
print!("End");
```

Here the compiler knows both the size of the array and the value of the index, because they are constants, and so it can foresee that the generated code will panic at runtime.

Therefore, when you compile this code, the compiler emits an error message containing the following sentences.

First:

```
error: this operation will panic at runtime
```

Then:

```
index out of bounds: the length is 1 but the index is 1
```

And then:

```
note: `#[deny(unconditional_panic)]` on by default
```

The first sentence states what the compiler has foreseen, as a compilation error.

The second sentence explains why this operation will panic.

The third statement explains that, by default, such condition generates a compile-time error. The identifier `unconditional_panic` means a condition in which, if this statement is executed, it will surely generate a panic at runtime; therefore it is probably wrong, or in any case it should be replaced by a more explicit error message.

You can obtain an executable program if you write, instead:

```
let x = ["a"];
#[warn(unconditional_panic)]
let _y = x[1];
print!("End");
```

It will generate the compilation message:

```
warning: this operation will panic at runtime
```

If you write the following code instead:

```
let x = ["a"];
#[allow(unconditional_panic)]
let _y = x[1];
print!("End");
```

you will get no compilation error or warning.

In both cases, when you run the program you will see on the terminal a message starting with this:

```
thread 'main' panicked at
'index out of bounds: the len is 1 but the index is 1'
```

After that, the process will terminate without printing the End word.

Notice that such abnormal termination is not caused by the operating system, like a *segmentation violation*, but it is caused by instructions inserted by the Rust compiler itself into the executable program.

Mutable Arrays

Now get back to what we can do with arrays.

The modification of the items of an array is possible only on mutable arrays:

```
let mut x = ["This", "is", "a", "sentence"];
x[2] = "a nice";
print!("{} {} {} {}.", x[0], x[1], x[2], x[3]);
```

This will print: This is a nice sentence.

The first statement contains the mut keyword, and the second statement assigns the new value to the third item of the array. This operation is allowed by the compiler, because the following three conditions hold:

- The x variable is mutable.

- The type of the new value assigned is the same as the other items of x. Actually, they are all strings.

- The index is a non-negative integer number.

In addition, at runtime, the operation is performed without panicking, because the index is less than the array size, that is, the condition 2 < 4 holds.

Instead, it is not allowed to add items to an array or to remove items from an array. Therefore, its length is a compile-time-defined constant.

A mutable variable of an array type, as any mutable variable, can be the target of an assignment from another array:

```
let mut x = ["a", "b", "c"];
print!("{}{}{}. ", x[0], x[1], x[2]);
x = ["X", "Y", "Z"];
print!("{}{}{}. ", x[0], x[1], x[2]);
let y = ["1", "2", "3"];
x = y;
print!("{}{}{}.", x[0], x[1], x[2]);
```

This will print: abc. XYZ. 123.

In the first line, an array is created and assigned to the x variable. In the third line, another array is created and assigned to the same x variable, therefore replacing all the three existing strings. In the fifth line, another array is created and assigned to the new y variable. In the sixth line, such array is assigned to the x variable, therefore replacing the three existing values.

If x weren't mutable, two compilation errors would be generated: one at the third line and one at the sixth.

The following code generates "mismatched types" compilation errors both at the second and at the third lines:

```
let mut x = ["a", "b", "c"];
x = ["X", "Y"];
x = [15, 16, 17];
```

Actually, because of the first line, x is of type "array of three elements of type string." The statement in the second line tries to assign to x a value of type "array of *two* elements of type string"; in this case, the number of elements is different, even if the type of each element is the same.

The statement in the third line tries to assign to x a value of type "array of three elements of type *integer number*"; in this case, the number of the elements is the same, but the type of each element is different.

In both cases, the type of the whole value that is being assigned is different from the type of the target variable.

Arrays of Explicitly Specified Size

We already saw how to create an array by listing the items initially contained.

If you want to handle many items, instead of writing many expressions, you can write

```
let mut x = [4.; 5000];
x[2000] = 3.14;
print!("{}, {}", x[1000], x[2000]);
```

That will print: `4, 3.14`.

The first statement declares the x variable as a mutable array of 5000 floating-point numbers, all initially equal to `4`. Notice the usage of a semicolon instead of a comma inside the square brackets.

The second statement assigns the value `3.14` to the item at position 2000 of such array.

Finally the value, which *never changed*, at position 1000, and the value, which *just changed*, at position 2000 are printed. Notice that the valid indexes for this array go from 0 to 4999.

To scan the items of an array, the `for`-statement is very useful:

```
let mut fib = [1; 12];
for i in 2..fib.len() {
    fib[i] = fib[i - 2] + fib[i - 1];
}
for i in 0..fib.len() {
    print!("{}, ", fib[i]);
}
```

This will print: `1, 1, 2, 3, 5, 8, 13, 21, 34, 55, 89, 144, `.

This program computes the first 12 numbers of the famous Fibonacci sequence and then it prints them. The sequence is defined in this way: the first two numbers are both 1, and every other number is the sum of the two preceding numbers.

Examine the program.

The first statement creates a variable named fib and initializes it using an array of 12 numbers with value 1.

The statement in the following three lines is a for loop, in which the i variable is initialized to 2, and it is incremented up to the length of the array. The body of the loop assigns to each item of the array, starting from the third one, the sum of the two preceding items. Given that, when each item is written, the preceding items have already received their correct value, such assignment always uses correct values.

Finally, there is another for loop, to print all the numbers; this time its index starts from 0.

Multidimensional Arrays

You can easily write arrays having several dimensions:

```
let mut x = [[[23; 4]; 8]; 15];
x[14][7][3] = 56;
print!("{}, {}", x[0][0][0], x[14][7][3]);
```

This will print: 23, 56.

The first statement declares an array of 15 items, each of them being an array of 8 items, each of them being an array of 4 items, each of them initialized with the integer number 23.

The second statement accesses the 15th and last item of the array, so referring an array; then it accesses the 8th and last item of the array, so getting an array; then it accesses the 4th and last item of such array, so getting an item of type integer number; finally, it assigns the integer number 56 to that item.

The third statement prints the content of the very first item and the content of the very last item of the array.

Because multidimensional arrays are no more than arrays of arrays, it is easy to get the sizes of a given array:

```
let x = [[[0; 4]; 8]; 15];
print!("{}, {}, {}.",
    x.len(), x[0].len(), x[0][0].len());
```

This will print: `15, 8, 4`.

A big limitation of arrays is the fact that their size must be defined at compilation time:

```
let length = 6;
let arr = [0; length];
```

The compilation of this code generates the error `attempt to use a non-constant value in a constant`. Actually, the expression `length` is a variable, and therefore conceptually it is not a compile-time constant, even if it is immutable and even if it has just been initialized by a constant. The size of an array cannot be an expression containing variables.

This is because, in general, immutable variables can have a value that is computed only at runtime, even if in this case it can be easily computed at compilation time. Instead, the size of an array must always be known by the compiler at compilation time.

Vectors

To create sequences of objects whose size is defined at runtime, the Rust standard library provides the Vec type, shorthand for *vector*:

```
let x = vec!["This", "is"];
print!("{} {}. Length: {}.", x[0], x[1], x.len());
```

This will print: `This is. Length: 2`.

The first statement looks like the creation of an immutable array, with the only difference being the appearance of the vec! clause.

Such a clause is an invocation of the vec macro of the standard library. vec is an abbreviation of *vector*.

The effect of such a macro is indeed to create a vector, initially containing the two strings specified between square brackets. Actually, when len() is invoked on such an object, 2 is returned.

Vectors allow us to do everything that is allowed for arrays, but they allow also us to change their size after they have been initialized:

```
let mut x = vec!["This", "is"]; print!("{}", x.len());
x.push("a"); print!(" {}", x.len());
```

```
x.push("sentence"); print!(" {}", x.len());
x[0] = "That";
for i in 0..x.len() { print!(" {}", x[i]); }
```

This will print: `2 3 4 That is a sentence`.

The first line creates a mutable vector, initially containing two strings, and prints its length, meaning the number of strings contained in the vector.

The second line invokes the `push` function on the just created vector, and prints its new length. Such a function adds its argument at the bottom of the vector. To be legal, it must have exactly *one* argument, and such argument must be of the same type of the items of the vector. The word `push` is the word commonly used for the operation of adding an item to a *stack* data structure.

The third line adds another string at the end of the vector, so making the vector contain four items, and it prints the new length of the vector.

The fourth line replaces the value of the first item of the vector. This operation and the two preceding ones are allowed only because the x variable is mutable.

The fifth line scans the four items of the vector, and prints them all on the terminal.

Let's see another example:

```
let length = 5000;
let mut y = vec![4.; length];
y[6] = 3.14;
y.push(4.89);
print!("{}, {}, {}", y[6], y[4999], y[5000]);
```

This will print: `3.14, 4, 4.89`.

The second line declares a variable having as value a vector containing a sequence of 5000 items, each one of them having value 4. The length of the sequence is specified by the variable `length`. This wouldn't be allowed with an array.

The third line changes the value of the seventh item of the vector.

The fourth line adds a new item at the end of the vector. Because the vector had 5000 items, the new item will get position 5000, that is, the last position of any vector having 5001 items.

Finally, three items are printed: the changed item, the item that was the last before the addition, and the just added item.

So we saw that, differing from arrays, you can create vectors with a length defined at runtime, and you can change their length at runtime, after initialization. Also vectors, like arrays, have generic types, but while the type of every array is defined by two parameters, a type and a length, the type of every vector is defined by a single parameter, the type of its elements. The length of every vector is variable at runtime, so it does not belong to the type, as in Rust all types are defined only at compile time.

Therefore, this program:

```
let mut _x = vec!["a", "b", "c"];
_x = vec!["X", "Y"];
```

is valid, as a vector of strings is assigned to a vector of strings, even if they have different lengths. However, this one:

```
let mut _x = vec!["a", "b", "c"];
_x = vec![15, 16, 17];
```

is illegal, as a vector of numbers cannot be assigned to a vector of strings.

As vectors can do all that arrays can do, what's the need to use arrays? The answer is that arrays are more efficient, so if at compile time you know how many items to put in your collection, you get a faster program by using an array instead of a vector.

Those who know the C++ language should have imagined that Rust arrays are equivalent to C++ `std::array` objects, while Rust vectors are equivalent to C++ `std::vector` objects.

Other Operations on Vectors

The standard library provides many operations regarding vectors. Here are some of them:

```
let mut x = vec!["This", "is", "a", "sentence"];
for i in 0..x.len() { print!("{} ", x[i]); } println!();
x.insert(1, "line");
for i in 0..x.len() { print!("{} ", x[i]); } println!();
x.insert(2, "contains");
for i in 0..x.len() { print!("{} ", x[i]); } println!();
x.remove(3);
for i in 0..x.len() { print!("{} ", x[i]); } println!();
```

```
x.push("about Rust");
for i in 0..x.len() { print!("{} ", x[i]); } println!();
x.pop();
for i in 0..x.len() { print!("{} ", x[i]); } println!();
```

This program will print the following lines:

```
This is a sentence
This line is a sentence
This line contains is a sentence
This line contains a sentence
This line contains a sentence about Rust
This line contains a sentence
```

Let's analyze it. The lines at position 2, 4, 6, 8, 10, and 12 print the current contents of the x vector.

The third line inserts the string "line" at position 1, that is, at the second place, just after the string This.

The fifth line inserts the string "contains" in the next position.

The seventh line removes the item that, after the last two insertions, is in position 3, that is, the string "is", which initially was in position 1.

At this point, we already have the vector we need, but just to show some other features of vectors, we add a string at the end, and next we remove it.

As it is shown, the vector.push(item); statement is equivalent to vector.insert(vector.len(), item);, while the statement vector.pop() is equivalent to vector.remove(vector.len() - 1).

Given that the push and pop functions operate only at the last position, while the insert and remove functions can operate at any position, someone could think that the former two statements are much less used than the latter ones, or even that they are useless. Well, he who thinks so would be wrong, because, using vectors, adding or removing items at the last position is quite typical; it is at least as common as adding or removing items at any other position. This is because inserting or removing items at the end of a vector is faster than adding or removing them at any other position. So, if a specific position is not required, the last position is the preferred one.

Notice that the insert library function operates on three arguments. One is the vector in which the item is to be inserted, and it is written before the name of the function. Another one is the position inside the vector, where the item is to be inserted, and it is passed as the first argument in the parentheses. The third one is the value to insert, passed as the second argument in the parentheses.

If it were written

```
let mut x = vec!["This", "is", "a", "sentence"];
x.insert("line", 1);
```

it would generate the compilation errors `mismatched types` at both arguments of the call to `insert`. This is because it would mean *insert into the vector* x *the number* 1 *at position* "line". This kind of logic error is reported by the compiler, because the `insert` function, like any Rust function, requires that its argument list has exactly the types specified by the function definition. The `insert` function applied to a vector of strings requires two arguments: the first one must be an integer number, and the second argument must be a string. Passing some more arguments, or fewer arguments, or some arguments of different types causes compilation errors.

Ambiguity is possible only with a vector of integer numbers:

```
let mut _x = vec![12, 13, 14, 15];
_x.insert(3, 1);
```

This code is valid, but at a glance it is not obvious if it is inserting the number 1 at position 3 (and it is indeed so), or if it is inserting the number 3 at position 1 (and it is not so). Therefore, only with vectors of integer numbers, the logic error of exchanging the two arguments wouldn't be detected by the compiler. In any other case, the compiler helps to avoid this kind of error.

Empty Arrays and Vectors

We saw that arrays and vectors have generic types, parameterized by the type of their items, and that such type is inferred by the type of the expressions used to initialize such arrays or vectors.

Now, let's assume we want to invoke a function `f`, in this way:

```
f(["help", "debug"], vec![0, 4, 15]);
```

It accepts two arguments: an array of options, where each option is a string; and a vector of options, where each option is an integer number.

However, if we want to tell such function that we don't want to pass any option, we could try to write:

```
f([], vec![]);
```

This is not allowed, though, because the compiler is not able to determine the type of the array nor the type of the vector. It needs some items to make such inference, and here we have no items.

Then how can we declare an empty array or an empty vector?

If we compile

```
let _a = [];
```

we get a compilation error with the message "`type annotations needed for `[_; 0]``" and then "`cannot infer type`".

Instead, if we write

```
let _a = [""; 0];
```

the compilation is successful, and creates an empty array whose type is that of an array of strings. The empty string specified is never used at runtime; it is used only by the compiler to understand that the expression is an array of strings.

Similarly, the code

```
let _a = vec![true; 0];
let _b = vec![false; 0];
```

declares two variables having the same type, and initially also the same value, as the `true` and `false` expressions are used only to specify the type as Boolean.

Therefore, our preceding function can be invoked in this way:

```
f([""; 0], vec![0; 0]);
```

Debug Print

As we saw, the `print` and `println` macros accept only a string as their first argument, but the possible further arguments can be of various types, including integer numbers, floating-point numbers, and Boolean values. However, if you want to print the contents of an array or of a vector, the following code is not allowed:

```
print!("{} {}", [1, 2, 3], vec![4, 5]);
```

This happens because both the array passed as second argument and the vector passed as third argument have no standard display format, and so two error messages are emitted.

When debugging a program, though, it is useful to display the contents of such structures without having to resort to for loops. For this purpose, you can write

```
print!("{:?} {:?}", [1, 2, 3], vec![4, 5]);
```

That will print: [1, 2, 3] [4, 5].

By inserting the characters :? enclosed in the braces of a placeholder, you are telling the print macro (and the println macro) to generate a debug format for the corresponding data. So, whenever you want to print the contents of any variable, if the simple placeholder "{}" does not work, you may hope that the debug placeholder "{:?}" works.

Copying Arrays and Vectors

If you want to copy an entire array or an entire vector, you are not required to write the code that scans its items:

```
let mut a1 = [4, 56, -2];
let a2 = [7, 81, 12500];
println!("{:?} {:?}", a1, a2);
a1 = a2;
println!("{:?} {:?}", a1, a2);
a1[1] = 10;
println!("{:?} {:?}", a1, a2);
```

This will print:

```
[4, 56, -2] [7, 81, 12500]
[7, 81, 12500] [7, 81, 12500]
[7, 10, 12500] [7, 81, 12500]
```

The first printed line shows the contents of the two arrays just after they are initialized.

The second printed line shows the contents of them just after a2 is copied onto a1. Indeed, the a1 array is exactly overwritten by the contents of the a2 array.

The third printed line shows the contents of the arrays just after the second item of a1 is changed. It appears that nothing else is changed.

Using vectors is not so simple, though.

This code will work correctly:

```
let mut a1 = vec![4, 56, -2];
let a2 = vec![7, 81, 12500];
println!("{:?} {:?}", a1, a2);
a1 = a2;
println!("{:?}", a1);
a1[1] = 10;
println!("{:?}", a1);
```

It will print the following lines:

```
[4, 56, -2] [7, 81, 12500]
[7, 81, 12500]
[7, 10, 12500]
```

Here, the previous program has been changed by replacing arrays with vectors, and by avoiding printing the a2 variable in the second and third printing statements.

This is because trying to also print a2 would generate a compilation error. For example, if the last line is replaced by this one:

```
println!("{:?} {:?}", a1, a2);
```

the error message borrow of moved value: `a2` is printed. It means that the a2 variable hasn't been simply *copied*. Actually it has been *moved*, which means *copied and destroyed*. So, differing from arrays, when a vector is assigned to another vector, the original vector exists no more.

CHAPTER 6

Using Primitive Types

In this chapter, you will learn:

- How to write numeric literals in hexadecimal, octal, or binary notation

- How to use the underscore character to make numeric literals easier to read

- How to use the exponential notation to write huge or tiny numbers in a compact form

- Which are the twelve primitive integer numeric types, and the two primitive floating-point numeric types; what are their ranges; and when it is better to use each of them

- How to specify numeric literals of concrete types or of unconstrained types

- How to convert a numeric value to another numeric type

- The other primitive types: Booleans, characters, and empty tuples

- How type inference works

- How to express the types of arrays and vectors

- How to assign a name to a compile-time constant

- How to use the compiler to discover the type of an expression

© Carlo Milanesi 2022
C. Milanesi, *Beginning Rust*, https://doi.org/10.1007/978-1-4842-7208-4_6

Nondecimal Numeric Bases

The way we write numbers every day uses the so-called *decimal notation* or *base-ten notation*. Though, sometimes it is handy to write numbers in a base different from ten:

```
let hexadecimal = 0x10;
let octal = 0o10;
let binary = 0b10;
let mut n = 10;
print!("{} ", n);
n = hexadecimal;
print!("{} ", n);
n = octal;
print!("{} ", n);
n = binary;
print!("{}", n);
```

This will print: 16 10 8 2.

It is so because, if a literal integer number starts with a zero digit followed by an "x" (that is the third letter of "hexadecimal"), that number is expressed in hexadecimal notation; if it starts instead with a zero followed by an "o" (that is the initial of "octal"), it is a number expressed in octal notation; and if it starts with a zero followed by a "b" (that is the initial of "binary"), it is a number expressed in binary notation. In every other case, the number is expressed in decimal notation.

The numbers of this example are expressed in different notations, but they are all of the same type: integer numbers.

The n variable could receive the assignments from the other variables, because they are all of the same type.

Instead, floating-point numbers can be expressed only in decimal notation.

Notice that such representations exist only in source code, as the machine code generated by the Rust compiler always uses a binary notation, both for integer numbers and for floating-point numbers.

For example, the program:

```
print!("{} {}", 0xA, 0b100000000);
```

and the program

```
print!("{} {}", 10, 256);
```

generate exactly the same executable program.

A last point: the letters used as hexadecimal digits may be indifferently uppercase or lowercase. For example, the number 0xAEf5b is equal to the number 0xaeF5B.

However, the letters used to indicate the numeric base must be lowercase. Therefore, the expressions 0X4, 0O4 and 0B4 are illegal.

The Underscore in Numeric Literals

We can write the integer number "one billion," as 1000000000. But are you sure that it contains exactly nine zeros?

The integer number "one billion" comes out to be more readable if you write it as 1_000_000_000. The underscore characters ("_") can be inserted in any literal number, even floating point, and they are ignored by the compiler.

Even the number 3___4_.56_ is a valid number, and it is equal to 34.56. Though usually the underscore characters are used only to group decimal digits or octal digits by three, or hexadecimal or binary digits by four, as in:

```
let hexadecimal = 0x_00FF_F7A3;
let decimal = 1_234_567;
let octal = 0o_777_205_162;
let binary = 0b_0110_1001_1111_0001;
print!("{} {} {} {}", hexadecimal, decimal, octal, binary);
```

This will print: 16775075 1234567 134023794 27121.

The Exponential Notation

Floating-point numbers can reach huge values, both positive and negative, like one billion of billions of billions of billions, and also hugely small values, that is, values very near to zero, like one billionth of a billionth of a billionth of a billionth. If we wrote the literals of such hugely large or small numbers using the notation used so far, we would have to write many zeros, and the resulting numbers would be hard to read, even using underscores.

But you can also write floating-point literal numbers in another way:

```
let one_thousand = 1e3;
let one_million = 1e6;
let thirteen_billions_and_half = 13.5e9;
let twelve_millionths = 12e-6;
print!("{}, {}, {}, {}", one_thousand, one_million,
    thirteen_billions_and_half, twelve_millionths);
```

It will print: 1000, 1000000, 13500000000, 0.000012.

The first line uses a literal meaning "one times ten raised to the third power." To get the usual decimal notation, it is enough to write the number before the "e" and then shift the decimal point *to the right* by as many places as are indicated after the "e", adding zeros if there are not enough digits. In our case, we write "1", then we shift the point by three places, adding as many zeros, and we get the number "1000".

The number before the "e" is named *mantissa*, while the number following it is named *exponent*. They are both signed decimal numbers. The mantissa may have also a decimal point, and it may be followed by a fractional part.

This notation is named *exponential*. The literals written in exponential notation are still floating-point numbers, even if they are written with no decimal point.

The second literal in the example, 1e6, means *one times ten raised to the sixth power*. It is equal to 1,000,000.

The third literal, 13.5e9, means *thirteen point five times ten raised to the ninth power*. There is already one decimal digit beyond which we have to shift the point, and after it we must add eight zeros, to get the value 13500000000. This number also could be written as 1.35e10, meaning *one point thirty-five times ten raised to the tenth power*, or as 135e8 or 13500e6, and in other ways, all generating the same machine code.

Finally, the fourth literal in the code example, 12e-6, means *twelve times ten raised to the sixth negative power*, or, equivalently, *twelve divided by ten raised to the sixth power*. Using a negative exponent of ten is equivalent to writing the mantissa and then shifting the point *to the left* by as many digits as are indicated after the minus sign of the exponent, adding the needed zeros. So, the number 12e-6 is equal to the number 0.000012.

The Various Kinds of Signed Integer Numbers

So far, we said that there are two types of numbers: integer numbers and floating-point numbers.

There are programming languages having only floating-point numbers, without having a specific type for integer numbers; with respect to such languages, having two distinct numeric types is more complicated. But Rust is much more complicated, as it can actually use twelve different integer numeric types and two floating-point numeric types. Having further numeric types can have performance advantages, so that many programming languages have several numeric types.

So far we used integer numbers and floating-numbers, without further specifications, but it is possible to be more precise when defining the internal format of such numbers.

Here an important aspect of Rust appears: efficiency. Actually, Rust has been designed to be extremely efficient.

A simple programming language could use only 32-bit integer numbers. But if we want to store a long sequence of small numbers, say between 0 and 200, and if every value were stored in a 32-bit object, some memory would be wasted, because it is possible to represent any number between 0 and 200 using only 8 bits, which is a quarter of 32 bits.

This is not only for saving RAM space or storage space, but also to optimize speed. That's because the larger our objects are, the more cache space they use, and cache space is strictly limited. If an object cannot be contained in cache, its access will slow down the program. To have a fast program, you should keep in cache as much processed data as possible. To this purpose, objects should be as small as possible. In our example, we shouldn't use more than 8 bits to store our numbers.

On the other hand, 32-bit numbers could be not large enough to represent all the values required by the application. For example, a program could need to store with accuracy a number larger than ten billion. In such a case, a type having more than 32 bits is needed.

Therefore, Rust provides the opportunity to use 8-bit integer numbers, 16-bit integer numbers, 32-bit integer numbers, 64-bit integer numbers, and also 128-bit integer numbers. And in case many of them are needed, like in an array or in a vector, it is advisable to use the smallest data type able to represent all the values required by application logic.

Let's see how we can use these numbers:

```
let a: i8 = 5;
let b: i16 = 5;
let c: i32 = 5;
let d: i64 = 5;
let e: i128 = 5;
print!("{} {} {} {} {}", a, b, c, d, e);
```

The ": i8" clause, inserted in the first statement, and the similar ones in the four following statements, define the *datatype* of the variable that is being declared, and also of the object represented by such variable.

The words i8, i16, i32, i64, and i128 are Rust keywords that identify, respectively, the type *8-bit signed integer number*, the type *16-bit signed integer number*, the type *32-bit signed integer number*, the type *64-bit signed integer number*, and the type *128-bit signed integer number*. The i letter is the initial of "integer."

Such types identify with precision how many bits will be used by the object. For example, the "a" variable will use eight bits, which will be able to represent 256 distinct values; being a *signed* number, such an object will be able to contain values between -128 and +127, extremes included.

The variables "a", "b", "c", "d", and "e" are of five different types, so if we append an assignment statement from one of these variables to another, like b = d;, we will get a compilation error.

We already saw that it is not possible to compute an addition between an integer number and a floating-point number, because they have different types. Similarly, it is not possible to sum two integer numbers having a different number of bits:

```
let a: i8 = 5;
let b: i16 = 5;
print!("{}", a + b);
```

This code generates two compilation error messages for the same error: mismatched types and cannot add `i16` to `i8`.

Maybe someone will wonder why the number of bits of an integer number must be exactly 8, 16, 32, 64, or 128, and not, for example, 19.

This is due to two reasons, both regarding efficiency:

- Every modern processor has instructions for arithmetic and data transfer that apply efficiently only to numbers having a number or bits that is a power of 2, starting from a minimum of 8 bits; that is the minimum addressable chunk of bits. A 19-bit number would be handled anyway by the same machine language instructions that handle 32-bit numbers, and therefore there is no advantage in distinguishing a 19-bit type from 32-bit type.

- Memory management is more efficient when manipulating objects having as size a power of two. Therefore, having objects of different sizes causes less efficient code or the need to allocate additional space to reach a power of two (this operation is named *padding*).

Unsigned Integer Number Types

If we had to define an object containing an integer number that can have values between 0 and 200, which type is best to use for that object? To minimize the space in cache, in RAM, and in storage, and also to minimize the time to access such memory, it should be better to use the smallest type among those that can represent all such values. The i8 type is the smallest, but it can only represent values between -128 and +127, and therefore it's no good. So, with the type encountered so far, we must use i16.

This is not optimal, as only eight bit could represent all the values between 0 and 255. Though, it is required to reinterpret such bits to mean such numbers; it happens that such reinterpretation is already included in the machine language of all modern processors, so it would be a pity (read "inefficient") to not use it.

Therefore, Rust allows the use of five other numeric types:

```
let a: u8 = 5;
let b: u16 = 5;
let c: u32 = 5;
let d: u64 = 5;
let e: u128 = 5;
print!("{} {} {} {} {}", a, b, c, d, e);
```

Here we introduced five other types of integer numbers. The "u" letter, shorthand for *unsigned*, indicates it is an unsigned integer number. The number after the "u" letter indicates how many bits are used by such object; for example, the "a" variable uses eight bits, using which it can represent 256 distinct values; therefore, being an unsigned number, such values will be the integer numbers from 0 to 255, extremes included.

But there is at least one other reason to prefer unsigned numbers to signed numbers. If we want to check if a *signed* integer number x is between zero included and a positive value n excluded, we should write the Boolean expression 0 <= x && x < n. But if x is an *unsigned* number, such a check can be done simply using the expression x < n.

Notice that the variables "a" "b", "c", "d", and "e" have five different types, which are distinct among them, and also from the corresponding signed types.

Target-Dependent Integer-Number Types

So far we have seen ten different types to represent integer numbers, but Rust still has other integer numeric types.

When you access an item in an array or in a vector, which type should have the index?

You could think that, if you have a small array you could use an i8 value or a u8 value, while if you have a somewhat larger array it would be required to use instead an i16 value or a u16 value.

It isn't so. It turns out that the most efficient type to use as index of an array or of a vector is as follows:

- On 16-bit computers, it is an unsigned 16-bit integer.

- On 32-bit computers, it is an unsigned 32-bit integer.

- On 64-bit computers, it is an unsigned 64-bit integer.

In other words, the index of an array or vector should be unsigned, and it should have the same size of a memory address.

At present, Rust supports one 16-bit system, several 32-bit systems, and many 64-bit systems. So, which type should we use to write some source code that should be optimal on all such systems?

Notice that it is not relevant on which system the compiler runs, but on which system the program generated by the compiler will run. Actually, by a so-called *cross-compilation*, a compiler can generate machine code for a system having a different architecture from the one where the compiler is run. The system for which machine code is generated is named *target*. So, there is a need to specify an integer numeric type having a size dependent on the target, which is a 16-bit integer if the target is a 16-bit system, a 32-bit integer if the target is a 32-bit system, and a 64-bit integer if the target is a 64-bit system.

To such purpose, Rust contains the isize type and the usize type:

```
let arr = [11, 22, 33];
let i: usize = 2;
print!("{}", arr[i]);
```

This will print: 33.

In the word usize, the "u" letter indicates it is an unsigned integer, and the size word indicates it is a type thought to measure the length of some (possibly very large) object.

The usize type is implemented by the compiler as the u16 type, if it is generating machine code for a 16-bit system; it is implemented as the u32 type, if it is generating machine code for a 32-bit system; and it is implemented as the u64 type, if it is generating machine code for a 64-bit system.

In general, the usize type is useful every time there is a need for an unsigned integer, having the same size of a memory address (aka pointer).

In particular, if you have to index an array:

```
let arr = [11, 22, 33];
let i: usize = 2;
print!("{}", arr[i]);
let i: isize = 2;
print!("{}", arr[i]);
let i: u32 = 2;
print!("{}", arr[i]);
let i: u64 = 2;
print!("{}", arr[i]);
```

This code will generate three compilation errors, one for each call to `print`, except the first one. The error messages are:

```
the type `[{integer}]` cannot be indexed by `isize`
the type `[{integer}]` cannot be indexed by `u32`
the type `[{integer}]` cannot be indexed by `u64`
```

Actually, only the `usize` type is allowed as an index of an array.

Similar error messages are printed if you use a vector instead of an array.

In such a way, Rust allows us to access arrays and vectors only in the most efficient way.

Notice that it is not allowed even to use an index of `u16` type on a 16-bit system, nor to use an index of `u32` type on a 32-bit system, nor to use an index of `u64` type on a 64-bit system. This guarantees source code portability.

For symmetry, there is also the `isize` type, which is a *signed* integer, having the same size of a memory address in the target system.

Type Inference

In the previous chapters we were declaring variables without specifying their type, and we were talking about the types "integer number," "floating-point number," and so on.

In this chapter we started to add to the variable declarations the data type annotations.

But if no type is specified, do variables still have a specific type, or are they of a generic type?

```
let a = [0];
let i = 0;
print!("{}", a[i]);
```

This program is valid. How come? Didn't we say that to index an array, only `usize` expressions are valid?

In fact, each variable and each expression always has a well-defined type, but it is not always required to specify *explicitly* such a type. In many cases the compiler is able to deduce it, or, as it is usually said, to *infer* it, from the way in which the variable or expression in question is used.

For instance, in the preceding example, after having assigned to "i" the integer value 0, the compiler infers that the type of "i" must be that of an integer number, but it has not yet determined exactly which one, among the twelve integer types available in Rust. We say that the type of such variable is that of a *generic*, or better, *unconstrained* integer number.

However, when the compiler realizes that such variable is used to index an array, an operation allowed only to the usize type, the compiler assigns the usize type to the "i" variable, as it is the only allowed type in that statement.

In this program,

```
let i = 0;
let _j: u16 = i;
```

the compiler first determines that "i" is of type "unconstrained integer number." Then it determines that "_j" is of type u16, as such type is explicitly annotated. Then, as "i" is used to initialize "_j", an operation allowed only to expressions of type u16, it determines that "i" is of such type.

But the compilation of this program

```
let i = 0;
let _j: u16 = i;
let _k: i16 = i;
```

generates an error at the third line, with the message expected `i16`, found `u16`.

Indeed, the compiler, following the preceding reasoning, has determined at the second line that "i" must be of type u16, but at the third line "i" is used to initialize a variable of type i16.

Conversely, this program is valid:

```
let i = 0;
let _j: u16 = i;
let _k = i;
```

In this case, it is the variable "_k" that is of type u16.

Notice that such reasoning is always performed at compile time. In the final stage of every successful compilation, every variable has one concrete, constrained type.

If the compiler cannot infer the type of a 0 variable, it generates the compilation error: type annotations needed.

Instead, if the compiler succeeds in inferring only that the type is an integer one but it cannot constrain it to a specific integer type, then, as *default* integer type, it takes the type i32.

For example, if you try to compile the following statement:

```
let _n = 8_000_000_000;
```

You get the error message: `literal out of range for `i32``.

This means that first the compiler has inferred i32 to be the type of the expression used to initialize the _n variable, and then it has noted that such literal has a value larger than the maximum value for the i32 type.

The Type Inference Algorithm

We saw that the compiler always tries to determine a concrete type for each variable and for each expression. For what we saw so far, the algorithm used is the following one:

If a type is explicitly specified, the type of the variable must be the specified one.

If the type of a variable or an expression hasn't yet been determined at all, and such variable or expression is used in an expression or in a declaration that can be valid only with a specific type, then that type is determined in this way for such variable or expression. Such determination may be of a constrained kind, or it may be of an unconstrained kind. A constrained type is a specific type, like i8 or u64, while an unconstrained type is a category of types, like {integer}. The word *constrained* is used to mean that the compiler finds that the Rust syntax allows only one specific type in that context. The word *unconstrained* means that the compiler finds that a family of types, like all the positive integers or all the integers, is allowed in that context.

If, at the end of the parsing, the compiler has determined only that a variable is of an unconstrained integer numeric type, that type is defined to be i32. Instead, if the type is completely undetermined, a compilation error is generated.

Floating-Point Numeric Types

Regarding the floating-point numeric types, the situation is similar to that of integer numbers, but much simpler: at present in Rust there are only two floating-point types.

```
let a: f64 = 4.6;
let b: f32 = 3.91;
print!("{} {}", a, b);
```

This program will print: 4.6 3.91.

The f64 type is that of 64-bit floating-point numbers, while the f32 type is that of 32-bit floating-point numbers. The "f" letter is shorthand for *floating-point*. Such types correspond exactly and respectively to the double and float types of the C language.

So far, Rust has no other numeric types, but if a 128-bit floating-point type were added, probably its name would be f128.

What we said about integer types holds also for these types. For example:

```
let a = 4.6;
let mut _b: f32 = 3.91e5;
_b = a;
```

This program is valid. The compiler, parsing the first line, determines that the variable "a" has an *unconstrained* floating-point numeric type. Then, it determines that the type of the variable "_b" is f32, because it is specified by a type annotation. Then, parsing the third line, it determines that the variable "a" is of type f32, because this is the only type allowed to assign a value to a variable of f32 type.

The default floating-point type is the 64-bit one. Therefore, if there wasn't the last line in this program, the "a" variable would have been of f64 type.

For floating-point numbers, the criteria to choose between 32-bit and 64-bit numbers are similar to those for integer numbers, but somewhat fuzzier. It is still true that 32-bit numbers occupy exactly half as much memory and cache as 64-bit numbers. And it is still true that the maximum value that can be represented by a 64-bit number is larger than the maximum value that can be represented by a 32-bit number. However, the latter is so large that it is rarely exceeded.

Instead, a more important fact is that 64-bit numbers have much more digits in mantissa, and that makes such numbers much more precise. Indeed, 32-bit numbers have a 24-bit mantissa, while 64-bit numbers have a 53-bit mantissa.

To give you an idea, 32-bit numbers can represent exactly all the integer numbers only up to around 16 million, while 64-bit numbers can represent exactly all the integer numbers up to around 9 million billions. Put in other words, each value of f32 type, expressed in decimal notation, has almost 7 significant digits, while every f64 has almost 16 significant digits.

Explicit Conversions

We have said several times that Rust performs a very strict checking of types: every time that the compiler expects an expression of a certain type, it generates an error if it finds an expression of another type, even if similar; and in every arithmetic expression, the compiler expects that its operands are of the same type.

These rules would seem likely to forbid any calculation involving objects of different types; but it isn't so:

```
let a: i16 = 12;
let b: u32 = 4;
let c: f32 = 3.7;
print!("{}", a as i8 + b as i8 + c as i8);
```

This will print: 19.

The variables "a", "b", and "c" are of three different types. The last one is not even an integer number. However, by using the "as" operator, followed by the name of a type, you can do many conversions, including the three just shown.

All of the three objects of the example are converted into objects of type i8, so such resulting objects can be summed up.

Notice that if the destination type is less *expressive* than the original type, you may lose information. For example, when you convert the fractional value 3.7 into the integer type i8, the fractional part is discarded, and 3 is obtained.

The following code generates three compilation errors:

```
let a = 500 as i8;
let b = 100_000 as u16;
let c = 10_000_000_000 as u32;
print!("{} {} {}", a, b, c);
```

The first one has the message: `literal out of range for `i8``. It happens because the value 500 is too large for the type i8.

Similar messages are emitted for the second and third lines.

But if you insert at the beginning of the program the following line:

```
#[allow(overflowing_literals)]
```

you can compile the program, which will print some possibly surprising numbers: `-12 34464 1410065408`.

The inserted attribute instructs the compiler to allow the use of literals that surely will cause arithmetic overflow at runtime.

The resulting values are understandable only when thinking about the binary code that is used to represent the integer numbers.

If we take the binary representation of the value 500, we extract its least significant 8 bits, and then we interpret such an 8-bit sequence as an "i8" object, when we print that object in decimal notation, we get -12.

Similarly, the least significant 16 bits of the binary representation of one hundred thousand, interpreted as an unsigned integer, are printed in decimal notation as 34464; and the least significant 32 bits of the binary representation of ten billions, interpreted as an unsigned number, are printed in decimal notation as 1410065408.

Therefore the "as" operator, if applied to an integer number object, extracts from that object enough least significant bits to represent the specified type, and it generates such value as the result of the expression.

Type Suffixes of Numeric Literals

So far, we used two kinds of numeric literals: the integer ones, like -150; and the floating-point ones, like 6.022e23. The former is of type *unconstrained integer number*, and the latter of type *unconstrained floating-point number*.

If you want to constrain a number, there are several ways:

```
let _a: i16 = -150;
let _b = -150 as i16;
let _c = -150 + _b - _b;
let _d = -150i16;
```

All these four variables are of type i16, and they have the same value.

The first one has a type annotation in the variable declaration. In the second line, the unconstrained integer numeric expression has been converted into a specific type. In the third line, the expression contains the subexpressions "_b" of a specific type, so the whole expression gets that type. At last, in the fourth line a new notation is used.

If a type is specified after an integer numeric literal, the literal gets such type, as if an "as" keyword were interposed. Notice that between the literal and the type, no blank is allowed. If you like, you can add some underscores, like in -150_i16 or 5__u32.

Similarly, you can add a type-specification suffix also to floating-point literals: 6.022e23f64 is a 64-bit floating-point number, while -4f32 and 0_f32 are 32-bit floating-point numbers. Notice that the decimal point is not needed if there is no fractional digit.

All the Numeric Types

In summary, here is an example that uses all the Rust numeric types:

```
let _: i8 = 127;
let _: i16 = 32_767;
let _: i32 = 2_147_483_647;
let _: i64 = 9_223_372_036_854_775_807;
let _: i128 = 170_141_183_460_469_231_731_687_303_715_884_105_727;
let _: isize = 100;
let _: u8 = 255;
let _: u16 = 65_535;
let _: u32 = 4_294_967_295;
let _: u64 = 18_446_744_073_709_551_615;
let _: u128 = 340_282_366_920_938_463_463_374_607_431_768_211_455;
let _: usize = 100;
let _: f32 = 1e38;
let _: f64 = 1e308;
```

All of them are initialized to the maximum value of their type, except for isize and usize, whose maximum value depends on the processor architecture; and except for f32 and f64, whose mantissa cannot be exactly represented in decimal notation. And here is the list of all Rust built-in integer numeric types.

Type	Occupied Bytes	Minimum Value	Maximum Value
I8	1	−128	+127
i16	2	−32,768	+32,767
i32	4	-2^{31}	$+2^{31} - 1$
i64	8	-2^{63}	$+2^{63} - 1$
i128	16	-2^{127}	$+2^{127} - 1$
isize	2 or 4 or 8	on a 16-bit target: -2^{15}; on a 32-bit target: -2^{31}; on a 64-bit target: -2^{63}	on a 16-bit target: $-2^{15} - 1$; on a 32-bit target: $-2^{31} - 1$; on a 64-bit target: $+2^{63} - 1$
u8	1	0	+255
u16	2	0	+65,535
u32	4	0	$+2^{32} - 1$
u64	8	0	$+2^{64} - 1$
u128	16	0	$+2^{128} - 1$
usize	2 or 4 or 8	0	on a 16-bit target: $+2^{16} - 1$; on a 32-bit target: $+2^{32} - 1$; on a 64-bit target: $+2^{64} - 1$

Instead, there are just two floating-point numeric types:

- f32, having 32 bits, is equivalent to the float type of the C language.

- f64, having 64 bits, is equivalent to the double type of the C language.

Booleans and Characters

In addition to numeric types, Rust defines some other primitive built-in types:

```
let a: bool = true; print!("[{}]", a);
let b: char = 'a'; print!("[{}]", b);
```

This will print: [true][a].

The bool type, which we saw already, is equivalent to the type of C++ language having the same name. It admits only the two values: false and true. It is used mainly for the condition in the if statements and in the while statements.

The char type, which actually we haven't seen yet, *looks like the type of C language having the same name, but in fact it differs a lot from it.* To start with, a C language char typically occupies only one byte, while an isolated Rust char occupies four bytes. This is due to the fact that Rust chars are Unicode characters, and the Unicode standard defines more than one million possible values.

Literal characters are enclosed in single quotes, and they can be also non-ASCII characters. For example, this code

```
let e_grave = 'è';
let japanese_character = 'さ';
println!("{} {}", e_grave, japanese_character);
```

in a terminal supporting Unicode, will print: è さ.

Notice that, differing from C language, neither bool nor char are in any way considered numbers. So, both of the following statements are illegal:

```
let _a = 'a' + 'b';
let _b = false + true;
```

For the first statement, the generated error is: cannot add `char` to `char`. For the other, the generated error is: cannot add `bool` to `bool`.

However, both types may be converted to numbers:

```
print!("{} {} {} {} {}", true as u8, false as u8,
    'A' as u32, 'à' as u32, '€' as u32);
```

This will print: 1 0 65 224 8364.

In this way, we just discovered that true is represented by the number 1, false by the number 0, the "A" character by the number 65, the grave "a" by the number 224, and the euro symbol by the number 8364.

If you want to convert numbers into Booleans or into characters, you can use these features:

```
let truthy = 1;
let falsy = 0;
```

```
print!("{} {} {} {}", truthy != 0, falsy != 0,
    65 as char, 224 as char);
```

This will print: true false A à.

But you cannot use the "as bool" clause with a number, because not every numeric value corresponds to a Boolean; in fact only zero and one have this property, so in general such a conversion would not be well defined.

So, if the zero value is meant to represent falsity for a number, to convert such number into a Boolean, which is to see if it corresponds to truth, it is enough to check if it is different from zero.

The situation of characters is similar. Each character is represented by a 32-bit number, so it may be converted to it. But not every 32-bit number represents a character, so some (actually, most) 32-bit numbers wouldn't be convertible into characters. Therefore, the expression "8364 as char" is illegal.

To convert any number into a character, you need to use the char::from_u32 standard library function, not described here.

However, for each number between 0 and 255, there is a Unicode character corresponding to it, so it is allowed to convert any number of u8 type into a character. Actually, that has been done, in the preceding example, for the numbers 65 and 224.

It may be interesting, for those who don't yet know Unicode, to see all the printable characters corresponding to the first 256 numbers. The characters having code from 0 to 31 and from 127 to 159 are control characters, which cannot be properly printed. Here is the code that prints the other ones:

```
for n in 32..127 {
    println!("{}: [{}]", n, n as u8 as char);
}
for n in 160..256 {
    println!("{}: [{}]", n, n as u8 as char);
}
```

This will print a line for each of the Unicode characters having code from 32 to 126 and from 150 to 255, as the ranges exclude the ending number.

Notice that n must be converted to u8 type before being able to convert it into a char.

The Empty Tuple

There is another primitive, weird type, whose name in Rust is "()", which is just a pair of parentheses. Such type has only one value, which is written in the same way as its type, which is "()". This type somewhat corresponds to the "void" type of the C language, or to the "undefined" type of JavaScript, as it represents the absence of type information. It is named *empty tuple*.

This type appears in several cases, like the following ones:

```
let a: () = ();
let b = { 12; 87; 283 };
let c = { 12; 87; 283; };
let d = {};
let e = if false { };
let f = while false { };
print!("{:?} {} {:?} {:?} {:?} {:?}",
    a, b, c, d, e, f);
```

This code will print: () 283 () () () ().

The first line declares a variable of empty tuple type, and initializes it using the only possible value. In the last line, the print macro cannot match such type with the placeholder "{}", so the debug placeholder "{:?}" must be used, as explained in the "Debug Print" section of Chapter 5.

The second line, let b = { 12; 87; 283 };, declares a variable and initializes it with the value of a block. From here, some new concepts appear.

The first concept is that a simple number like 12 or 87 can be used in place of any statement, by putting a semicolon character after it, because any expression can be used in place of a statement. Of course such a statement does nothing, so it will generate no machine code.

The second concept is that the value of a block is defined to be the value of its last expression, if there is such an expression; so, in the case of the second line, the value of the block is the integer number 283, and such value is used to initialize the "b" variable, which therefore will be of i32 type.

The third line, let c = { 12; 87; 283; };, shows the case where the contents of a block ends with the statement terminator, the semicolon character. In such case, the value of the block is the empty tuple, and that value is used to initialize the "c" variable, which therefore will be of empty tuple type.

The fourth line, `let d = {};`, declares the "d" variable, and it initializes it with the value of an empty block. Also, empty blocks have empty tuples as their values.

In the fifth line, `let e = if false { };`, there is a conditional expression without the "`else`" branch. When the "`else`" branch is missing, the "`else { }`" clause is implied. Therefore, the statement is meant to be "`let e = if false { } else { }`". Such a conditional expression is valid, as both branches have the same type.

The sixth line, `let f = while false { };`, shows that the `while`-statement also has the value of an empty tuple. Actually both the `while` statement block and the `while` statement itself must always have an empty tuple as value, and therefore it makes little sense to use the `while` construct as an expression. This also holds for `loop` statements and `for` statements.

Array and Vector Types

When presenting arrays and vectors, we said that if we change the type of the contained items, we implicitly also change the type of the containers, both arrays and vectors; and if we change the number of the contained items, we implicitly also change the type of arrays but not the type of vectors.

If you want to make explicit the type of arrays or vectors, you should write:

```
let _array1: [char; 3] = ['x', 'y', 'z'];
let _array2: [f32; 200] = [0f32; 200];
let _vector1: Vec<char> = vec!['x', 'y', 'z'];
let _vector2: Vec<i32> = vec![0; 5000];
```

As it is shown, the expression that represents the type of an array contains both the type of the items and their number, separated by a semicolon and enclosed in square brackets.

The type of a vector is written as the word `Vec` (with an uppercase initial), followed by the type of the contained items, enclosed in angular brackets.

Constants

The following program is illegal:

```
let n = 20;
let _ = [0; n];
```

It generates the error `attempt to use a non-constant value in a constant`, because arrays must be of a length known at compile time. Even if "n" is immutable, and so, in a sense, it is constant, its initial value could be determined at runtime, therefore we are not allowed to use it to specify the size of an array.

But the following program is valid:

```
const N: usize = 20;
let _ = [0; N];
```

The "`const`" keyword allows us to declare an identifier having a value defined at compile time, and of course not changeable at runtime. In its declaration, it is required to specify its type.

Rust constants correspond to C language macros with no arguments. The C code that corresponds to the previous Rust code is this:

```
#define N 20
int _[N];
```

A Rust constant can be considered a name that at compile time is associated to a value, not to an object. The compiler replaces such value in every place in the program where the constant's name is used.

Discovering the Type of an Expression

You will often come across an expression, and wonder what the type of that expression is.

This could be answered by an interpreter, an integrated development environment, or the written documentation, but there is a trick to answering such kind of questions using only the compiler.

Say we want to know the type of the expression `4u32 / 3u32`, which in some languages is a floating-point number.

We just add a statement that tries to use that expression to initialize an empty tuple variable. If the program compiles with no errors, that means that the value of our expression is an empty tuple. But in our case we have:

```
let _: () = 4u32 / 3u32;
```

The compilation of this program generates the error `mismatched types`, and the detail of the error message explains expected `()`, found `u32`. From this explanation, we learn that our expression is of `u32` type.

Sometimes, the error message is vaguer:

```
let _: () = 4 / 3;
```

For this program the error explanation is expected `()`, found `integer`. That word `integer` does not indicate a concrete type; it indicates a still unconstrained type, which the compiler has determined to be an integral type but not yet which of the several existing integral types.

CHAPTER 7

Enumerations and Matching

In this chapter, you will learn:

- How enums help in defining variables that can take on values only from a finite set of cases

- How enums can be used to implement discriminated union types

- How to use the match pattern-matching construct to handle enums

- How to use the match construct to handle other data types, like integer numbers, strings, and single characters

- How to define enumerations containing fields of data and how to match them with literals

- How to define variables in patterns of match statements

- How to use match expressions

- How to use Boolean guards to generalize the pattern-matching of the match construct

- How to use the if-let and the while-let constructs

Enumerations

Instead of writing the following code:

```
const EUROPE: u8 = 0;
const ASIA: u8 = 1;
const AFRICA: u8 = 2;
```

© Carlo Milanesi 2022
C. Milanesi, *Beginning Rust*, https://doi.org/10.1007/978-1-4842-7208-4_7

```
const AMERICA: u8 = 3;
const OCEANIA: u8 = 4;
let continent = ASIA;
if continent == EUROPE { print!("E"); }
else if continent == ASIA { print!("As"); }
else if continent == AFRICA { print!("Af"); }
else if continent == AMERICA { print!("Am"); }
else if continent == OCEANIA { print!("O"); }
```

It is better to write the following equivalent code:

```
#[allow(dead_code)]
enum Continent {
    Europe,
    Asia,
    Africa,
    America,
    Oceania,
}
let contin = Continent::Asia;
match contin {
    Continent::Europe => print!("E"),
    Continent::Asia => print!("As"),
    Continent::Africa => print!("Af"),
    Continent::America => print!("Am"),
    Continent::Oceania => print!("O"),
}
```

They both print: As.

The "**enum**" keyword introduces the new Continent type, specified just after it. Such a type is called *enumerative*, because it lists a set of items, internally associating a unique number to each item. In the example, the allowed values for the type Continent are Europe, Asia, Africa, America, and Oceania, which respectively are represented internally by the values 0u8, 1u8, 2u8, 3u8, and 4u8. Such allowed values are named *variants*.

In the simplest cases, like the one just shown, this type is similar to the construct of the C language having the same name.

After having defined an enumerative type, it is possible to create objects of such type, named *enumerations*, or *enums* for short. In the example, the `contin` enum variable, of `Continent` type, has been defined.

The first line of the program is an attribute. We have seen attributes in the section "Rust Attributes" in Chapter 5. Its purpose is the following one.

The compiler includes a useful check: every variant must be constructed at least one time in an application, otherwise it is useless, and the compiler will emit a warning about it. In the preceding program only the Asia variant is constructed, so the compiler would emit four warnings about the unused variants. To avoid them, the attribute `#[allow(dead_code)]` has been added. Actually, the creation of an enum variant is some kind of code. The compiler reckons that this code will never be run, so it is *dead code*. We are warned of the existence of such dead code.

Notice that the use of a variant must be qualified by the name of its type, like in `Continent::Asia`.

The following code

```
enum T {A, B, C, D}
let n: i32 = T::D;
let e: T = 1;
```

generates a compilation error at the second line, and another one at the third line, both of the kind `mismatched types`. The first error is described as `expected `i32`, found enum `T``, and the second error is described as `expected enum `T`, found integer`. Therefore, enums cannot implicitly be converted to numbers, and numbers cannot implicitly be converted to enums.

The `match` Construct

In the example introducing the `enum` construct, the just created enum is used by a new kind of statement, beginning with the "`match`" keyword.

The `match` statement is the basic Rust tool to use enumerations, similarly to the `switch` statement in C language, even if they differ about many aspects.

In the first place, notice that the expression following the `match` keyword doesn't have to be enclosed in parentheses.

Then, the various cases, also called *arms*, are made of a pattern, followed by the symbol "`=>`" (named *fat arrow*), followed by an expression. Such arms are separated by commas.

Both in the declaration of the enumerative type, and in the `match` statement, after the last item, it is optional to put another comma. That is, you can write a comma after the last variant of an enum declaration, or you can omit it; and you can write a comma after the last arm of a `match` statement, or you can omit it. Usually, if you put each item in a different line, the comma is written, so that every line containing items ends with a comma. However, the comma is usually omitted just before a closed brace, like in `enum CardinalPoint { North, South, West, East };`.

The behavior of our `match` statement is as follows.

First, the statement following `match` is evaluated, thereby obtaining a value, which in our example is `Continent::Asia`. Then, that value is compared with each one of the (five) patterns, in the order that they appear written. As soon as a pattern matches, the right side of its arm is evaluated and the statement is ended.

Notice that the right side of every arm must be a single expression. So far, we always used `print!` as if it were a statement, but actually it is an expression.

In fact, **any valid expression becomes a valid statement, if you add a semicolon character after it**. For example, consider this:

```
let a = 7.2;
12;
true;
4 > 7;
5.7 + 5. * a;
```

This code is valid, although, of course, it does nothing. Actually, for the last two statements, these warnings are generated: `unused comparison that must be used`, and `unused arithmetic operation that must be used`. This happens because the compiler thinks that such senseless expressions probably are programming errors. To avoid these warnings, write this code:

```
let a = 7.2;
12;
true;
let _ = 4 > 7;
let _ = 5.7 + 5. * a;
```

Given that an invocation of the `print!` macro is a valid expression, when we added a ";" character after it, we transformed it into a statement.

However, notice that there are statements that aren't valid expressions. For example, "fn empty() {}" is a statement that isn't a valid expression. If for an arm we wrote:

```
Continent::Africa => fn aaa() {},
```

we would have gotten the error message: expected expression, found keyword `fn`, because at the right of the fat arrow, there isn't a valid expression.

And what can you do if, in an arm, you wish to execute a statement that isn't also an expression, or several expressions? In such cases you can use a block:

```
#[allow(dead_code)]
enum Continent {
    Europe,
    Asia,
    Africa,
    America,
    Oceania,
}
let mut contin = Continent::Asia;
match contin {
    Continent::Europe => {
        contin = Continent::Asia;
        print!("E");
    },
    Continent::Asia => { let a = 7; print!("{}", a); }
    Continent::Africa => print!("Af"),
    Continent::America => print!("Am"),
    Continent::Oceania => print!("O"),
}
```

This will print: 7.

Here contin has been declared as mutable, and then, in case its value was Europe, it would be changed to Asia and the letter E would be printed. But in case its value was Asia, another variable would be declared, initialized, printed, and then destroyed.

Such two arms have a block as their right side, and, because any block is an expression, this syntax is valid.

Relational Operators and Enums

Enums are not comparable using the "==" operator. Actually, the following program is illegal:

```
enum CardinalPoint { North, South, West, East }
let direction = CardinalPoint::South;
if direction == CardinalPoint::North { }
```

For the last statement the compiler generates the message "`binary operation `==` cannot be applied to type `CardinalPoint``". Consequently, to check the value of an enum, you are required to use a `match` statement.

Enums are important, as they are used in many places in the standard library and also in other Rust libraries. And the `match` construct is important, because it is required to use enums, even if often it is encapsulated in other constructs.

With enums, not only the "==" operator is forbidden, but also the other relational operators: "!=", "<", "<=", ">", and ">=". Therefore, the following code will also generate a compilation error:

```
enum CardinalPoint { North, South, West, East }
if CardinalPoint::South < CardinalPoint::North { }
```

Handling All the Cases

If you try to compile the following program:

```
#[allow(dead_code)]
enum CardinalPoint { North, South, West, East }
let direction = CardinalPoint::South;
match direction {
    CardinalPoint::North => print!("NORTH"),
    CardinalPoint::South => print!("SOUTH"),
}
```

you will get the error: `non-exhaustive patterns: `West` and `East` not covered`. The compiler complains that among the allowed values for the expression `direction`, only two of them were considered, and the cases in which the expression's value would be `West` or `East` weren't considered. This happens because Rust requires that the `match` statement explicitly handles every possible case.

However, the following program is valid, as it considers all the possible values of the argument of match:

```
#[allow(dead_code)]
enum CardinalPoint { North, South, West, East }
let direction = CardinalPoint::South;
match direction {
    CardinalPoint::North => print!("NORTH"),
    CardinalPoint::South => print!("SOUTH"),
    CardinalPoint::East => {},
    CardinalPoint::West => {},
}
```

However, here the last two variants (East and West) do nothing, and it is annoying to list them anyway. To avoid having to list all the variants that do nothing, it is possible to use an underscore sign in the following way:

```
#[allow(dead_code)]
enum CardinalPoint { North, South, West, East }
let direction = CardinalPoint::South;
match direction {
    CardinalPoint::North => print!("NORTH"),
    CardinalPoint::South => print!("SOUTH"),
    _ => {},
}
```

The underscore sign always matches with any value, so it avoids the compilation error, because in this way all cases have been handled. Of course, such a "catch-all" case must be the last one, to avoid catching cases that should be handled differently:

```
#[allow(dead_code)]
enum CardinalPoint { North, South, West, East }
let direction = CardinalPoint::South;
match direction {
    CardinalPoint::North => print!("NORTH"),
    _ => {},
    CardinalPoint::South => print!("SOUTH"),
}
```

This program does not print anything, because the matching `CardinalPoint::South` case is never reached, but the compiler notices that the last case can never be reached, and it emits the warning: `unreachable pattern`.

The "_" pattern corresponds to the "`default`" case of the C language.

Using `match` with Numbers

The `match` construct, in addition to being needed with enums, is also usable and useful with other data types:

```
match "value" {
    "val" => print!("value "),
    _ => print!("other "),
}
match 3 {
    3 => print!("three "),
    4 => print!("four "),
    5 => print!("five "),
    _ => print!("other "),
}
match '.' {
    ':' => print!("colon "),
    '.' => print!("point "),
    _ => print!("other "),
}
```

This will print: `other three point`.

The first `match` statement has a string as its argument, so it expects strings as left sides of its arms. In particular, no arm matches exactly, so the default case is taken.

The second `match` statement has an integer number as its argument, so it expects integer numbers as left sides of its arms. In particular, the pattern of the first arm matches, so it is taken.

The third `match` statement has a character as its argument, so it expects single characters as left sides of its arms. In particular, the pattern of the second arm matches, so it is taken.

Also for `match` statements with arguments that aren't enums, it is required that all possible cases are handled. However, except for enums and Booleans, it is not feasible to specify all single cases; therefore, it is required to use the underscore "catch-all" case.

Enumerations with Data

Rust enumerations aren't always as simple as the one seen previously. Here is a more complex example:

```
#[allow(dead_code)]
enum Result {
    Success(u8),
    Failure(u16, char),
    Uncertainty,
}
// let outcome = Result::Success(1);
let outcome = Result::Failure(20, 'X');
match outcome {
    Result::Success(0) => print!("Result: 0"),
    Result::Success(1) => print!("Result: 1"),
    Result::Success(_) => print!("Result: other"),
    Result::Failure(10, 'X') => print!("Error: 10 X"),
    Result::Failure(10, _) => print!("Error: 10"),
    Result::Failure(_, 'X') => print!("Error: X"),
    Result::Failure(_, _) => print!("Error: other"),
    Result::Uncertainty => {},
}
```

It will print: `Error X`.

Instead, if the commented out line that declares the `outcome` variable is reactivated, and the next line is commented out, the program will print: `Result: 1`.

In this code, in the definition of the `Result` enumerative type, the first variant specifies a data type enclosed in parentheses (`u8`); the second variant specifies two data types in parentheses (`u16` and `char`); and the third variant does not specifies any data type (and does not use parentheses).

The effect of such a declaration is that every object having such a Result type, like the variable outcome in the example, can have the following values:

- Result::Success, and in addition it also contains a field of type u8;

- Result::Failure, in addition it also contains a field of type u16 and a field of type char;

- Result::Uncertainty, and it contains no further data.

There is no other possibility.

Therefore, **with respect to the C language, Rust enumerative types combine the enum feature with the union feature**.

You can see that to assign a value to the outcome variable, the name of the variant (Result::Success or Result::Failure) is specified, and such name is followed by some comma-separated values, enclosed in parentheses, like in a function call ((1) in the first case and (20, 'X') in the second case).

When you assign a value to an enumeration of such a type, you must specify in parentheses the arguments having the same types specified in the fields of that variant. In the example, in the Success case, an integer is passed; in the Failure case, an integer and a character are passed; and in the Uncertainty case, no parameter is passed. If you pass arguments of other types or in different numbers, you'll get a compilation error.

The match statement extends the concept of pattern matching to the variant fields. You can see that in the example code there are seven different patterns. The first three of them require a Result::Success variant; the next three require a Result::Failure variant; and the last one requires a Result::Uncertainty variant.

These patterns contain some literals in parentheses. For example, the first arm contains the "0" literal. In case the value to match is a Success variant containing the "0" value, the pattern matches, so this arm is taken and the string "Result: 0" is printed. In case the value is different, this arm is skipped.

The second arm matches only with the value Success(1). If the value to match is still different, even this arm is skipped. The third arm contains an underscore, which is a catch-all pattern, meaning that any Success pattern will match.

In case the value to match is a Failure variant, the fourth arm checks whether the values of the fields to match are 10 and 'X'. In case both fields match, the arm is taken.

Otherwise, the fifth arm is checked. It checks that the value of the first field is 10, and it allows any value for the second field. If the first field is not 10, this arm is skipped.

The sixth arm allows any value for the first field, but requires that the value of the second field is `'X'`.

The seventh arm allows any value for both fields of the `Failure` variant.

The last arm is taken only for an `Uncertainty` variant.

So, in every pattern there must be as many arguments as the fields defined in their respective declaration. In addition, the types of the literals must be the same of the respective fields. Here too, doing it differently causes compilation errors.

In addition, a compilation error is emitted if a possible case is not considered by any pattern.

The equivalent program in C language is this:

```c
#include <stdio.h>
int main() {
    enum eResult {
        Success,
        Failure,
        Uncertainty
    };
    struct sResult {
        enum eResult r;
        union {
            char value;
            struct {
                unsigned short error_code;
                char module;
            } s;
        } u;
    } outcome;
    /*
    outcome.r = Success;
    outcome.u.value = 1;
    */
    outcome.r = Failure;
    outcome.u.s.error_code = 20;
    outcome.u.s.module = 'X';
```

```c
switch (outcome.r) {
    case Success:
        switch (outcome.u.value) {
            case 0:
                printf("Result: 0");
                break;
            case 1:
                printf("Result: 1");
                break;
            default:
                printf("Result: other");
                break;
        }
        break;
    case Failure:
        switch (outcome.u.s.error_code) {
            case 10:
                switch (outcome.u.s.module) {
                    case 'X':
                        printf("Error: 10 X");
                        break;
                    default:
                        printf("Error: 10");
                        break;
                }
                break;
            default:
                switch (outcome.u.s.module) {
                    case 'X':
                        printf("Error: X");
                        break;
                    default:
                        printf("Error: other");
                        break;
                }
```

```
            break;
        }
        break;
    case Uncertainty:
        break;
    }
    return 0;
}
```

As you can see, it is much more verbose.

match Statements with Variables in Patterns

We saw how to use literals in match statements patterns. Rust also allows the use of variables in these patterns, like in this example:

```
#[allow(dead_code)]
enum Result {
    Success(u8),
    Failure(u16, char),
    Uncertainty,
}
// let outcome = Result::Success(13);
let outcome = Result::Failure(20, 'X');
match outcome {
    Result::Success(0) => print!("Result: 0"),
    Result::Success(1) => print!("Result: 1"),
    Result::Success(n) => print!("Result: {}", n),
    Result::Failure(10, 'X') => print!("Error: 10 X"),
    Result::Failure(10, m) => print!("Error: 10 in module {}", m),
    Result::Failure(code, 'X') => print!("Error: n.{} X", code),
    Result::Failure(code, module) =>
        print!("Error: n.{} in module {}", code, module),
    Result::Uncertainty => {},
}
```

This will print: `Error: n.20 X`.

Activating the first declaration of the `outcome` variable, instead of the second one, it will print: `Result: 13`.

In the `match` statement, the patterns of the third, fifth, sixth, and seventh arms contain identifiers never declared. They are `n`, `m`, `code`, and `module`. Such identifiers are declared as new variables in this way.

Their type is inferred by the type of the corresponding field. So, the type of `n` is `u8`; the type of code is `u16`; and the type of `m` and of `module` is `char`.

Such variables always match with the corresponding field, and, in case the complete pattern matches, they are initialized by the matching value.

The scope of such variables is only the arm in which they are declared. So, if a variable with the same name exists before, it will be shadowed just for the body of the arm.

match Expressions

Similarly to the `if`-expressions, there are also `match`-expressions:

```
#[allow(dead_code)]
enum CardinalPoint { North, South, West, East }
let direction = CardinalPoint::South;
print!("{}", match direction {
    CardinalPoint::North => 'N',
    CardinalPoint::South => 'S',
    _ => '*',
});
```

This will print: `S`.

We already saw that if the "if" keyword is used to create an `if` expression, it must also have an `else` block, and its returned type must be the same as the block before the `else` keyword.

The same applies for `match` expressions: all the arms of any `match` expressions must have the right sides of the same type. In the example, the three arms have the values `'N'`, `'S'`, and `'*'`, so they are all of `char` type.

If the third arm were replaced by "`_ => {},`", you would get the compilation error "`match arms have incompatible types.`" Indeed, as two arms are of char type, and one of empty tuple type, it is impossible to determine the type of the whole match expression.

Use of Guards in match Constructs

Let's assume we want to classify the integer numbers in the following categories: all the negative numbers, the zero number, the one number, and all the other positive numbers. Here is the code to perform such classification:

```
for n in -2..5 {
    println!("{} is {}.", n, match n {
        0 => "zero",
        1 => "one",
        _ if n < 0 => "negative",
        _ => "plural",
    });
}
```

This program will print:

```
-2 is negative.
-1 is negative.
0 is zero.
1 is one.
2 is plural.
3 is plural.
4 is plural.
```

The for statement iterates the integer numbers from -2 included to 5 excluded.

For each processed number, that number is printed, followed by its classification. Such classification is performed by the match construct, which here is used as an expression having a string as its value. Indeed, each of its arms has a literal string as its value.

The third arm differs from the others, though. Its pattern is an underscore, so such an arm should always match, but the pattern is followed by a clause made by the "`if`" keyword followed by a Boolean condition. Such a clause causes this pattern to match only if that Boolean condition is true. It is named *guard*, as it *protects* the expression by an arbitrary Boolean condition, in addition to the pattern to match.

The last arm is the real catch-all pattern.

if-let and while-let Constructs

Sometimes you just need to check whether an enum value is a certain variant, and in that case you need to extract its fields. It can be accomplished by the following code:

```
enum E {
    Case1(u32),
    Case2(char),
    Case3(i64, bool),
}
let v = E::Case3(1234, true);
match v {
    E::Case3(n, b) => if b { print!("{}", n) }
    _ => {}
}
```

In this code, we need to check whether the value of v is a Case3 variant, and in such a case we need to use its two fields.

In addition to this code, the Rust language supports the following syntax, which replaces the preceding match statement:

```
if let E::Case3(n, b) = v {
    if b { print!("{}", n) }
}
```

Here the construct let E::Case3(n, b) = v tries to match the value of the expression v with the pattern E::Case3(n, b). If the match is successful, the n and b variables get the value of the two fields of v, and they can be used inside the following block. Instead, if the match is unsuccessful, the condition of the if-expression is considered false, and the following expression is not evaluated; if there is an else clause, it is evaluated.

A similar construct exists for `while` statements, like in the following code:

```
enum E {
    Case1(u32),
    Case2(char),
}
let mut v = E::Case1(0);
while let E::Case1(n) = v {
    print!("{}", n);
    if n == 6 { break; }
    v = E::Case1(n + 1);
}
```

It will print: 0123456.

At any iteration, the value of `v` is matched against the pattern `E::Case1(n)`. As long as the match is successful, the loop is repeated.

CHAPTER 8

Using Heterogeneous Data Structures

In this chapter you will learn how to define and use other composite types:

- Tuples
- Structs
- Tuple-structs

They are useful to group objects of different types.

At the end of the chapter, you'll see some code style conventions.

The Tuples

Arrays and vectors can contain several items, yet such items must all be of the same type. If you wish to store in a single object several subobjects of different types, you can do it in this way:

```rust
let data = (10000000, 183.19, 'Q');
let copy_of_data = data;
print!("{}, {}, {}",
    data.0, copy_of_data.1, data.2);
```

This will print: 10000000, 183.19, Q.

The "data" variable is a composite object, as it is composed of three objects. Even arrays are composite objects, but they are constrained to be composed of objects of the same type, while the "data" variable is composed of objects of different types: an integer number, a floating-point number, and a character.

© Carlo Milanesi 2022
C. Milanesi, *Beginning Rust*, https://doi.org/10.1007/978-1-4842-7208-4_8

Therefore, our object is not an array but a *tuple*.

The declaration of tuples looks like that of arrays. The only difference is that round parentheses are used instead of square brackets.

Each item of a tuple is named *field*.

Also the type of tuples can be made explicit:

```
let data: (i32, f64, char) = (10000000, 183.19, 'Q');
```

The type has the same format as the expression giving the value, where, for each field, the expression giving the value is replaced by its type.

As shown in the second statement, an entire tuple may be used to initialize another tuple of the same type.

You can access the fields of a tuple by their position, using the dot notation. When accessing the seventh item of the "arr" array, you must write "arr[6]"; to access the seventh field of the "data" tuple, you must write "data.6".

Also, tuples can be mutable:

```
let mut data = (10000000, 183.19, 'Q');
data.0 = -5;
data.2 = 'x';
print!("{}, {}, {}", data.0, data.1, data.2);
```

This will print: -5, 183.19, x.

Similarly to arrays, tuples can also have any number of fields, including zero. Because to write the type of a tuple you write the sequence of the types of its fields, enclosed in parentheses, then, if there are no fields, only the parentheses remain. Therefore, to write the type of a tuple with no fields, you just write "()."

But in Chapter 6, we already saw this type and this value. So now it is explained why they are named *empty tuples*.

A difference between tuples and arrays is that tuples cannot be accessed by a variable index. Consider this code:

```
let array = [12, 13, 14];
let tuple = (12, 13, 14);
let i = 0;
print!("{}", array[i]);
print!("{}", tuple.i);
```

The compiler generates, at the last line, the error: no field `i` on type `({integer}, {integer}, {integer})`. There is no way to get the value of a field of a tuple using an index determined at runtime.

The Structs

Tuples are useful as long as they contain no more than a handful of items, but when they have many fields, it is too easy to mistake them, and the code that uses them is hard to understand:

```
let data = (10, 'x', 12, 183.19, 'Q', false, -9);
print!("{}", data.2 + data.6);
```

Is it clear that this code will print 3?

In addition, the type of any tuple is defined only by the sequence of the types of its fields, and if there are many fields, the types are too long to specify and hard to understand:

```
let data1 = (10, 'x', 12, 183.19, 'Q', false, -9);
let mut data2: (u16, char, i16, f64, bool, char, i16);
data2 = data1;
```

This code is illegal. Can you spot the error?

In addition, if a field is added at the beginning of a tuple, all the indexes to objects of such a type must be incremented in source code. For example, data.2 must become data.3. For instance, the first example of this section would become:

```
let data = ("first", 10, 'x', 12, 183.19, 'Q', false, -9);
print!("{}", data.3 + data.7);
```

Therefore, it comes out very useful to have a specific statement to declare the type of a structure, giving it a name, and labeling all the fields of that structure. Here is an example of it:

```
struct SomeData {
    integer: i32,
    fractional: f32,
```

```
    character: char,
    five_bytes: [u8; 5],
}
let data = SomeData {
    integer: 10_000_000,
    fractional: 183.19,
    character: 'Q',
    five_bytes: [9, 0, 250, 60, 200],
};
print!("{}, {}, {}, {}",
    data.five_bytes[3], data.integer,
    data.fractional, data.character);
```

This will print: `60, 10000000, 183.19, Q`.

The first statement occupies six lines: it starts with the `struct` keyword and proceeds with a block. Its effect is to declare the `SomeData` type. Any object of that type is a sequence of four fields. For each field, its name and its type are declared, separated by a colon. The list of field declarations is comma separated, with an optional ending comma. Let's name *struct* such a kind of data type.

Also the second statement occupies six lines. It declares the variable "`data`" and initializes it with an object of the type just declared. Notice that the initialization syntax looks like the type declaration syntax, where the `struct` keyword is removed, and each field type is replaced by an expression whose value is to be assigned to such a field. Let's name *struct-object* such kind of an object, which is any object whose type is a struct.

The third statement accesses the fields of the just-defined struct-object, using the so-called dot notation. This notation consists of an expression representing the struct-object, followed by a dot, followed by the name of the field to access.

This code is similar to the following C language program:

```
#include <stdio.h>
int main() {
    struct SomeData {
        int integer;
        float fractional;
        char character;
        unsigned char five_bytes[5];
    };
```

```
struct SomeData data = {
    10000000,
    183.19,
    'Q',
    {9, 0, 250, 60, 200},
};
printf("%d, %d, %g, %c",
    data.five_bytes[3], data.integer,
    data.fractional, data.character);
return 0;
}
```

Let's see where this C code differs from the preceding Rust code.

While in C the fields are separated by semicolons, in Rust they are separated by commas.

In Rust, the type is written after the name of the field, like in the Pascal language.

In C you can declare several fields of the same type, by specifying the type just once, that is, in this way: int a, b;. In Rust, instead, you must specify the type once for every field, in this way: a: i32, b: i32,.

In C the initialization of "data" is done simply by listing the values, similarly to Rust tuples. In Rust, instead, for each field you must specify also the name of that field.

Both in C and in Rust, the dot notation is used.

If you declare a variable as mutable, you can also change the values of its fields, using the same dot notation:

```
struct SomeData {
    integer: i32,
    fractional: f32,
}
let mut data = SomeData {
    integer: 10,
    fractional: 183.19,
};
data.fractional = 8.2;
print!("{}, {}", data.fractional, data.integer);
```

This will print: `8.2, 10`.

Like tuples, structs may be empty also, so you can declare a struct containing no fields, and then a variable of such type:

```
struct NoData {}
let _no_data = NoData {};
```

The Tuple-Structs

We already saw that if you want to define a structure containing objects of different types, you have two possibilities:

- Create a tuple, whose type has no name, it was not previously declared, and whose fields have no name.

- Create a struct, whose type has a name, it must have been previously declared, and whose fields have a name.

So, there are several differences between these two kinds of structures. Yet sometimes something halfway is needed: a kind of structure whose types have names and must be previously declared, like structs, but whose fields have no name, like tuples. Because they are a hybrid between tuples and structs, they are named *tuple-structs*:

```
struct SomeData (
    i32,
    f32,
    char,
    [u8; 5],
);
let data = SomeData (
    10_000_000,
    183.19,
    'Q',
    [9, 0, 250, 60, 200],
);
print!("{}, {}, {}, {}",
    data.2, data.0, data.1, data.3[2]);
```

This will print: Q, 10000000, 183.19, 250.

As shown in the example, the tuple-struct is defined before instantiating it, by using the keyword `struct` like for structs, but enclosing its fields in parentheses instead of braces, and without specifying the names of the fields, like for tuples. The initialization starts with the name of the type, like for structs, but it goes on like for tuples.

Its fields are accessed like those of tuples, because they have no name.

Differing from both tuples and structs, empty tuple-structs are not allowed.

Actually, tuple-structs are not used often.

Lexical Conventions

Now that we have seen a good deal of different Rust constructs (but not yet all of them), it is a good time to think about some lexical conventions adopted by almost every Rust programmer, so they are strongly recommended to everyone. Such conventions are so entrenched, that even the compiler emits a warning if they are violated.

Here is a program showing them:

```
const MAXIMUM_POWER: u16 = 600;
#[allow(dead_code)]
enum VehicleKind {
    Motorcycle,
    Car,
    Truck,
}
#[allow(dead_code)]
struct VehicleData {
    kind: VehicleKind,
    registration_year: u16,
    registration_month: u8,
    power: u16,
}
let vehicle = VehicleData {
    kind: VehicleKind::Car,
    registration_year: 2003,
```

```
    registration_month: 11,
    power: 120,
};
if vehicle.power > MAXIMUM_POWER {
    println!("Too powerful");
}
```

The conventions shown in this example are:

- Names of constants (for example: MAXIMUM_POWER) contain only uppercase characters, with words separated by underscore. This convention is usually named *screaming snake case*, or *upper snake case*, or simply *upper case*.

- Type names defined by application code or by the standard library (for example: VehicleKind and VehicleData) and enum variant names (for example: Car) are comprised of words stuck together, where every word has an uppercase initial letter, followed by lowercase letters. This convention is usually named *upper camel case* or *PascalCase*.

- Any other name (for example, keywords like let, primitive types like u8, and field identifiers like registration_year) use only lowercase letters, with words separated by underscores. This convention is usually named *snake case*.

CHAPTER 9

Defining Functions

In this chapter you will learn:

- How to define your own procedures (better known as "functions") and how to invoke them

- When and how you can have several functions with the same name

- How to pass arguments to a function, by value or by reference

- How to return simple and composite values from a function

- How to exit prematurely from a function

- How references to objects can be manipulated

Defining and Invoking a Function

If it happens that you write the same code several times, you can encapsulate that code in a block, and then give that block a name. In this way you define a *function*. Then you can execute that code by invoking that function by name:

```
fn line() {
    println!("----------");
}
line();
line();
line();
```

This will print:

```
----------
----------
----------
```

© Carlo Milanesi 2022
C. Milanesi, *Beginning Rust*, https://doi.org/10.1007/978-1-4842-7208-4_9

To define a function, you write the fn keyword, followed by the name you want to associate to that function, followed by a pair of parentheses, followed by a block.

That block is named the *body* of the function, and all that precedes the body is named the *signature* of the function.

This syntax should look quite familiar by now, as all the programs we have written so far are nothing but definitions of a function named main.

Although the main function is a special function, as it is invoked by the program startup machine code, our line function is executed only when our code invokes it.

Indeed, the second part of our small program invokes the line function three times. To invoke (or *call*) it, it is enough to write its name, followed by a pair of parentheses.

Notice that we defined the line function inside the main function. Actually, differing from C language, in Rust you can define functions inside the body of other functions. And you can also invoke functions defined externally of the main function. Here is a complete Rust program (not to be inserted in a main function):

```rust
fn f1() { print!("1"); }
fn main() {
    f1();
    fn f2() { print!("2"); }
    f2(); f1(); f2();
}
```

This will print: 1212.

Functions Defined After Their Use

This code is illegal (generating the error: cannot find value `a` in this scope):

```rust
a;
let a = 3;
```

because it uses the a variable before having defined it.

The following one is valid instead:

```rust
f();
fn f() {}
```

because you may invoke a function even before defining it, as long as it is defined in the current scope or in an enclosing scope.

Functions Shadowing Other Functions

We already saw that after having defined a variable, you can define another variable having the same name, and that second variable will shadow the first one. With functions you cannot do that, inside the same scope:

```
fn f() {}
fn f() {}
```

This will generate the compilation error that the name `f` is defined multiple times.

However, you can define several functions with the same name, as long as they are in distinct independent blocks:

```
{
    fn f() { print!("a"); }
    f(); f();
}
{
    fn f() { print!("b"); }
    f();
}
```

This will print: aab.

Every function is valid only in the block where it is defined, so you cannot invoke it from the outside of that block:

```
{
    fn f() { }
}
f();
```

This will generate, on the last line, the compilation error: "cannot find function `f` in this scope."

Finally, a function can shadow another function defined in an outer block. Here is a complete program:

```
fn f() { print!("1"); }
fn main() {
    f(); // Prints 2
    {
        f(); // Prints 3
        fn f() { print!("3"); }
    }
    f(); // Prints 2
    fn f() { print!("2"); }
}
```

It will print: 232.

Indeed, externally to the main function, a function that prints 1 is defined, but inside the main function another function is defined, having the same name, and printing 2; so the first statement in the main function invokes the function declared inside the main function, even if it is defined six lines below. In the nested block, still another function with the same name is defined and invoked, and it prints 3. Then that block ends, so the function printing 2 gets back to being the active one. The external function, which would print 1, is never invoked, so the compiler reports that in the warning: function is never used: `f`.

Passing Arguments to a Function

A function that always prints the same text every time it is invoked is not very useful. A function that prints the sum of any two numeric values that are passed to it is more interesting:

```
fn print_sum(addend1: f64, addend2: f64) {
    println!("{} + {} = {}", addend1, addend2,
        addend1 + addend2);
}
print_sum(3., 5.);
print_sum(3.2, 5.1);
```

This will print:

```
3 + 5 = 8
3.2 + 5.1 = 8.3
```

Now you can understand the use of parentheses for function definition and invocation. In a function definition, they enclose the arguments expected by the function; and in a function invocation, they enclose the expressions whose values are passed as arguments to the function.

The definitions of the arguments of a function behave much like definitions of variables.

So, the preceding program above is to be interpreted as if it were the following one:

```
{ // First invocation of `print_sum`
    let addend1: f64 = 3.; let addend2: f64 = 5.;
    println!("{} + {} = {}", addend1, addend2,
        addend1 + addend2);
}
{ // Second invocation of `print_sum`
    let addend1: f64 = 3.2; let addend2: f64 = 5.1;
    println!("{} + {} = {}", addend1, addend2,
        addend1 + addend2);
}
```

The main difference between the definition of a variable and the definition of an argument of a function is that, in function argument definitions, the type specification is required, that is, you cannot rely only on type inference.

Type inference is used anyway by the compiler to check that the value received as the argument is actually of the type declared for that argument. Indeed, this code

```
fn f(a: i16) {}
f(3.);
f(3u16);
f(3i16);
f(3);
```

generates an error at the first invocation of f, as a floating-point number is passed to an integer argument; and it generates an error also at the second invocation, as a value of u16 type is passed to an argument of i16 type.

The last two invocations, instead, are allowed. Actually, the third invocation passes a value that has exactly the type expected by the function; while the fourth invocation passes an argument of unconstrained integer type, which is constrained to the i16 type by the invocation itself. This constraint to a concrete type of a previously unconstrained integer type was explained, for variable initialization, in the section "Type Inference" of Chapter 6.

Passing Arguments by Value

Notice also that arguments are not simply new names for the passed objects, that is, they are not aliases; instead they are *copies* of such objects. Such copies are created when the function is invoked, and they are destroyed when the function ends and the control returns to the caller code. This example clarifies this concept:

```
fn print_double(mut x: f64) {
    x *= 2.;
    print!("{}", x);
}
let x = 4.;
print_double(x);
print!(" {}", x);
```

This will print: 8 4.

Here, apparently, a variable named x is declared and initialized in the fifth line, and then it is passed to the function print_double, where it keeps its name x. The value of such variable is changed to 8, its new value is correctly printed, the function ends, returning to the caller, and the value of our variable is printed with the value it had before the function invocation!

Actually, it is not *the variable* that is passed to the function, but *the value* of the variable. It is a so-called *pass-by-value* argument passing mechanism, like in C language. The value of the x variable is used to initialize a new variable, which accidentally here is also named x, which is the argument of the function. The new variable is then changed and printed inside the function body, and it is destroyed by the ending of the function. The variable declared in the caller function has never changed its value.

Notice that in the signature of print_double, before the argument x, there is the mut keyword. This is required to allow the first statement inside the function body to change the value of that argument; yet, as said before, such a statement changes only the value of the argument of the function, not the variable defined externally to the function, which indeed had no need of the mut specification.

Returning a Value from a Function

Functions, in addition to being able to receive values to process, can send back to the caller a result of the computation:

```
fn double(x: f64) -> f64 { x * 2. }
print!("{}", double(17.3));
```

This will print: 34.6.

The value returned by a function is normally the value of its body.

We already saw that the body of any function is a block, and that the value of any block is the value of its last expression, if there is a last expression, or otherwise an empty tuple.

The content of the body of the double function in the preceding code is x * 2.. The value returned by the function is actually the value of such expression.

The type of the value returned by functions, which in C language is written before the name of the function, is written afterward in Rust, separated by a thin arrow symbol "->." The double function just shown, according to its signature, returns an f64 value.

If no return value type is specified, it is implied to be the empty tuple type, that is "()."

```
fn f1(x: i32) {}
fn f2(x: i32) -> () {}
```

These functions f1 and f2 are equal, as they both return an empty tuple.

The value returned by any function must be of the same type specified by the function signature as the return value type, or an unconstrained type that may be constrained to that type.

So, this code is valid:

```
fn _f1() -> i32 { 4.5; "abc"; 73i32 }
fn _f2() -> i32 { 4.5; "abc"; 73 }
fn _f3() -> i32 { 4.5; "abc"; 73 + 100 }
```

While this code is not:

```
fn _f1() -> i32 { 4.5; "abc"; false }
fn _f2() -> i32 { 4.5; "abc"; () }
fn _f3() -> i32 { 4.5; "abc"; {} }
fn _f4() -> i32 { 4.5; "abc"; }
```

It generates four `mismatched type` errors: for the _f1 function, the error expected `` `i32` ``, found `` `bool` ``; for the _f2, _f3, and _f4 functions, the error expected `` `i32` ``, found `` `()` ``.

Early Exit

So far, to exit from a function, we had to get to the end of its body. However, if you write a function containing many statements, often you realize in the middle of the function that you have no more computations to do, and so you want to quickly get out of the function.

A possibility is to break out from a loop; another one is to create a large if-statement enclosing the rest of the statements of the function; a third possibility is to set a Boolean variable indicating that no more processing is necessary, and checking the value of such variable using if statements every time you must do something.

Typically, though, the most convenient way is to ask the compiler to get out immediately from the function, returning a value of the type required by the function signature:

```
fn f(x: f64) -> f64 {
    if x <= 0. { return 0.; }
    x + 3.
}
print!("{} {}", f(1.), f(-1.));
```

It will print: 4 0.

The return statement evaluates the expression that follows it, and the resulting value is immediately returned to the caller.

The return keyword is the same as in C language, with the difference that in Rust it is not normally used as a last statement, but only for early exits. Yet, you can write:

```rust
fn f(x: f64) -> f64 {
    if x <= 0. { return 0.; }
    return x + 3.;
}
print!("{} {}", f(1.), f(-1.));
```

This program is equivalent to the preceding one, but it is considered bad style. The following program is also equivalent, and it is usually considered better:

```rust
fn f(x: f64) -> f64 {
    if x <= 0. { 0. }
    else { x + 3. }
}
print!("{} {}", f(1.), f(-1.));
```

The return statement is considered convenient only when it allows you to decrease the number of lines of code or the indentation level.

Also for the return statement, the return value type must be equal to the one declared in the function signature.

If the function signature specifies the empty tuple as a return value type, that value may be omitted in the return-statement. Therefore, this is a valid program:

```rust
fn f(x: i32) {
    if x <= 0 { return; }
    if x == 4 { return (); }
    if x == 7 { return {}; }
    print!("{}", x);
}
f(5);
```

It will print: 5. Any function invocation may be considered a valid statement, even if the returned value is not used:

```
fn f() -> i32 { 3 }
f();
```

In such a case, the returned value is ignored and immediately destroyed.

Instead, if the returned value is used, like in this valid code,

```
fn f() -> i32 { 3 }
let _a: i32 = f();
```

then it must be of the proper type. As a counterexample, the following program is illegal:

```
fn f() -> i32 { 3 }
let _a: u32 = f();
```

Returning Several Values

If you want to return several values from a function, you can use a tuple:

```
fn divide(dividend: i32, divisor: i32) -> (i32, i32) {
    (dividend / divisor, dividend % divisor)
}
print!("{:?}", divide(50, 11));
```

This will print: (4, 6).

Or you can return an enum, a struct, a tuple struct, an array, or a vector:

```
#[allow(dead_code)]
enum E { E1, E2 }
#[allow(dead_code)]
struct S { a: i32, b: bool }
struct TS (f64, char);
fn f1() -> E { E::E2 }
fn f2() -> S { S { a: 49, b: true } }
fn f3() -> TS { TS (4.7, 'w') }
fn f4() -> [i16; 4] { [7, -2, 0, 19] }
fn f5() -> Vec<i64> { vec![12000] }
```

```
print!("{} ", match f1() { E::E1 => 1, _ => -1 });
print!("{} ", f2().a);
print!("{} ", f3().0);
print!("{} ", f4()[0]);
print!("{} ", f5()[0]);
```

This will print: `-1 49 4.7 7 12000`.

Let's explain these five numbers.

The invocation of f1 in the first `print!` invocation returns the enumeration E2, which tries to match with E1; as it doesn't match, the catch-all case is taken, so `-1` is printed.

The invocation of f2 returns a struct object containing the fields a and b, and from it the a field is extracted.

The invocation of f3 returns a tuple-struct containing two fields, and from it the first field is extracted.

The invocation of f4 returns an array containing four items, and from it the first item is extracted.

The invocation of f5 returns a vector containing just one item, and from it the first and only item is extracted.

How to Change a Variable of the Caller

Let's assume we have an array containing ten numbers, and we want to double the value of such numbers.

We can do that in this way:

```
let mut arr = [5, -4, 9, 0, -7, -1, 3, 5, 3, 1];
for n in 0..10 {
    arr[n] *= 2;
}
print!("{:?}", arr);
```

This will print: `[10, -8, 18, 0, -14, -2, 6, 10, 6, 2]`.

Now let's assume we want to encapsulate such an operation into a function. We could incorrectly write:

```
fn double(mut a: [i32; 10]) {
    for i in 0..10 {
        a[i] *= 2;
    }
}
let mut arr = [5, -4, 9, 0, -7, -1, 3, 5, 3, 1];
double(arr);
print!("{:?}", arr);
```

This will print: [5, -4, 9, 0, -7, -1, 3, 5, 3, 1]. Our array hasn't changed at all.

Indeed, when passing this array by value, the entire array has been copied into another array, created by the function invocation. This last array has been changed inside the function, and then it has been destroyed when the function ended.

The original array was never changed, and the compiler is aware of that, as it reports the warning variable does not need to be mutable. That is, given that arr is never changed, you may also remove the mut clause from its declaration.

To ensure that our array is changed, you can make the function return the changed array:

```
fn double(mut a: [i32; 10]) -> [i32; 10] {
    for n in 0..10 {
        a[n] *= 2;
    }
    a
}
let mut arr = [5, -4, 9, 0, -7, -1, 3, 5, 3, 1];
arr = double(arr);
print!("{:?}", arr);
```

This will print the expected result, that is: [10, -8, 18, 0, -14, -2, 6, 10, 6, 2]. However, this solution has one drawback: all the data is copied twice. First, at function invocation, the entire array is copied into the function; then the function works on the local copy of the data; and at last all the local data is copied back in place of the original data. These copies have a computational cost, which can be avoided.

Passing Arguments by Reference

To optimize the passing of a (long) array to a function, you can pass to that function only the address of the array, letting the function work directly on the original array:

```
fn double(a: &mut [i32; 10]) {
    for n in 0..10 {
        (*a)[n] *= 2;
    }
}
let mut arr = [5, -4, 9, 0, -7, -1, 3, 5, 3, 1];
double(&mut arr);
print!("{:?}", arr);
```

This program prints the expected result, but without copying arrays.

You obtain this result through the so-called *pass-by-reference* argument passing mechanism. The syntax is quite similar to the *pass-by-pointer* technique of C language.

Let's see it in detail.

The new symbols "&" and "*" have appeared. They have the same meaning in Rust as in C language. The "&" symbol, in the expression &a, means *the (memory) address of the object a*, and the "*" symbol, in the expression *a, means *the object that is present at the (memory) address a*.

The a argument of the double function is of type &mut [i32; 10]. By putting an & symbol before the type specification, it is specified as an *address* (also known as *pointer*, or *reference*) of an object of the type specified just afterward. We want to let the function modify the value of the referenced object, so the mut keyword is required for this reference. Therefore, in this case, a is of type *address of a mutable array of ten 32-bit signed integer numbers*.

In the function body, we are not interested in handling the address itself, but in handling the object referred to by such address. So, we use the * symbol to access such object. In general, given a reference "a," the "*a" expression indicates the object referred to by such reference.

In the second line of the function, the "*a" expression access the object positioned at the address received as argument by the function. Such an object is an array, and so you can access its item at position n.

The parentheses around the "*a" expression are required, because square brackets have precedence over the star operator; the *a[n] expression would be taken as *(a[n]), which means: *take the* n*th item of the object* a, *and then, considering such item as an address, take the object having such address*. This is not what we want to do, and it would generate the compilation error type `i32` cannot be dereferenced, which means: *you cannot get the object whose memory address is contained in a value of type* i32.

Using this kind of argument passing, the double function receives only the address of an array, by which it can read and write the items of such array.

After having declared this function, we can use it. The array must be declared and initialized as mutable, because its contents will have to be changed. Then the function is invoked without expecting a returned value, but passing as argument the address of the array. Notice that it is required to repeat the mut keyword also where the argument is passed, to make explicit that the referred object is expected to be changed by the function.

In fact, this function may be simplified as the following equivalent version:

```
fn double(a: &mut [i32; 10]) {
    for n in 0..10 {
        a[n] *= 2;
    }
}
```

We removed the asterisk before the use of the "a" argument, which actually is not required, and we also removed its surrounding parentheses, which have become useless. Let's see why we could make such a simplification.

Most Rust operators, like +, +=, and [ ], are actually *syntactic sugar* of function calls. Our function is equivalent to the following one:

```
fn double(a: &mut [i32; 10]) {
    use std::ops::IndexMut;
    use std::ops::MulAssign;
    for n in 0..10 {
        (*(*a).index_mut(n)).mul_assign(2);
    }
}
```

In this function, there are two use directives that declare the intention to use some library modules. The standard library contains the module `ops`, short for operators, that defines the operators of the language and also defines an implementation of such operators for the primitive types.

The `IndexMut` module defines the use of square brackets to access a collection in a mutable way. It provides the `index_mut` function such that the expression `collection.index_mut(index)` is equivalent to the expression `collection[index]`, when it appears as a destination of an assignment.

The `MulAssign` module defines the use of the operator `*=`. It provides a `mul_assign` function, such that the expression `number1.mul_assign(number2)` is equivalent to the expression `number1 *= number2`.

After such directives, it is allowed to write the following expression.

If you have a reference, named `collection`, and you want to call a function on the referenced object, say the `index_mut` function, you can use the syntax `(*collection).index_mut(index)`. However, in general, in Rust you can use the simplified syntax `collection.index_mut(index)`. In such a case, Rust automatically implies that the reference is dereferenced, that is, the function is applied to the referenced object and not to the reference itself. This allows saving an asterisk and a pair of parentheses. Such simplification is not applied for function arguments, though.

This automatic simplification is also applied to the possible corresponding operators. So, you can write `(*collection)[index]`, but you can also equivalently write `collection[index]`.

This explains why we could use the "a" argument inside the function body as if it were an object instead of a reference.

The resulting syntax is that of C++ references, with the difference that in Rust it is also allowed to apply an explicit dereference. That is, before a reference, you are allowed to write or to omit the asterisk, while in C++, to get the referenced object, you must put it before a pointer and must not put it before a reference.

Using References

References are used mainly as function arguments, but you may use them elsewhere too:

```
let a = 15;
let ref_a = &a;
print!("{} {} {}", a, *ref_a, ref_a);
```

This will print: `15 15 15`.

Actually, the same object is printed three times.

The "a" variable simply contains a 32-bit object whose value is the number 15.

The `ref_a` variable contains the memory address of such object, that is, of the "a" variable. Therefore, it is a reference to a number.

In the last statement, first the value of "a" is printed. Then, the object referred by `ref_a` is taken and printed. Finally, the compiler attempts to directly print the `ref_a` variable, but it is not allowed to directly print a reference in this way, so the referred object is taken and printed. This happens because internally the `print` macro calls a function on that expression, so the dereferencing is implied.

Using references, you can demonstrate some virtuosity:

```
let a = &&&7;
print!("{} {} {} {}", ***a, **a, *a, a);
```

It will print: `7 7 7 7`.

In the first statement, the 7 value is taken, and it is put in memory in a nameless object. Then, the address of that object is taken, and the address is put in memory in a second nameless object. Then, the address of such object is taken, and it is put in memory in a third nameless object. Then the address of such object is taken, and it is put in memory in a fourth object, and the name `a` is associated to such object. This fourth object is the "a" variable, which therefore is a reference to a reference to a reference to a number.

In the second statement, first the ***a expression is printed. Here, considering that "a" is a reference, the object referenced by "a" is taken by using the rightmost asterisk of the three. Next, considering that this object is also a reference, the object referenced by it is taken by using the middle asterisk. Then, considering that this object is also a reference, the object referenced by it is taken by using the leftmost asterisk. Finally, considering that this object is a number, it is printed as a number.

Here a table shows a possible memory layout of such values in a 32-bit system.

Addresses	1000	1004	1008	1012
Memory contents	**7**	**1000**	**1004**	**1008**

All these values are in decimal notation.

The leftmost cell contains the nameless numeric object, whose value is 7. Its memory address is 1000, but it occupies four bytes. In Rust code, it is represented by the expression ***a.

The second cell from the left, at address from 1004 to 1007, is the address of the first cell, and so its value is 1000. It is represented by the expression **a.

The third cell from the left, at address from 1008 to 1011, is the address of the second cell, and so its value is 1004. It is represented by the expression *a.

The rightmost cell, at address from 1012 to 1015, is the address of the third cell, so its value is 1008. It is directly represented by the a variable.

If you added one or more additional asterisks, a compilation error would result, because it is not allowed to dereference an object that is not a reference.

After having printed the first 7 using a completely explicit syntax, the same object is printed three other times, using expressions that imply, respectively, one, two, or three asterisks. The expression **a represents a reference to a number; the expression *a represents a reference to a reference to a number; and the expression a represents a reference to a reference to a reference to a number. Such expressions are passed to the print macro, which is expecting values that are not references, so it converts such references to their referenced object.

Mutability of References

Let's see how to use the mut keyword with references:

```
let mut a: i32 = 10;
let mut b: i32 = 20;
let mut p: &mut i32 = &mut a; // line 3
print!("{} ", *p);
*p += 1; // line 5
print!("{} ", *p);
p = &mut b; // line 7
```

```
print!("{} ", *p);
*p += 1; // line 9
print!("{} ", *p);
```

It will print: 10 11 20 21 .

Here, we have the two numeric variables "a" and "b," and the reference "p," initially referring to "a."

For a moment ignore all those mut words.

Initially, the value of "a" is 10, and "p" refers to "a." So, by printing *p, 10 is printed.

Then, at line 5, the object referred to by "p" is incremented, becoming 11. So, by printing *p, 11 is printed.

Then, at line 7, "p" is made to refer to "b," whose value is 20. Indeed, by printing *p, 20 is printed.

Then, at line 9, the object now referred to by "p" is also incremented, becoming 21. So, by printing *p, 21 is printed.

Notice that, at line 5, "p" indirectly increments the "a" variable, so "a" must be mutable; at line 9, "p" indirectly increments the "b" variable, so "b" must be mutable too; and at line 7, "p" itself is changed, so "p" must also be mutable. But the reasoning of the compiler is different.

The actual reasoning is as follows.

At line 5 and line 9, the objects referred to by "p" are incremented, that is, they are read and written. This is allowed only if *p is mutable. So "p" cannot be of type &i32; it must be of type &mut i32, which is "reference to a mutable i32."

Regarding line 3, the expression &a is of type &i32, and so it cannot be assigned to "p," which is of type &mut i32. Instead, the expression &mut a has the correct type, as it has the same mutability of "p."

But the expression &mut a, which can be read "reference to a mutable a," allows us to change "a," and Rust allows this only if "a" is mutable. Therefore, the initialization at line 3 is allowed only if the "a" variable is declared as mutable in the first line. Similarly, the initialization at line 7 is allowed only if the "b" variable is mutable, as declared in the second line.

Then, notice that at line 7, "p" itself is changed, that is, it is made to refer to some other object. This is allowed only if the "p" variable is mutable, as declared in the third line.

And with this, any use of mut in this program has been explained.

However, it is better to insist that at line 3 the first occurrence of the mut word has a different meaning than the two other occurrences.

The first mut word means that the p variable can be changed, meaning it can be reassigned, making it refer to another object, as has been done at line 7. Without such mut word, p would refer always to the same object.

The second and third mut words mean that the type of "p" allows it to change the value of the referred object. Without such mut words, "p" wouldn't be able to change the value of its referred object.

CHAPTER 10

Defining Generic Functions and Types

In this chapter, you will learn:

- How to write a single function definition, whose invocations can efficiently handle different data types

- How to use type inference to avoid the need to specify the types used by generic functions

- How to write a single struct, tuple-struct, or enum type, whose instances can efficiently contain different data types

- How to use two important standard generic enums, `Option` and `Result`, to represent optional data or fallible functions results

- How some standard functions ease the handling of `Option` and `Result`

Need of Generic Functions

Rust performs a strict data type check, so when you define a function that uses an argument of a certain type, say `fn square_root(x: f32) -> f32`, the code that invokes such a function must pass to it an expression of exactly that type, like in `square_root(45.2f32)`, or it must perform explicit conversions every time that function is used, like in `square_root(45.2f64 as f32)`. You cannot pass a different type, like in `square_root(45.2f64)`.

This is inconvenient for those who write the code that invokes the function, but also for whoever writes the function itself. As Rust has many different numeric types, when you write a function, you must cope with the problem of which type to choose. For example, if you decide to specify that an argument of your function must be of `i16` type,

© Carlo Milanesi 2022
C. Milanesi, *Beginning Rust*, https://doi.org/10.1007/978-1-4842-7208-4_10

but then in a program you must call this function many times, and in most such calls you want to pass an expression of i32 type, you must perform many type conversions. Such type conversions are verbose, and they may incur a performance overhead.

In addition, consider this code:

```
// Library code
fn f(ch: char, num1: i16, num2: i16) -> i16 {
    if ch == 'a' { num1 }
    else { num2 }
}
// Application code
print!("{}", f('a', 37, 41));
```

It will print: 37.

The first part of the code is a definition of a function, designed to be invoked in several places, so this section is nicknamed *library code*.

The second part is an invocation of that function, so this section is nicknamed *application code*.

In the application code, if you replace 37 with 37.2, and 41 with 41., you would get a compilation error; moreover, if you add as i16 after each number, obtaining the statement

```
print!("{}", f('a', 37.2 as i16, 41. as i16));
```

the program would still print 37 instead of the desired 37.2.

If you decide to change the f function, that is, the library code, replacing i16 with f32 or with f64, the program will work correctly in all the preceding cases, but will force all the callers to use floating-point numbers.

As far as we have seen, the only way for the library writer to satisfy all the application developers using that library code is to write several functions, one for each supported type. As Rust has many primitive data types, and other types may be defined by libraries and by application code, many similar functions should be written.

Defining and Using Generic Functions

The idiomatic way to solve this problem in Rust is to write the following code:

```
// Library code
fn f<T>(ch: char, num1: T, num2: T) -> T {
    if ch == 'a' { num1 }
    else { num2 }
}
// Application code
let a: i16 = f::<i16>('a', 37, 41);
let b: f64 = f::<f64>('b', 37.2, 41.1);
print!("{} {}", a, b);
```

This will print 37 41.1.

In the function definition, just after the name of the function, there is the T word enclosed in angular brackets. This symbol is a *type parameter* of the function declaration.

It means that what is being declared is not a concrete function, but a *generic function*, which is parameterized by the T type parameter. That function will become a concrete function only when, still at compile time, a concrete type is specified for such T parameter.

The T parameter is defined only in the scope of the function definition. Indeed it is used three times, only in the signature of the function. It also could have been used in the body of the function, but not elsewhere.

While the ch argument is of char type, the num1 and num2 arguments, as well as the function returned value, are of the T generic type. When such a function is used, you must replace such T parameter with a concrete type, so obtaining a concrete function.

The first line of the application code, instead of using the f generic function, uses a function whose name is f::<i16>; this is the name of the concrete function obtained from the generic function by replacing the T parameter with the i16 type. Similarly, the second line of the application code invokes the f::<f64> function; this is the concrete function obtained by replacing the T parameter with the f64 type.

Notice that in the first call, in which the i16 type has been specified in angle brackets, two integer values, which may be constrained to the i16 type, are passed as second and third arguments of the function; and the value returned by the function is assigned to a variable having type i16.

Instead, in the second call, in which the f64 type has been specified, two floating-point values, which may be constrained to the f64 type, are passed as second and third arguments of the f generic function; and the value returned by the function is assigned to a variable having type f64.

If you swapped the arguments in such function calls, passing integers to the function that specifies a floating-point parameter, or passing floating-point numbers to the function that specifies an integer parameter, some mismatched types compilation errors would have been obtained.

In such a way, by writing library code without useless repetitions, it is possible to write application code that uses two distinct types without having to change the existing library code. Other data types could be used just as well.

C language does not allow generic functions, but C++ language allows them: they are the function templates.

Inferring the Parametric Types

The preceding application code may be further simplified, though, as show in this program:

```
// Library code
fn f<T>(ch: char, num1: T, num2: T) -> T {
    if ch == 'a' { num1 }
    else { num2 }
}
// Application code
let a: i16 = f('a', 37, 41);
let b: f64 = f('b', 37.2, 41.1);
print!("{} {}", a, b);
```

As it appears, the ::<i16> and ::<f64> clauses have been removed, obtaining anyway an equivalent program. Here, the compiler, when it sees that the f function is invoked with 37 and 41 as arguments, in places where expressions of the T generic type are expected, *infers* that the T type is that of such numbers, that is, i32. And when the function is invoked with 37.2 and 41.1 as arguments, it infers that the T type is f64.

Indeed, when the compiler is parsing an invocation of a generic function, it infers the type parameter using the types of the function arguments.

Of course, the various types used must be consistent:

```
fn f<T>(a: T, _b: T) -> T { a }
let _a = f(12u8, 13u8);
let _b = f(12i64, 13i64);
let _c = f(12i16, 13u16);
let _d: i32 = f(12i16, 13i16);
```

This code generates a compilation error at the last-but-one statement, and two other errors at the last statement.

Indeed, the first statement defines a function expecting a first argument of any type, named T, but expecting a second argument of the same type, as it is also named T. Also the returned value must have the same type.

The first and second invocations of that function pass two numbers of the same type, so they are valid. But the third invocation passes two values of different types.

In the last statement, the two arguments have the same type, but the returned value is assigned to a variable of a different type.

If you need to parameterize a function with several values of different types, you can do that by specifying several type parameters:

```
fn f<Param1, Param2>(_a: Param1, _b: Param2) {}
f('a', true);
f(12.56, "Hello");
f((3, 'a'), [5, 6, 7]);
```

This program is valid, even if it does nothing.

In the second statement, the generic parameter Param1 is inferred to be the char type, and the generic parameter Param2 is inferred to be the bool type.

Defining and Using Generic Structs

Parametric types are useful also for declaring generic structs and generic tuple-structs:

```
#[allow(dead_code)]
struct S<T1, T2> {
    c: char,
    n1: T1,
```

```
    n2: T1,
    n3: T2,
}
let _s = S { c: 'a', n1: 34, n2: 782, n3: 0.02 };
struct SE<T1, T2> (char, T1, T1, T2);
let _se = SE ('a', 34, 782, 0.02);
```

The first statement declares the generic struct S, parameterized by the two types T1 and T2. The first one of such generic types is used by two fields, while the second one is used by only one field.

The second statement creates an object having a concrete version of such generic type. The parameter T1 is implicitly replaced by i32, because the two unconstrained integers 32 and 782 are used to initialize the two fields n1 and n2. The parameter T2 is implicitly replaced by f64, because an unconstrained floating-point number 0.02 is used to initialize the field n3.

The third and fourth statements are similar, but they use a tuple-struct instead of a struct.

Also for structs, the type parameter concretizations can be made explicit:

```
#[allow(dead_code)]
struct S<T1, T2> {
    c: char,
    n1: T1,
    n2: T1,
    n3: T2,
}
let _s = S::<u16, f32> { c: 'a', n1: 34, n2: 782, n3: 0.02 };
struct SE<T1, T2> (char, T1, T1, T2);
let _se = SE::<u16, f32> ('a', 34, 782, 0.02);
```

C language does not allow generic structs, but C++ language allows them: they are the class templates and the struct templates.

Genericity Mechanics

To better understand how genericity works, you should take the role of the compiler and follow the process of compilation. Indeed, conceptually, generic code compilation happens in several stages.

Let's follow the conceptual mechanics of compilation, applied to the following code, which includes the main function:

```
fn swap<T1, T2>(a: T1, b: T2) -> (T2, T1) { (b, a) }
fn main() {
    let x = swap(3i16, 4u16);
    let y = swap(5f32, true);
    print!("{:?} {:?}", x, y);
}
```

In the first stage, the source code is scanned, and every time the compiler finds a generic function declaration (in the example, the declaration of the swap function), it loads in its data structures an internal representation of such function, in all its genericity, checking only that there are no syntax errors in the generic code.

In the second stage, the source code is scanned again, and every time the compiler encounters an invocation of a generic function, it loads in its data structures an association between such usage and the corresponding internal representation of the generic declaration, of course after having checked that such correspondence is valid.

Therefore, after the first two stages in our example, the compiler has a generic swap function and a concrete main function, with this last function containing two references to the generic swap function.

In the third stage, all the invocations of generic functions are scanned (in the example, the two invocations of swap). For each of such usages, and for each generic parameter of the corresponding definition, a concrete type is determined. Such a concrete type may be specified explicitly, or (as in the example) it may be inferred from the type of the expression used as the argument of the function. In the example, for the first invocation of swap, the parameter T1 is associated to the i16 type, and the parameter T2 is associated to the u16 type; in the second invocation of swap, the parameter T1 is associated to the f32 type, and the parameter T2 is associated to the bool type.

After having determined the concrete type by which the generic parameters are to be replaced, a concrete version of the generic function is generated. In such a concrete version, every generic parameter is replaced by the concrete type determined for the specific function invocation, and the invocation of the generic function is replaced by an invocation of the just generated concrete function.

For the example, the generated internal representation corresponds to the following Rust code:

```
fn swap_i16_u16(a: i16, b: u16) -> (u16, i16) { (b, a) }
fn swap_f32_bool(a: f32, b: bool) -> (bool, f32) { (b, a) }
fn main() {
    let x = swap_i16_u16(3i16, 4u16);
    let y = swap_f32_bool(5f32, true);
    print!("{:?} {:?}", x, y);
}
```

As you can see, there are no more generic definitions or generic function invocations. The generic function definition has been transformed into two concrete function definitions, and the two function invocations now each invoke a different concrete function.

The fourth stage consists of compiling this code.

Notice that it was needed to generate two different concrete functions, as the two invocations of the generic swap function specified different types.

But this code:

```
fn swap<T1, T2>(a: T1, b: T2) -> (T2, T1) { (b, a) }
let x = swap('A', 4.5);
let y = swap('g', -6.);
print!("{:?} {:?}", x, y);
```

is internally translated to this code:

```
fn swap_char_f64(a: char, b: f64) -> (f64, char) { (b, a) }
let x = swap_char_f64('A', 4.5);
let y = swap_char_f64('g', -6.);
print!("{:?} {:?}", x, y);
```

Even if there are several invocations of the generic function swap, only one concrete version is generated, because all the invocations required the same types for the parameters.

In general, it always applies the optimization of generating only one concrete version of a generic function declaration, when several invocations specify exactly the same type parameters.

The fact that the compiler can generate, in a single program, several concrete versions of machine code corresponding to a single function has consequences:

- This multistage compilation is somewhat slower, with respect to compiling nongeneric code.

- The generated code is highly optimized for each specific invocation, as it uses exactly the types used by the caller, without needing conversions or decisions. Therefore, the runtime performance of each invocation is optimized.

- If many invocations with different data types are performed for a generic function, a lot of machine code is generated, and that can impact performance because of bad code locality. To lessen this phenomenon, named *code bloat*, it may be better to reduce the number of distinct types used to call a generic function.

All that was said in this section about generic functions also holds for generic structs and tuple-structs.

Generic Arrays and Vectors

Regarding arrays and vectors, there is no news. We saw from Chapter 5, where they were introduced, that they are generic types.

Actually, while arrays are part of the Rust language, vectors are structs defined in the Rust standard library.

Generic Enums

In Rust, even enums can be generic.

```
enum Result1<SuccessCode, FailureCode> {
    Success(SuccessCode),
    Failure(FailureCode, char),
    Uncertainty,
}
```

```
let mut _res = Result1::Success::<u32, u16>(12u32);
_res = Result1::Uncertainty;
_res = Result1::Failure(0u16, 'd');
```

The preceding program is valid, but the following one causes a compilation at the last line:

```
enum Result1<SuccessCode, FailureCode> {
    Success(SuccessCode),
    Failure(FailureCode, char),
    Uncertainty,
}
let mut _res = Result1::Success::<u32, u16>(12u32);
_res = Result1::Uncertainty;
_res = Result1::Failure(0u32, 'd');
```

Here, the first argument of `Failure` is of type `u32`, while it should be of type `u16`, according to the initialization of `_res`, two lines before.

Generic enums are used a lot in the Rust standard library.

The `Option<T>` Standard Enum

One of the most used enums defined in the Rust standard library solves the following common problem. If a function *can fail*, what should it do, when it fails?

For example, the function `pop` removes the last item from a vector, and returns the removed item, if that vector contains some items. But what should the expression `vec![0; 0].pop()` do? It is removing an item from an empty vector!

Some languages leave this *behavior undefined*, possibly leading to unpredictable results. Rust avoids undefined behavior as much as possible.

Some languages raise an *exception*, to be handled by an enclosing block or by the callers of the current function, or leading to a crash. Rust implements the concept of *exception*, with the *panic* concept. Usually, though, a panic is raised only in very exceptional situations, and it is prevented whenever possible.

Some languages return a specific *null* value. But a vector can contain almost any possible type, and many types have no null value.

Here is the Rust idiomatic solution:

```
let mut v = vec![11, 22, 33];
for _ in 0..5 {
    let item: Option<i32> = v.pop();
    match item {
        Some(number) => print!("{}, ", number),
        None => print!("#, "),
    }
}
```

This will print: `33, 22, 11, #, #,` .

The `v` variable is a vector, initially containing three numbers.

The loop performs five iterations. Each of them tries to remove an item from `v`. If the removal is successful, the removed item is printed; otherwise the # character is printed.

The `pop` function applied to an object of `Vec<T>` type returns a value of `Option<T>` type.

Such a generic type is defined by the Rust standard library as this:

```
enum Option<T> {
    Some(T),
    None,
}
```

This enum means: "This is an optional value of T type. It has the option of being a T, and the option of being nothing. It can be something or nothing. If it is something, it is a T."

Probably such a definition would have been clearer if it had been:

```
enum Optional<T> {
    Something(T),
    Nothing,
}
```

It should be thought as such. However, Rust always tries to abbreviate names, so the previous definition is the valid one.

Getting back to the example, at the first iteration of the loop, the value of the variable `item` is `Some(33)`; at the second iteration, it is `Some(22)`; at the third iteration it is `Some(11)`. Then the `v` vector has become empty, so `pop` can only return `None`, which is assigned to `item` at the fourth and fifth iterations.

The `match` statement discriminates when `Some` number has been popped, and when there was `None`. In the former case, that number is printed, and in the latter case, just a # is printed.

The Result<T, E> Standard Enum

The Rust standard library also defines a generic enum to handle the case in which a function cannot return a value of the expected type, because of an error condition:

```
fn divide(numerator: f64, denominator: f64) -> Result<f64, String> {
    if denominator == 0. {
        Err(format!("Divide by zero"))
    } else {
        Ok(numerator / denominator)
    }
}
print!("{:?}, {:?}", divide(8., 2.), divide(8., 0.));
```

This will print: `Ok(4), Err("Divide by zero")`.

The `divide` function should return the result of the division of the first number by the second number, but only if the second number is not zero. In this latter case, it should return an error message.

The `Result` type is similar to the `Option` type, but while the `Option` type represents as `None` the case of a missing result, the `Result` type can add a value that describes such an anomalous condition.

The definition of this generic enum in the standard library is:

```
enum Result<T, E> {
    Ok(T),
    Err(E),
}
```

In our example, T was f64, because that is the type resulting from the division of two f64 numbers, and E was String because we wanted to print a message.

We used the results of the invocations only to print them as debug information, using the `{:?}` placeholder. In a production program, though, that is not acceptable, because such results can be used in further computations. This is obviously true for the success result (the Ok variant), but also the failure result (the Err variant) can be used to display a clear explanation of how the error happened or to take a branch of the algorithm that handles such case. A more appropriate code would be the following one:

```
fn divide(numerator: f64, denominator: f64) -> Result<f64, String> {
    if denominator == 0. {
        Err(format!("Divide by zero"))
    } else {
        Ok(numerator / denominator)
    }
}
fn show_divide(num: f64, den: f64) {
    match divide(num, den) {
        Ok(val) => println!("{} / {} = {}", num, den, val),
        Err(msg) => println!("Cannot divide {} by {}: {}",
            num, den, msg),
    }
}
show_divide(8., 2.);
show_divide(8., 0.);
```

This will print:

```
8 / 2 = 4
Cannot divide 8 by 0: Divide by zero
```

Enum Standard Utility Functions

The Option and Result standard generic types allow us to capture in a flexible and efficient way all the cases that happen in real-world code; though, to use a match statement to get the result is quite inconvenient.

Therefore, the standard library contains some utility functions to ease the decoding of an Option or Result value:

```
fn divide(numerator: f64, denominator: f64) -> Result<f64, String> {
    if denominator == 0. {
        Err(format!("Divide by zero"))
```

```
    } else {
        Ok(numerator / denominator)
    }
}
let r1 = divide(8., 2.);
let r2 = divide(8., 0.);
println!("{} {}", r1.is_ok(), r1.is_err());
println!("{} {}", r2.is_ok(), r2.is_err());
println!("{}", r1.unwrap());
println!("{}", r2.unwrap());
```

This program first prints

```
true false
false true
4
```

and then panics with the message: `thread 'main' panicked at 'called `Result::unwrap()` on an `Err` value: "Divide by zero"'`.

The `is_ok` function returns `true` if it is applied to an `Ok` variant. The `is_err` function returns `true` if it is applied to an `Err` variant. As they are the only possible variants, `is_err()` is equivalent to `!is_ok()`.

There are similar functions for the `Option` generic type:

```
let mut a = Some(12);
print!("{} {}; ", a.is_some(), a.is_none());
a = None;
print!("{} {}", a.is_some(), a.is_none());
```

It will print: `true false; false true`.

The `unwrap` function returns the value of the `Ok` variant, if it is applied to an `Ok` variant, and it panics otherwise. The meaning of this function is "I know that this value is a value probably wrapped in an `Ok` variant, so I just want to get that contained value, getting rid of its wrapping; in the strange case it is not an `Ok` variant, an irrecoverable error has happened, so I want to immediately terminate the program."

There is also an unwrap function for the Option enum. For example, to print all the values in a Vec, you can write:

```
let mut v = vec![11, 22, 33];
for _ in 0..v.len() {
    print!("{}, ", v.pop().unwrap())
}
```

This will print: 33, 22, 11, . The invocation of unwrap gets the number inside the Ok enum returned by pop(). We avoided calling pop() on an empty vector; otherwise pop() would have returned a None, and unwrap() would have panicked.

The unwrap function is much used in quick-and-dirty Rust programs, where it is OK that a possible errors generates a panic. To create a robust application, in which errors are handled in a user-friendly way, any possible None or Err values must be properly handled.

CHAPTER 11

Allocating Memory

In this chapter, you will learn:

- The various kinds of memory allocation, their performance characteristics, and their limitations

- How to specify in Rust which memory allocation to use for an object

- The difference between a reference and a Box

The Various Kinds of Allocation

To understand the Rust language, but also any other systems programming language, like C language, it is important to understand well the various concepts of memory allocation, like static allocation, stack allocation, and heap allocation.

This chapter is entirely dedicated to such issues. In particular, we'll see the four kinds of memory allocation:

- In processor registers

- Static

- In the stack

- In the heap

In C and C++ languages, static allocation is that of the global variables and the variables declared using the `static` keyword; the stack allocation is the one used for all non-`static` local variables, and also for function arguments; while heap allocation is the one used by invoking the `malloc` function of the C language standard library or the `new` operator of the C++ language.

151

© Carlo Milanesi 2022
C. Milanesi, *Beginning Rust*, https://doi.org/10.1007/978-1-4842-7208-4_11

Linear Addressing

In any computer hardware, there is a readable and writable kind of memory, also known as RAM, which is comprised of a long sequence of bytes, accessible by their position. The first byte of memory has position *zero*, while the last byte has a position equal to the size of installed memory minus one.

Simplifying, in our era there are two kinds of computers:

- Those where a single process at a time can run, and where such a process directly uses the physical memory addresses. These are called *real-memory systems*.

- Those with a multiprogramming operating system, which offers a virtual address space to each of the running processes. These are called *virtual-memory systems*.

In the computers of the first kind, now used only as controllers, there could be no operating system (and so they are known also as *bare-metal systems*), or there could be an operating system residing in the first part of the memory. In this last case, the addresses greater than a certain value are available to the application program.

In the computers of the second kind, the capability to access any part of system memory is reserved for the operating system, which runs in a privileged mode (also known as *protected mode*, or *kernel mode*), and such software assigns portions of memory to the various running processes.

Yet, in multiprogramming systems, the processes *see* their memory differently from how the operating system *sees* it. Consider this: a process asks the operating system for permission to use 200 more memory bytes, and the operating system satisfies such a request by reserving for that process, say, the portion of memory from machine location 300 to machine location 499, extremes included. Then the operating system communicates to the process that it has allocated 200 bytes, but it does not communicate to it that the starting address of such portion of memory is 300. Indeed, every process has a distinct address space, properly called *virtual*, which the operating system maps to the physical memory, properly called *real*.

Actually, when a process asks the operating system for some memory, the operating system just reserves a portion of the address space of the process, and no real memory is actually reserved for the process. As a result, such allocation is extremely fast even for very large memory portions.

As long as the process tries to access such memory, even if only to initialize it to zero, the operating system realizes that the process is accessing portions of virtual memory not yet mapped to real memory; it immediately performs the mapping of the accessed virtual memory portion to a corresponding real memory portion.

Therefore, processes do not operate directly on real memory, but on the virtual memory that the operating system has made available to them and that it has mapped to real memory.

In fact, often the virtual memory of a single process is even larger than the whole real memory of the computer. For example, you could have a computer with one gigabyte of physical (real) memory, and four processes running on that computer, with each process having a virtual memory space of three gigabytes. If all the virtual memory were mapped to the real memory, twelve gigabytes of memory would be required to handle such a situation. Instead, most bytes of the virtual memory are not mapped to real memory; only the bytes actually used by a process are mapped to real memory. As long as the processes begin to use portions of their address space not yet mapped to real memory, the operating system maps such portions of virtual memory to corresponding portions of real memory.

Therefore, every time a process accesses, for reading or for writing, an address, if that address belongs to a virtual memory portion (called *page*) reserved and mapped to a corresponding portion of real memory, the process immediately accesses such real memory. If, instead, the page is reserved but not presently mapped, the operating system, before allowing such access, kicks in, in a mechanism called *page fault*, by which it allocates a real memory page and maps that page to the virtual memory page referenced by the accessed address. But if the accessed address does not belong to a page reserved by the operating system as part of the address space of the process, an addressing error happens (often called *segmentation fault*). This is quite rare in programs written in Rust or in higher level languages, like Java, JavaScript, or Python, because the statements in these languages can access only the memory previously reserved to the process. Instead, this kind of error is common in low-level languages, like Assembly and C, because in such languages any number can be converted into a memory address, and if the address is computed wrongly, it may be outside the address space of the program. Usually, addressing errors cause the immediate termination of the process.

Of course, if programs use memory too liberally, the operating system could take a lot of time to do such mappings, resulting in huge slowdowns of the processes or even their termination for memory shortage.

Therefore, in modern computers, both single-programmed and multiprogrammed ones, every process *sees* its memory like an array of bytes. In one case, it is real memory, and in the other case, it is virtual memory; anyway, it is a contiguous address space, or, as is usually said, *linear addressing* is used. This differs from old computer systems that used a *segmented* address space, more cumbersome to use by application programmers.

All this has been said to clarify that, in a virtual-memory system, the operating system manages a kind of memory allocation, which is the mapping from virtual memory to real memory. Though, from now on, we'll never talk anymore about such memory allocation, and we will define memory allocation as the operation of reserving a portion of the memory *seen* by the process, and associating such memory portion to a Rust object.

Static Allocation

There are various allocation policies, though.

The simplest allocation policy is the *static* allocation. According to that policy, the compiler determines how many bytes are needed by an object of the program, and takes from the address space the corresponding byte sequence. All the objects allocated statically are laid out consecutively. Therefore, the address of each variable is determined at compile time. Here is an example in Rust:

```
static _A: u32 = 3;
static _B: i32 = -1_000_000;
static _C: f64 = 5.7e10;
static _D: u8 = 200;
```

The static keyword is similar to the let keyword. Both are used to declare a variable and optionally to initialize it.

The differences between static and let are:

- static uses the static allocation, while let uses stack allocation, introduced in the next section.

- static requires the explicit specification of the type of the variable, which is optional using let.

- Normal code cannot change the value of a static variable, even if it has the mut specification. Therefore, in Rust, static variables are normally immutable, for safety reasons.

- The style guidelines require that the names of static variables contain only uppercase letters, with words separated by underscore. If that rule is violated, the compiler reports a warning.

Of these four aspects, here we'll see only the first one, regarding the allocation kind.

The _A and _B variables take up 4 bytes each, _C takes 8 bytes, while _D takes just 1 byte. If the address of the process would start at zero (that usually does not happen), the compiler would assign to _A the address 0, to _B the address 4, to _C the address 8, and to _D the address 16, for a total of 17 bytes allocated at compile time.

When the program is launched, the process asks the operating system to use 17 bytes of memory. Then, during execution, no further memory requests are performed. When the process terminates, all the process memory is automatically released to the operating system.

A drawback of static allocation is the impossibility of creating recursive functions, which are functions that, directly or indirectly, invoke themselves. Indeed, if the arguments and local variables of a function are allocated statically, there is just one copy of them, and when the function invokes itself, it cannot have another copy of its arguments and local variables.

Another drawback of static allocation is that all the variables of all the subroutines are allocated at the start of the program. If the program contains many variables, but each particular execution uses only a small fraction of them, many variables are allocated uselessly, making the program memory hungry.

In addition, `static` variables are unsafe to modify.

Therefore, in Rust, they are not used a lot.

However, static allocations are used extensively for two other kinds of data: all the executable binary code (which actually is not really "data"), and all the string literals.

Stack Allocation

Because of the shortcomings of static allocation, Rust uses *stack* allocation a lot. Every time a variable is declared using the `let` keyword, and every time an argument is passed to a function invocation, Rust allocates an object in a portion of the address space named *stack*. Every process has its own stack.

In fact, there is a stack for every thread, not only one for every process. If the operating system supports threads, then every time a program is launched, that is, every time a process is created, a thread is created and launched inside such process.

Afterward, inside the same process, other threads may be created and launched. Every time a thread is created, including the main thread of the process, the operating system is requested to allocate a portion of address space, which is the stack of that thread. In real-memory systems, only one stack is created at the beginning of the execution of the program.

Each thread keeps stored the addresses of the ends of its stack. Typically, the end having a higher value is considered the base of the stack, and the end having the lower value is considered the top of the stack.

Let's consider the following code, similar to the previous one but using stack allocation instead of static allocation:

```
let _a: u32 = 3;
let _b: i32 = -1_000_000;
let _c: f64 = 5.7e10;
let _d: u8 = 200;
```

This program has only one thread. Now assume, quite unrealistically, that this thread has a stack of only 100 bytes, with addresses going from 500 included to 600 excluded. When this program is run, the four variables are allocated going down from the base address, which is 600.

Therefore, as shown in Figure 11-1, the _a variable will occupy the 4 bytes having addresses from 596 to 599, the _b variable will occupy the 4 bytes having addresses from 592 to 595, the _c variable will occupy the 8 bytes having addresses from 584 to 591, and the _d variable will occupy just the byte having address 583.

Addresses	Memory
500	stack
501	
.	
.	
.	
583	d: u8
584	
585	
586	
587	_c: f64
588	
589	
590	
591	
592	
593	_b: i32
594	
595	
596	
597	_a: u32
598	
599	
600	

Figure 11-1.

However, when you need to indicate the address of an object, you must always specify the lower address. So, we say that _a is at the address 596, _b at the address 592, _c at the address 584, and _d at the address 583.

The word *stack* refers to the fact that if we got a stack of China dishes, we shouldn't insert a dish in the middle of the stack, nor remove a dish from the middle of the stack. We are only allowed to add a dish to the top of the stack, if it has not reached the ceiling yet, or remove a dish from the top of the stack, if the stack is not empty.

157

Similarly, the characteristic of stack allocation is that you can add an item only at the top of the stack, and you can remove an item only from the top of the stack.

Stack allocation and deallocation are very fast, because they consist, respectively, of decrementing or incrementing the address of the last item inserted and not yet removed, which is the address of the *top* of the stack. That address is named *stack pointer*, and it is kept constantly in a processor register. When there is a context switch, and control passes to another thread, the stack pointer of that thread is loaded into the processor register.

The stack limitation of acting only on the top applies only to allocations and deallocations, not to other kinds of access. Indeed, once an object is added to a stack, that object can be read and written even if other objects have been added, as long as such writing does not increase or decrease the size of that object.

When a function is invoked, enough stack space for all its arguments and all its local variables is allocated. The allocation is performed by decrementing the stack pointer by the sum of the sizes of all such objects. When the execution of the function terminates, the stack space is deallocated by incrementing the stack pointer by the same value. So, after a function returns, the stack pointer is restored to the value it had just before the function invocation.

However, a function may be invoked from several points in a program, and in such points the stack could have contents of different sizes. So, arguments and local variables of any function are allocated in different positions according to where such function is invoked. Here is an example:

```
#[allow(unused_variables)]
fn f1(x1: i32) {
    let y1 = 2 + x1;
}
fn f2(x2: i32) {
    f1(x2 + 7);
}
let k = 20;
f1(k + 4);
f2(30);
```

Let's follow the execution of this program. This table shows, after each operation, the contents of the first four positions of the stack.

Operation	1	2	3	4	Description
k →	20				The invocation of main adds the value 20 of its local variable k to the stack.
x1 →	20	24			The invocation of f1 from main adds the value 24 of its argument x1 to the stack.
y1 →	20	24	26		The beginning of the execution of f1 adds the value 26 of its local variable y1 to the stack.
← y1	20	24			The termination of f1 removes the value 26 of its local variable y1 from the stack.
← x1	20				The termination of f1 removes the value 24 of its argument x1 from the stack.
x2 →	20	30			The invocation of f2 from main adds the value 30 of its argument x2 to the stack.
x1 →	20	30	37		The invocation of f1 from f2 adds the value 37 of its argument x1 to the stack.
y1 →	20	30	37	39	The beginning of the execution of f1 adds the value 39 of the local variable y1 to the stack.
← y1	20	30	37		The termination of f1 removes the value 39 of its local variable y1 from the stack.
← x1	20	30			The termination of f1 removes the value 37 of its argument x1 from the stack.
← x2	20				The termination of f2 removes the value 30 of its argument x2 from the stack.
← k					The termination of main removes the value 20 of its local variable k from the stack.

Actually, whenever a function is invoked, further data is added to the stack, and whenever that function terminates, such data is removed from the stack, but here we can ignore that additional data. As you can see in the preceding table, the f1 function is invoked twice. The first time, its argument x1 is represented by an object having value 24, put at the second place of the stack, and its local variable y1 is represented by an object having value 26, put at the third place of the stack. The second time f1 is invoked, its argument x1 is represented by an object having value 37, put at the third place of the stack, and its local variable y1 is represented by an object having value 39, put at the fourth place of the stack.

Therefore, the machine code generated for the function f1 cannot use absolute addresses to refer to its arguments and its local variables. Instead, it uses addresses relative to the stack pointer. Initially, the stack pointer contains the base address of the stack. In machine code, the addresses of the stack-allocated variables are all relative to the stack pointer. Let's see again the previous example.

This table shows, after each operation, the contents of the first four positions of the stack, the value of the stack pointer, and the absolute addresses of the objects associated to the variables x1 and y1, where SP means "stack pointer."

Operation	1	2	3	4	Stack Pointer	x1	y1
					base		
k →	20				base − 4		
x1 →	20	24			base − 12	SP + 4	SP
y1 →	20	24	26		base − 12	SP + 4	SP
← y1	20	24			base − 12		
← x1	20				base − 4		
x2 →	20	30			base − 8		
x1 →	20	30	37		base − 16	SP + 4	SP
y1 →	20	30	37	39	base − 16	SP + 4	SP
← y1	20	30	37		base − 16		
← x1	20	30			base − 8		
← x2	20				base − 4		
← k					base		

At the beginning of the program, the stack pointer value is the stack base address, the contents of the stack are undefined, and the variables x1 and y1 have not yet been defined.

When the main function is invoked by the system, the stack pointer becomes base - 4, as the main function has no arguments and has just one local variable, k, which occupies 4 bytes.

When the f1 function is invoked for the first time, the stack pointer becomes base - 12, as the f1 function has one argument, x1, and one local variable, y1, each occupying 4 bytes.

The creation and destruction of y1 does not change the stack pointer, as its appropriate value has already been set at function invocation.

When the function f1 terminates, the stack pointer is restored at the value it had before the function invocation, which is base - 4.

When the function f2 is invoked, the stack pointer is incremented by the size of its argument x2, setting it to the value of base - 8.

When the f1 function is invoked for the second time, the stack pointer becomes base - 16, as it is decremented by the same amount as for the first invocation, which is 8 bytes.

As each of the f1, f2, and main functions terminate, the stack pointer is incremented, first to base - 8, then to base - 4, and then to base.

As shown in the last two columns of the table, in the f1 function, the address of the argument x1 is always the value of the stack pointer minus 4; and the address of the local variable y1 is always the value of the stack pointer itself.

Limitations of Stack Allocation

The stack allocation is very convenient and efficient, but it has some limitations:

- The stack usually has a quite limited size. Such size depends on the operating system, and it can be further reduced for some applications, but it is around a few megabytes in order of magnitude.

- Rust allows us to allocate in the stack only objects whose size is known at compilation type, like primitive types and arrays, and does not allow us to allocate in the stack objects whose size is determined only at runtime, like vectors.

- It is not allowed to allocate explicitly objects in the stack, or
to deallocate explicitly objects from the stack. Any variable is
automatically allocated when the function in which it is declared is
invoked, even if it is declared in an inner block inside that function,
and it is deallocated when the execution of that function terminates.
You cannot override such behavior.

Regarding the second limitation, we actually declared local variables of Vec<_> type,
so the corresponding object was allocated in the stack, but under the hood such objects
also allocate some memory outside of the stack.

Regarding the first limitation, it is easy to build an example program that exceeds the
stack capacity.

Caution   The following programs in this chapter will surely crash the running
program, but may also cause malfunction in the whole system. So, you'd better
run them in a virtual machine, and save any pending changes before running such
examples, because they may force you to reboot your system.

Here is an example of a program exceeding the stack capacity, causing the so-called
stack overflow:

```
const SIZE: usize = 100_000;
const N_ARRAY: usize = 1_000_000;
fn create_array() -> [u8; SIZE] { [0u8; SIZE] }
fn recursive_func(n: usize) {
    let a = create_array();
    println!("{} {}", N_ARRAY - n + 1, a[0]);
    if n > 1 { recursive_func(n - 1) }
}
recursive_func(N_ARRAY);
```

This program will probably crash, typically emitting a message like "Segmentation
fault," or something similar. Indeed, it tries to allocate more than 100 GB of data on the
stack.

Assuming your target is not a microcontroller, its stack should be larger than 100KB; therefore it can allocate at least one 100KB array. However, it probably cannot allocate one million such arrays.

Let's examine this program.

After the declaration of the constants SIZE and N_ARRAY, and the declarations of the functions create_array and recursive_func, there is just one statement, which is an invocation of the recursive_func function, with N_ARRAY as the argument.

The recursive_func function first declares the a variable, and initializes it with the result of the invocation of the create_array function; then it prints two numbers; then, if the argument n is greater than 1, it invokes itself, and so it is really a recursive function.

Notice that every recursive invocation passes an argument decremented by one, so eventually the argument becomes no greater than one, and the recursion eventually ends.

If N_ARRAY were 3, the argument n would be 3 for the first invocation, it would be 2 for the second invocation, it would be 1 for the third invocation, and then there would be no further invocations. Therefore, in this case, recursive_func would be invoked three times in all.

Indeed, the number of invocations is equal to the value of the argument of the original invocation, which is one million.

Now, look at the function create_array. It simply returns an array of 100,000 bytes. Such an array is then assigned to the variable a, which therefore is inferred to be of type [u8; 100000].

Remember that the variable a is allocated when the recursive_func function is invoked, and deallocated only when that function terminates. Therefore, at every recursive invocation, a new copy of a is allocated, without previously deallocating the existing copies. As a consequence, this program tries to allocate in the stack one million arrays of one hundred thousand bytes each. Of course it cannot do that, and after having printed some lines, it terminates, usually showing an error message like "Segmentation fault" or "Stack overflow."

The last line printed could be something like 83 0.

The first number indicates how many levels of recursion have been performed, and so, how many arrays have been allocated. If the number printed is 83, it means that more than 8.3 million bytes were successfully allocated in the stack before exceeding the available space.

The second number, which is the first item of the array, is there just to prevent a possible compiler optimization. Indeed, if the variable a were never read, the compiler, after emitting a warning, could remove it completely, as such removal would improve the performance of the program without changing its behavior (before crashing).

Heap Allocation

It's a pity to have a program that crashes for stack overflow, when there is so much more memory available. But heap allocation comes to the rescue:

```
const SIZE: usize = 100_000;
const N_ARRAY: usize = 1_000_000;
fn create_array() -> Box<[u8; SIZE]> { Box::new([0u8; SIZE]) }
fn recursive_func(n: usize) {
    let a = create_array();
    println!("{} {}", N_ARRAY - n + 1, a[0]);
    if n > 1 { recursive_func(n - 1) }
}
recursive_func(N_ARRAY);
```

Eventually, even this program crashes for stack overflow or for insufficient memory, but only after having printed many more lines than the previous program, and that means that it has successfully allocated much more memory.

In this program, with respect to the previous program, only the third line has changed.

Now, the create_array function, instead of returning an array, returns a value of type Box<[u8; SIZE]>.

That type is a *boxed* array of SIZE bytes.

In Rust you can box objects of most data types, not only arrays. The Rust standard library contains the generic struct type Box<T>. An object of type Box<T> is a reference to another object, which has type T, and that is placed in a part of memory named *heap*, different both from the static area and the stack.

The body of the create_array function is Box::new([0u8; SIZE]). This expression is an invocation of the new function declared in the Box scope. Such function receives as an argument an array of SIZE bytes, all of them equal to zero. The behavior and purpose of the Box::new function are to allocate an object in the heap that must be large enough to contain a copy of the received argument, then to copy the value of the received argument into such newly allocated object, and then to return the address of such object.

Therefore, the stack space occupied by the a variable is just that of one pointer. The actual array is allocated in the heap. Well, actually the Box::new function allocates that array temporarily in the stack, but it deallocates it as soon as it returns. So, it is enough that the stack can contain one instance of that array, which occupies one hundred thousand bytes.

Heap Management

Let's see how the heap memory is managed.

When a program starts, its heap is virtually empty (or very small).

At any time, each byte of the heap may be in two possible states: *reserved* (a.k.a. *used*) or *free* (a.k.a. *unused*).

When the program needs to allocate an object in the heap, first it searches whether the heap contains some sequence of free bytes that is at least as long as the size of the object to allocate. If there is such a sequence of bytes, the program reserves from it a subsequence as long as the object size. Instead, if the heap does not contain a long enough sequence, a request is made to the operating system to enlarge the size of the heap, so that the object can be allocated.

When an object allocated in the heap is not needed anymore, it can be explicitly deallocated, returning the memory space it used to the state of *free*.

Notice that usually the size of the heap of a process is never shrunk.

A serious problem of heap management is that it may become fragmented. If a million f64 objects are allocated in a heap, that heap must become as large as at least 8MB. If then every object having an odd position (1, 3, 5, ...) is deallocated from that heap, we get to a situation in which the heap contains half a million free spaces, for a total of 4MB, interleaved with half a million reserved spaces. There is a lot of free space, but if you need to allocate an object larger than 8 bytes, there is no free space that is large enough for it. So, you need to enlarge that heap.

In addition, a naive algorithm that searches a large enough space in a heap can be very costly. There are smarter search algorithms that can improve the performance of heap allocation, but they cause the heap deallocation to become more costly.

Therefore, stack allocation is always more efficient than heap allocation, both in time and in space. You get a heap allocation nearly as efficient as stack allocation only when you never deallocate, or when you deallocate only the last allocated object. Of course, often the application requirements do not allow this allocation/deallocation pattern.

The Behavior of Box

As we said, for any variable of type Box<T>, a pointer is allocated in the stack as soon as the function declaring such variable is invoked. Instead, the heap allocation happens only when the function Box::new is invoked. So, the allocation of Box<T> happens in two steps: first the pointer is allocated in the stack, and then the referenced object is allocated in the heap.

Similarly, the deallocation also happens in two steps. The deallocation from the stack of the pointer of a Box object happens only when the function containing the variable terminates, but the deallocation of the referenced object from the heap happens when the Box object exits its scope, as shown by the following program:

```
fn f(p: &f64) {
    let a = Box::new(*p);
    {
        let b = Box::new([1, 2, 3]);
        print!("{} {:?}", *a, *b);
    }
    let c = Box::new(true);
    print!(" {} {}", a, c);
}
f(&3.4);
```

This will print: 3.4 [1, 2, 3] 3.4 true.

When the function main is invoked, the value 3.4, of type f64, is allocated on the stack without being associated to any variable.

When the function f is invoked, four pointers are allocated in the stack, one for the argument p, and one for each of the three variables a, b, and c.

When the first statement of this function is executed, an f64 object is allocated in the heap, and it is initialized with the value of the expression *p, which is 3.4.

When the second statement of the function is executed, an array of three i32 values is allocated and initialized in the heap, and its address is used to initialize the b variable. The third statement prints the values referenced by a and b. The dereference operator used for Box objects is the same used for simple references. The c variable could not be printed here, because it is not yet visible. Immediately after this statement, the scope of b ends, so the array referenced by b is deallocated from the heap, freeing the space it used, making it available for other allocations.

This last action is important. When b exits its scope, it becomes available no more; and *automatically*, the heap object referred to by it is deallocated.

When the fourth statement of the function is executed, a Boolean object is allocated and initialized in the heap, and its address is used to initialize the c variable. It may be that such Boolean object overlaps that of the previous array in the heap, as the space used by the array was freed. The fifth statement prints the values referenced by a and c. Also for boxes, like for simple references, the asterisks are optional and omitted. The b variable could not be printed here, because it is no more visible. Immediately after this statement, the scope of both a and c ends, so the objects they are referencing are deallocated from the heap. This is also the end of the function execution, so the four pointers are also deallocated from the stack.

Finally, the main function ends, so the 3.4 unnamed object is deallocated from the stack.

Here it is rather pointless, but it is worth noting that if several variables are declared in the same scope, they exit their scope in reverse order of declaration. In our example, a has been declared before c, so a exits its scope after c. This causes the object referenced by a to be deallocated from the heap after the object referenced by c. This is quite reasonable, considering that it is a stack, so the top item is always the next to be removed.

Notice that here no deallocation function is invoked. Actually the Rust language and its standard library have no deallocation functions to call. This prevents forgetting to call them, or calling them twice for the same object.

Similarity with C and C++

Even in C and in C++ you can use the heap. In C language, you have the malloc, calloc, and realloc functions to allocate a buffer in the heap, and the free function to deallocate a previously allocated buffer. In addition, in the C++ language, you have the new and the new[ ] operators to allocate, respectively, an object or an array of objects in the heap; and you have the delete and delete[ ] operators to deallocate what has been allocated by, respectively, the new or the new[ ] operators.

Actually, the Rust Box<T> generic type is quite different from all the aforementioned kinds of heap allocation. But since 2011, in standard C++ there has existed a type that is quite similar to Box<T>: it is the unique_ptr<T> class template. It is a so-called *smart pointer*, which, like Box<T>, allocates an object in the heap and deallocates it automatically when it exits from its scope.

Boxing and Unboxing

So, for a given T generic type, both Box<T> and &T are kinds of references. Let's see how they can interact:

```
let a = 7;
let a_box: Box<i32>;
let mut a_ref: &i32 = &a;
print!("{} {};", a, *a_ref);
a_box = Box::new(a + 2);
a_ref = &*a_box;
print!(" {} {} {}", a, *a_ref, *a_box);
```

This will print: 7 7; 7 9 9. Let's examine it.

The stack will contain three objects: the number 7, represented by the a variable; and two pointers, represented by the a_box and a_ref variables. The pointer declared in the second line, a_box, is initialized only at the fifth line, while the other variables are initialized in the same statements in which they are declared.

Both pointer variables are type annotated, but such annotations are optional and could be removed, because their types can be inferred from their usage. However, they show that a_box is a *smart* pointer, while a_ref is a *dumb* pointer, meaning that a_box takes care of allocating and deallocating its referred object, while a_ref does not take care of either allocation or deallocation of its referred object.

In the two print macro invocations, the three asterisks are optional and could be removed.

In the fifth and sixth lines, the two pointers are assigned a value. But for a_box, it's an initialization, so the variable does not have to be mutable; however, a_ref had already been initialized, and so, to be reassigned it had to be declared with the mut clause.

The third line just set the a_ref variable value as the address of the a variable. But the fifth line does something more complex. It allocates an i32 object in the heap, initializes that object using the value of the expression a + 2, which is the value 9, and then it sets the a_box variable value as the address of that object.

In the sixth line, the value of a_box (not the value referred to by a_box), which is a pointer, is copied to the variable a_ref; in other words, the dumb pointer is made to point to the same object pointed to by the smart pointer. This is confirmed by the last print statement. However, this assignment cannot be simply a_ref = a_box;, because the two variables have different types, and also the statement a_ref = a_box as &i32; would be illegal. Instead, the trick of dereferencing using *, and then referencing using & allows us to convert a Box into a reference. Better said, it allows us to take the address of the object referenced to by the box.

Notice that the inverted operation would be illegal: a_box = &*a_ref;. Actually, the expression &*a_ref is still of type &i32, and so it cannot be assigned to a variable of type Box<i32>.

Finally, at the end of the program, first a_ref exits from its scope, doing nothing; then a_box exists from its scope, deallocating its referenced object from the heap; then a exits from its scope, doing nothing; and at last the three objects are deallocated from the stack.

This program is similar:

```
let a = 7;
let mut a_box: Box<i32>;
let a_ref: &i32 = &a;
print!("{} {};", a, a_ref);
a_box = Box::new(a + 2);
print!(" {} {} {};", a, a_ref, a_box);
a_box = Box::new(*a_ref);
print!(" {} {} {}", a, a_ref, a_box);
```

It will print 7 7; 7 7 9; 7 7 7.

Here it is a_box to be mutable, while a_ref is immutable.

The last-but-one statement reassigns the box. Conceptually, that causes the previously referenced object, whose value is 9, to be deallocated from the heap, and a new object is allocated in the heap. The value of the new object is taken from the value referenced by a_ref, which is 7.

Register Allocation

In Assembly language, and sometimes also in C language, the concept of *processor register allocation* is used. In Rust language, this concept is absent, because it would constrain the code to specific target hardware architectures. However, the code optimizer can move the location of a stack-allocated object into a processor register, as long as the resulting behavior of the program is equivalent. Therefore, what at source code level appears to be a stack-allocated object, at machine code level may turn out to be a register-allocated object. This of course depends on the target architecture, because the more registers the target processor has, the more variables can be allocated into registers.

This register allocation is usually irrelevant for the programmer. But if you use a source-level debugger to examine the contents of the memory of a highly optimized program, you will find that some stack-allocated variables have disappeared. So, when debugging, you should instruct your compiler to generate nonoptimized executable code, unless you want to directly debug machine code.

CHAPTER 12

Data Implementation

In this chapter, you will learn:

- How to know how many bytes of stack are taken by objects of various types
- How to shorten the path to access functions declared in external modules
- How bits are stored in primitive type objects
- How to know where an object is stored in memory
- Why padding can increase the size taken by some objects
- How vectors are implemented

Discovering the Size of Objects

Given a source file, the Rust compiler is free to generate any machine code, as long as it behaves in the way specified by the Rust language for that source code.

Therefore, for example, given a variable, how many memory bits it uses, and where it is located in memory are not defined. The compiler could even remove that variable from memory because it is never used, or because it is kept in a processor register.

However, it is instructive to see a possible typical implementation of the arrangement of the data used by a Rust program.

For such a purpose, some Rust features are available:

```
print!("{} ", std::mem::size_of::<i32>());
print!("{} ", std::mem::size_of_val(&12));
```

This will print: 4 4 .

© Carlo Milanesi 2022
C. Milanesi, *Beginning Rust*, https://doi.org/10.1007/978-1-4842-7208-4_12

In the first statement, the compiler enters the standard library module std (shorthand for *standard*), then it enters its submodule mem (shorthand for *memory*), and then it takes its generic function size_of.

The compiler concretizes such a generic function using the type i32, and then it generates the invocation of such resulting concrete function without passing any arguments. Such a function will return the number of octets of bits occupied by any object of the specified type. For more than four decades, such octets have been unambiguously named *bytes*. In the first years of computer technology, there were computers for which the name *byte* was used for shorter sequences of bits. Anyway, such very old computer architectures are not supported by Rust.

Typically, such function invocation will be inlined, and so the code generated is just a constant number. Actually, a 32-bit number occupies 4 bytes.

Notice that you may invoke this function even if in the program there is no object of the specified type.

In the second statement, the compiler enters in the same library module, but it accesses the generic function size_of_val (meaning *size of value*). In this case, the type of the parameter needed to concretize the generic function is inferred from the argument, so it wasn't required to specify it explicitly. Instead, in the first statement there were no arguments, so the type parameter was required.

When the concretized function size_of_val is invoked, an immutable reference to an object is passed to it. The function returns the size in bytes of that object.

The use Directive

If the path to reach a library function must be specified several times, it is convenient to *import* all or part of such path into the current scope, using the use directive.

The previous example can be rewritten in this way:

```
use std::mem;
print!("{} ", mem::size_of::<i32>());
print!("{} ", mem::size_of_val(&12));
```

or in this way:

```
use std::mem::size_of;
use std::mem::size_of_val;
```

```
print!("{} ", size_of::<i32>());
print!("{} ", size_of_val(&12));
```

The Rust use keyword is similar to the C++ using keyword.

There is an even more compact form of it:

```
use std::mem::*;
print!("{} ", size_of::<i32>());
print!("{} ", size_of_val(&12));
```

The asterisk is a wildcard that causes all the names at that level to be imported.

The Sizes of the Primitive Types

Now you should imagine the sizes of the objects having a primitive type:

```
use std::mem::*;
print!("{} {} {} {} {} {} {} {} {} {} {} {} {} {}",
    size_of::<i8>(),
    size_of::<u8>(),
    size_of::<i16>(),
    size_of::<u16>(),
    size_of::<i32>(),
    size_of::<u32>(),
    size_of::<i64>(),
    size_of::<u64>(),
    size_of::<i128>(),
    size_of::<u128>(),
    size_of::<f32>(),
    size_of::<f64>(),
    size_of::<bool>(),
    size_of::<char>());
```

In any computer, this will print: 1 1 2 2 4 4 8 8 16 16 4 8 1 4.

Some other data types have sizes that depend on the target platform of the compiler:

```
use std::mem::*;
print!("{} {} {} {}",
    size_of::<isize>(),
    size_of::<usize>(),
    size_of::<&i8>(),
    size_of::<&u32>());
```

In a 64-bit system, this will print: 8 8 8 8, while in a 32-bit system, it will print: 4 4 4 4.

The last two printed values are references. Independently from the referenced object, a reference (a.k.a. *pointer*) has the size of a memory address.

The Representation of Primitive Types

Rust discourages accessing the internal representation of objects, so it is not easy to do; but there is a trick to do that:

```
fn as_bytes<T>(o: &T) -> &[u8] {
    unsafe {
        std::slice::from_raw_parts(
            o as *const _ as *const u8,
            std::mem::size_of::<T>())
    }
}
println!("{:?}", as_bytes(&1i8));
println!("{:?}", as_bytes(&2i16));
println!("{:?}", as_bytes(&3i32));
println!("{:?}", as_bytes(&(4i64 + 5 * 256 + 6 * 256 * 256)));
println!("{:?}", as_bytes(&'A'));
println!("{:?}", as_bytes(&true));
println!("{:?}", as_bytes(&&1i8));
```

In an x86_64 system, this could print:

```
[1]
[2, 0]
[3, 0, 0, 0]
```

```
[4, 5, 6, 0, 0, 0, 0, 0]
[65, 0, 0, 0]
[1]
[129, 165, 54, 102, 23, 86, 0, 0]
```

The generic function as_bytes uses some Rust constructs we haven't seen yet, and that will not be explained here, because their knowledge is not required to understand what it does. It simply takes a reference to an argument of any type, and returns an object that represents the sequence of bytes contained in such an object. By printing such an object, you can see the representation of any object as the sequence of bytes it stores in memory.

First, an i8 having value 1 is stored in a single byte. And that is just the same in any supported hardware architecture.

Then, an i16 having value 2 is stored as a pair of bytes, of which the first one is 2 and the second one is 0. This happens both on 32-bit and 64-bit processors, but only in the so-called *little-endian* hardware architectures, which are those that store multibyte numbers placing the least significant byte at the lowest address. Instead, a *big-endian* hardware architecture would have printed [0, 2].

Similar behavior appears in the following printed lines.

Notice that a char is stored as a 32-bit number containing the Unicode value of such character, and a bool is stored as a single byte, which is 1 for true and 0 for false.

Finally, the last statement prints the address of an i8 number. Such an address occupies eight bytes for a 64-bit processor, and differs from run to run.

Location of Bytes in Memory

You can also discover the (virtual) memory location of any object, which is its address:

```
let b1 = true;
let b2 = true;
let b3 = false;
print!("{} {} {}",
    &b1 as *const bool as usize,
    &b2 as *const bool as usize,
    &b3 as *const bool as usize);
```

In a 64-bit system, this will print three huge numbers, resembling 140729279188109 140729279188110 140729279188111. But in a 32-bit system, it will print three numbers smaller than five billion.

Also, the constructs to get such numbers will not be explained here.

However, there is a simpler way to print the address of any object, in hexadecimal notation:

```
let b1 = true;
let b2 = true;
let b3 = false;
print!("{:p} {:p} {:p}", &b1, &b2, &b3);
```

The p format specifier is shorthand for *pointer*.

It will print something like:

```
0x7ffe16b20c8d 0x7ffe16b20c8e 0x7ffe16b20c8f
```

Here is a representation of the location of the three objects in the preceding code.

Absolute Address	Binary Value	Variable Name	Type
140729279188109	0000_0001	b1	bool
140729279188110	0000_0001	b2	bool
140729279188111	0000_0000	b3	bool

Each one of the three objects occupies just one byte. The first printed number is the address of the b1 variable; the second one is the address of the b2 variable; and the third one is the address of the b3 variable. As it appears, the three numbers are consecutive, and that means that the three objects are allocated in contiguous virtual memory locations.

The first number contains the true Boolean value, which is represented by the 1 byte, which in turn consists of seven bits having zero value and one bit having one value. Also the second object contains the true value. Instead, the third object contains the false value, represented by eight bits having zero value.

When allocating single bytes, the Rust compiler usually lays them out sequentially and contiguously, but when allocating larger objects, their position in memory is not easily predictable.

Almost all modern processors require that elementary data have particular memory locations, so Rust places its objects so that they are easily accessible by the processors.

The typical alignment rule is this: "Every object of a primitive type must have an address that is a multiple of its own size."

So, while the objects occupying just one byte can be placed anywhere, the objects occupying two bytes can be placed only at even addresses; the objects occupying four bytes can be placed only at addresses that are divisible by four; and the objects occupying eight bytes can be places only at addresses that are a multiple of eight.

In addition, larger objects often have addresses that are a multiple of sixteen.

Therefore, such alignment requirements can create unused spaces, the so-called *padding*.

Sizes of Composite Data Types

The effect of padding appears when there is a sequence of composite objects:

```
enum E1 { E1a, E1b }
enum E2 { E2a, E2b(f64) }
use std::mem::*;
print!("{} {} {} {} {} {}",
    size_of_val(&[0i16; 80]),
    size_of_val(&(0i16, 0i64)),
    size_of_val(&[(0i16, 0i64); 100]),
    size_of_val(&E1::E1a),
    size_of_val(&E2::E2a),
    size_of_val(&vec![(0i16, 0i64); 100]));
```

This will print: 160 16 1600 1 16 24.

This means that:

- An array of 80 16-bit numbers occupies 160 bytes, which is 80 * 2, so there is no waste.

- A tuple of a 16-bit number and a 64-bit number occupies 16 bytes, as if both numbers would occupy 8 bytes, so a padding of 6 bytes has been added.

- An array of 100 16-byte tuples occupies 1600 bytes, so there is no padding between array items, but the size of every item is multiplied by the length of the array.

- An enum having all its variants without data fields occupies just one byte; as long as there are no more than 256 variants, a single byte can contain a value that identifies a variant; such hidden value is usually named *tag*.

- An enum whose largest variant contains an 8-byte number occupies 16 bytes, even if the current value has no data; this is because any value of a variant must occupy the same size, that is, the size of the largest possible value of that enum. In this case, the second variant has a 1-byte tag and an 8-byte numeric field; the address of this field must be a multiple of 8, so a 7-byte padding is added between the tag and the field.

- A vector of 100 16-byte tuples looks like it occupies just 24 bytes, but of course something is missing from this measure.

Let's see just the case of the vector.

The data placed in the stack must have a size known at compile time, so arrays can be fully allocated in the stack; while for vectors only a fixed-size header can be placed in the stack, and the remaining data must be allocated in the heap.

Vector Allocation

We saw that vectors must be implemented as a two-object structure: a stack-allocated fixed-size header, and a heap-allocated variable-length buffer.

There are theoretically several possible ways to implement a vector data structure.

One way would be to keep in the header only a pointer to the buffer.

That has the disadvantage that every time the length of the array is desired, an indirection level would be required. The length of arrays is needed quite often, implicitly or explicitly, so it is better to keep such information in the header.

A naive way to implement the buffer would be to size it just large enough to keep the desired data. For example, if a vector of 9 `i32` items is requested, a buffer of 9 * 4 bytes would be allocated in the heap.

As long as the vector does not grow, this is good. But if another item is pushed into the vector, the buffer must be reallocated, and heap allocations and deallocation are costly. In addition, the old buffer contents must be copied to the new buffer.

If a 1,000-item vector is constructed, an item at a time, by creating an empty vector and calling the push function 1,000 times, there will be 1,000 heap allocations, 999 heap deallocations, and 1000 * 999 / 2 == 499_500 copies of items.

To improve such awful performance, a larger buffer may be allocated, so that a reallocation is performed only when that buffer is not enough.

Therefore, there is the need to track both the number of places in the allocated buffer and the number of used places in that buffer.

The number of places in the allocated buffer is usually called capacity, and that is also the name of the function used to access such number. Here is some code that displays the size of the buffer of a vector:

```
let mut v = vec![0; 0];
println!("{} {}", v.len(), v.capacity());
v.push(11);
println!("{} {}", v.len(), v.capacity());
v.push(22);
println!("{} {}", v.len(), v.capacity());
v.push(33);
println!("{} {}", v.len(), v.capacity());
v.push(44);
println!("{} {}", v.len(), v.capacity());
v.push(55);
println!("{} {}", v.len(), v.capacity());
```

This will possibly print:

```
0 0
1 4
2 4
3 4
4 4
5 8
```

When an empty vector is created, it contains zero items, and it hasn't even allocated a heap buffer, so its capacity is also zero.

When the first item is added, the vector object allocates in the heap a buffer capable of containing four 32-bit numbers (i.e., a 16-byte buffer), so its capacity is 4, but it effectively contains just one item, so its length is 1.

When three other items are added to the vector, there is no need to allocate memory, as the preallocated buffer is large enough to contain them.

But when the fifth item is added to the vector, a larger buffer must be allocated. The new buffer has a capacity of 8 items.

Notice that this growing strategy of the buffer is an implementation detail, and it may change in future implementations of the standard library.

The v object stores three subobjects in the stack: a pointer to the heap-allocated buffer, which is a memory address; the capacity of such buffer as a number of items, which is a usize number; and the length of the vector as a number of items, which is a usize number that is less than or equal to the capacity.

For this reason, the header of any vector occupies 3 * 8 == 24 bytes in any 64-bit system, and 3 * 4 == 12 bytes in any 32-bit system.

Let's see what happens if we add one thousand items to a vector of 32-bit numbers:

```
let mut v = vec![0; 0];
let mut prev_capacity = std::usize::MAX;
for i in 0..1_000 {
    let cap = v.capacity();
    if cap != prev_capacity {
        println!("{} {} {}", i, v.len(), cap);
        prev_capacity = cap;
    }
    v.push(1);
}
```

This could print:

```
0 0 0
1 1 4
5 5 8
9 9 16
17 17 32
33 33 64
65 65 128
129 129 256
257 257 512
513 513 1024
```

Well, it also will print the same for vectors whose items are of most other types.

The variable `cap` stores the current capacity of the vector; the variable `prev_capacity` stores the previous capacity of the vector, and it is initialized to a huge value.

At each iteration, before adding an item to the vector, it is checked to see if the capacity has changed. Each time the capacity changes, both the number of inserted items and the current capacity are printed.

It appears that the capacity is always a power of two, and all the powers of two are passed, just skipping the value 2. In this way, there are just 9 allocations, 8 deallocations, and $4 + 8 + 16 + 32 + 64 + 128 + 256 + 512 == 1020$ copies. So, the actual standard library algorithm is much more efficient than the naive version described at the beginning of this section.

In general, filling a vector by pushing one item at a time causes a number of allocations and deallocation that is a logarithm of the total number of items, so a number that is much smaller than the number of items, for a rather large number of items.

So, adding an item at a time is quite efficient. Though, if you can estimate the number of items that will be contained in the vector, you can improve this efficiency by preallocating the required buffer, like this code does:

```
let mut v = Vec::with_capacity(800);
let mut prev_capacity = std::usize::MAX;
for i in 0..1_000 {
    let cap = v.capacity();
    if cap != prev_capacity {
        println!("{} {} {}", i, v.len(), cap);
        prev_capacity = cap;
    }
    v.push(1);
}
```

It will print:

```
0 0 800
801 801 1600
```

This program is identical to the previous one, except for the first line. The function `Vec::with_capacity` creates a vector with a preallocated buffer, large enough to contain the specified number of items. It specified a capacity of 800 items, so until such capacity is exceeded, no allocation happens after the initialization. When the 801st item is pushed, the capacity is bumped to 1600.

CHAPTER 13

Defining Closures

In this chapter, you will learn:

- Why there is a need for anonymous inline functions, with type inference for the arguments and the return value type, without having to write braces, and which can access the variables that are alive at the function definition point

- How such lightweight functions, named "closures," can be declared and invoked

The Need for *Disposable* Functions

The Rust way to sort an array in ascending order is this:

```
let mut arr = [4, 8, 1, 10, 0, 45, 12, 7];
arr.sort();
print!("{:?}", arr);
```

This will print: [0, 1, 4, 7, 8, 10, 12, 45].

But if you want to sort it in descending order, or use some other criterion, there are no prepackaged functions; you must invoke the sort_by function, passing to it a reference to a comparison function. Such comparison function receives two items, and it returns an indication of which of them must precede the other one:

```
let mut arr = [4, 8, 1, 10, 0, 45, 12, 7];
use std::cmp::Ordering;
fn desc(a: &i32, b: &i32) -> Ordering {
    if a < b { Ordering::Greater }
    else if a > b { Ordering::Less }
```

© Carlo Milanesi 2022
C. Milanesi, *Beginning Rust*, https://doi.org/10.1007/978-1-4842-7208-4_13

```
    else { Ordering::Equal }
}
arr.sort_by(desc);
print!("{:?}", arr);
```

This will print: [45, 12, 10, 8, 7, 4, 1, 0].

The desc function returns a value whose type is defined by the standard library in the following way:

```
enum Ordering { Less, Equal, Greater }
```

This works, but it has several drawbacks.

First, the desc function is defined only to be used in one point, in the statement that follows it. Usually you don't create a very small function to be used only in one point; rather, the body of that function is expanded where it is needed. However, the library function sort_by requires a function. What is needed is an inline anonymous function, which is a function that is declared in the same point where it is used.

Moreover, while the type specification is optional for variable declarations, it is required for the arguments and the return value for function declarations. These specifications, like the name of the function, are convenient when such function is invoked from faraway statements, and possibly by other programmers. But when you have to write a function to be invoked just where it has been declared, such type specifications are mostly annoying. So it would be a convenient feature to declare and invoke inline an anonymous function with type inference of its arguments and its return value.

Another drawback regards the need to enclose the function body in braces. Usually, functions contain several statements, so it is not at all annoying having to enclose such statements in braces. But anonymous functions often consist of a single expression, which would be convenient to be able to write without having to enclose it in braces. Given that a block is still an expression, it would be nice to have an inline anonymous function with type inference and a single expression as body.

Capturing the Environment

All that's been said so far in this chapter is also valid in many other languages, C included. But Rust functions have an additional unusual limitation: they cannot access any variable that is declared outside of them. You can access `static` items, and also `const` items, but you cannot access stack-allocated (that is "let-declared") variables. For example, this program is illegal:

```
let two = 2.;
fn print_double(x: f64) {
    print!("{}", x * two);
}
print_double(17.2);
```

Its compilation generates the error: `can't capture dynamic environment in a fn item`. By *dynamic environment*, it means the set of the variables that happen to be valid where the function is defined. For instance, in the previous example, the variable `two` is still defined when the `print_double` function is defined. The ability to access the variables of that dynamic environment is named *capturing the environment*.

Instead, this is valid:

```
const TWO: f64 = 2.;
fn print_double(x: f64) {
    print!("{}", x * TWO);
}
print_double(17.2);
```

and this is too:

```
static TWO: f64 = 2.;
fn print_double(x: f64) {
    print!("{}", x * TWO);
}
print_double(17.2);
```

This code is valid because `const` items and `static` items can be captured by functions, but variables cannot.

Such a limitation has a good reason: `const` items and `static` items have fixed values, while the value of variables can change. So, if a function cannot access external variables, its behavior will change only if the value of its arguments changes. The ability to access external variables effectively introduces them into the programming interface of the function; though, they are not apparent from the function signature, so they are misleading for understanding code.

But when a function can be invoked only where it has been defined, the fact that it accesses external variables does not cause it to be less understandable, because those external variables are available anyway where the function is invoked.

Therefore, the requirements of our desired feature are the following: an inline anonymous function, with type inference; a single expression as body; and the capture of any valid variable.

Closures

Because of its great usefulness, in Rust there actually is such a feature, which is named *closure*.

A closure is just a handier kind of function, fit to define small anonymous functions, and to invoke them just where they have been defined.

In fact, you can also define a closure; assign it to a variable, so giving it a name; and then invoke it later using its name. This is not the most typical usage of closures, though. Even type annotation is possible.

Here is the earlier descending order sorting example, replacing the desc function with a closure, and keeping the code as similar to the previous one as possible:

```
let mut arr = [4, 8, 1, 10, 0, 45, 12, 7];
use std::cmp::Ordering;
let desc = |a: &i32, b: &i32| -> Ordering {
    if a < b { Ordering::Greater }
    else if a > b { Ordering::Less }
    else { Ordering::Equal }
};
arr.sort_by(desc);
print!("{:?}", arr);
```

The only differences with respect to the previous example are:

- The let keyword was used instead of fn.

- The = symbol has been added after the name of the closure.

- The (and) symbols, which enclose the function arguments, have been replaced by the | (pipe) symbol.

- A semicolon has been added after the closure declaration.

So far, there are no advantages, but we saw that the closure can be defined where it has to be used, and that the types and the braces are optional. Therefore, the previous code can be transformed into this one:

```
let mut arr = [4, 8, 1, 10, 0, 45, 12, 7];
use std::cmp::Ordering;
arr.sort_by(|a, b|
    if a < b { Ordering::Greater }
    else if a > b { Ordering::Less }
    else { Ordering::Equal });
print!("{:?}", arr);
```

This is already a nice simplification. But there is more.

The standard library already contains the cmp function (shorthand for *compare*); this function returns an Ordering value according to which of its two arguments is greater. The two following statements are equivalent:

```
arr.sort();
arr.sort_by(|a, b| a.cmp(b));
```

Therefore, to obtain the inverted order, you can use, indifferently, each one of the following statements:

```
arr.sort_by(|a, b| (&-a).cmp(&-b));
arr.sort_by(|a, b| b.cmp(a));
```

Here is a complete example:

```
let mut arr = [4, 8, 1, 10, 0, 45, 12, 7];
arr.sort_by(|a, b| b.cmp(a));
print!("{:?}", arr);
```

Also the use directive has been removed, because it is not required anymore.

The other way to write it is this:

```
let mut arr = [4, 8, 1, 10, 0, 45, 12, 7];
arr.sort_by(|a, b| (-*a).cmp(&-*b));
print!("{:?}", arr);
```

Let's explain the closure passed to the sort_by function. This closure receives two references; the type of both a and b is &i32. To apply the minus sign, we must dereference such references, to get numbers; so we write *a and *b. The cmp function expects a reference as argument, so we add the & symbol. The expression -*a could be written &-*a just as well, but in this case the reference symbol is implicit.

Rust closures are very efficient because they do not allocate heap memory, and because they are usually expanded inline by the compiler, thereby eliminating all temporary objects. They are actually quite similar to C++ lambdas. The C++ program corresponding to the previous Rust program is this:

```cpp
#include <array>
#include <algorithm>
#include <iostream>
#include <iterator>
using namespace std;
int main() {
    auto arr = array<int, 8> {
        4, 8, 1, 10, 0, 45, 12, 7 };
    stable_sort(
        arr.begin(), arr.end(),
        [](int a, int b) { return b < a; });
    copy(
      arr.begin(),
      arr.end(),
      ostream_iterator<int>(cout, ", "));
}
```

Closure Invocation Syntax

Here is another example that shows six ways to invoke a closure:

```rust
let factor = 2;
let multiply = |a| a * factor;
print!("{}", multiply(13));
let multiply_ref = &multiply;
```

```
print!(
    " {} {} {} {} {}",
    (*multiply_ref)(13),
    multiply_ref(13),
    (|a| a * factor)(13),
    (|a: i32| a * factor)(13),
    |a| -> i32 { a * factor }(13));
```

This will print: 26 26 26 26 26 26.

This program contains six identical closure invocations. Each of them performs these steps:

- It takes an i32 argument named a.

- It multiplies the argument by the captured variable factor, whose value is 2.

- It returns the result of such multiplication.

The argument is always 13, so the result is always 26.

In the second line, the first closure is declared, using a type inference both for the argument a and for the return value. The body of the closure accesses the external variable factor, declared by the previous statement, so such variable is captured inside the closure with its current value. The closure is then used to initialize the variable multiply, whose type is inferred.

In the third line, the closure assigned to the multiply variable is invoked. This shows that closures are invoked just like any function.

In the fourth line, the address of the just declared closure is used to initialize the multiply_ref variable, whose type is that of a reference to a closure.

In the seventh line, the reference to a closure is dereferenced, obtaining a closure, and that closure is invoked.

In the eighth line, that closure is invoked without dereferencing the reference, as the dereference operation is implicit for a function invocation.

In the last three statements, three anonymous closures are declared and invoked. The first one infers both the type of the argument and the type of the return value; the second one specifies the type of the argument and infers the type of the return value; and the third one infers the type of the argument and specifies the type of the return value.

Notice that the argument 13 is passed to the closure always enclosed in parentheses. To avoid confusing that expression (13) with the expression preceding it, which specifies the closure, in some cases such closure expression must be enclosed in parentheses too. In the last case, instead, the body of the closure had to be enclosed in braces, to separate it from the return value type specification.

The braces are also required when the closure contains several statements, like in this case:

```
print!(
    "{}",
    (|v: &Vec<i32>| {
        let mut sum = 0;
        for i in 0..v.len() {
            sum += v[i];
        }
        sum
    })(&vec![11, 22, 34]));
```

This will print 67, which is the sum of the numbers contained in the vector.

In this case, it was necessary to specify the type of the argument, as otherwise the compiler couldn't infer it, and it would emit the error message "type annotations needed."

CHAPTER 14

Using Changeable Strings

In this chapter, you will learn:

- How static strings are implemented

- How dynamic strings are implemented

- How you can add characters to or remove characters from a dynamic string

- How to convert a static string to a dynamic string, and conversely

- How to concatenate strings

Static Strings

Are the strings that we have used so far changeable?

They may be mutable and so, in a sense, we can change them, like in this code:

```
let mut a = "Hel";
print!("{}", a);
a = "lo";
print!("{}", a);
```

This will print: Hello. But in what sense did we change it? We abruptly changed all the content of the string, not just some characters. In fact, so far we changed strings only by assigning to a string variable a string literal or another string variable.

But if we wanted to create a string either algorithmically, or by reading it from a file, or by letting the user type it in, how could we do it? Simply stated, using the kind of strings we have used so far, we cannot do that. Indeed, although these string objects can be changed to refer to other string content, they have an immutable *content*, that is, it

© Carlo Milanesi 2022
C. Milanesi, *Beginning Rust*, https://doi.org/10.1007/978-1-4842-7208-4_14

is not possible to overwrite some characters or to add or remove characters in a string. Because of this, they are called *static* strings. The following example helps to clarify:

```
use std::mem::*;
let a: &str = "";
let b: &str = "0123456789";
let c: &str = "abcdè";
print!("{} {} {}",
    size_of_val(a),
    size_of_val(b),
    size_of_val(c));
```

This program will print: 0 10 6.

First, notice that we specified the type of the three variables. That type is &str, which means *reference to* str.

The str word is defined in the standard library as the type of an unmodifiable array of bytes representing a UTF-8 string. Each time the compiler parses a literal string, it stores in a static program area the characters of that string, and that area is of str type. Then the compiler uses a reference to that area as the value of the literal string expression, so any string literal is of type &str.

In the example, the size_of_val generic function is invoked on the three string variables. Remember that such a function returns the size of the object *referenced* by its argument. If the argument is a, which is of type &str, this function returns the size of the string buffer referenced by a, which is of type str.

So the sizes of the three buffers referred to by the variables a, b, and c are printed. Such sizes are, respectively, 0, 10, and 6 bytes. Indeed, the first string was empty, so its buffer occupies no bytes; the second string contained exactly ten digits, and each digit is a character that occupies one byte, so that string buffer occupies ten bytes; the third string contained only five characters, but the number six was printed as its length. This is because of the UTF-8 notation. In that notation, every character is represented by one or more bytes, depending on the character. The ASCII characters are represented by a single byte, while the "grave e" character, that is, è, is represented by two bytes. So, the whole string of five characters is represented by six bytes.

Notice that the buffers referred to by the a, b, and c variables are of the same type, which is str, but they have different lengths: 0, 10, and 6. So here, for the first time, we see a type that hasn't an associated length.

Such types are not very common, and they have some limitations. One is that you cannot declare a variable or a function argument of the type. Another obvious limitation is that you cannot ask the size of the type.

Here is an example of what you cannot do with the str type:

```
let a: str;
fn f(a: str) {}
print!("{}", std::mem::size_of::<str>());
```

All the three previous statements are illegal, so for each of them the compiler emits the error message: the size for values of type `str` cannot be known at compilation time.

But then, how can the previous program get the sizes of the buffers? In C language, string terminators are used to mark the end of strings, but Rust has no string terminators.

Actually the &str type is not a normal Rust reference, containing just a pointer, rather it is a pair of a pointer and a length. The pointer value is the address of the beginning of the string buffer, and the length value is the number of bytes of the string buffer.

Let's explore this strange type in more depth, with this code:

```
use std::mem::*;
let a: &str = "";
let b: &str = "0123456789";
let c: &str = "abcdè";
print!("{} {} {}; ",
    size_of_val(&a),
    size_of_val(&b),
    size_of_val(&c));
print!("{} {} {}",
    size_of_val(&&a),
    size_of_val(&&b),
    size_of_val(&&c));
```

This program in a 64-bit system will print: 16 16 16; 8 8 8, while in a 32-bit system it will print: 8 8 8; 4 4 4.

The first print statement prints the sizes of the variables themselves, which are of type &str. Such variables result in sizes that are twice as large as that of a normal reference, as they contain a pointer object and a usize object.

The second `print` statement prints the sizes of references to the variables themselves, which are of type `&&str`. They are normal references.

When we invoke the `len` function on a static string, we just read the second field of that pair, without even accessing the string buffer, so this function is quite efficient.

Dynamic Strings

So if we want to create or change the contents of a string at runtime, the `&str` type, which we always used so far, is unfit.

But Rust also provides another kind of strings, *dynamic strings*, whose content can be changed. Here is some code that uses a dynamic string:

```
let mut a: String = "He".to_string();
a.push('l');
a.push('l');
a.push('o');
print!("{}", a);
```

This will print: `Hello`.

The a variable is of type `String`, which is the type Rust uses for dynamic strings.

In Rust there are no literal dynamic strings; literal strings are always static. But a dynamic string may be constructed from a static string in several ways. One is to invoke the `to_string` function on a static string. The name of this function should be thought of as if it were `to_dynamic_string` or `to_String`. But the first alternative would be too long, and the second one would violate the convention of never using uppercase letters in the name of functions.

A dynamic string can be printed like any static string, as shown by the last statement of the example. But it is capable of something a static string cannot do: it can grow.

Each of the second, third, and fourth statements add a character at the end of the string.

It is also possible to add characters in other positions inside a dynamic string, or to remove any character, as is shown by this code:

```
let mut a: String = "Xy".to_string(); // "Xy"
a.remove(0); // "y"
a.insert(0, 'H'); // "Hy"
```

```
a.pop(); // "H"
a.push('i'); // "Hi"
print!("{}", a);
```

This prints: Hi.

The a variable is initialized to contain "Xy". Then the character at position 0 is removed, leaving "y". Then an "H" is inserted at position 0, obtaining a "Hy". Then the last character is popped from the end, leaving "H". Then an "i" is pushed at the end, obtaining the final "Hi".

Implementation of String

While a Rust static string is somewhat similar to a C language string, without a string terminator but with an additional counter, a Rust dynamic string is quite similar to a C++ std::string object. Both Rust and C++ dynamic string types contain a dynamically allocated array of bytes, which contains the characters of the string.

The main difference between Rust and C++ dynamic string types is that while for C++ strings each byte of the buffer represents exactly one character, the buffer of any Rust dynamic string, like that of any Rust static string, is guaranteed to use the UTF-8 encoding; so a byte of it does not necessarily correspond to a character.

Remaining in the Rust language, there are similarities of strings with arrays, and with vectors. While static string buffers are similar to arrays, that is, the str type is similar to the generic [u8; N] type, dynamic strings are similar to vectors of bytes, that is, the String type is similar to the Vec<u8> type.

Indeed, the functions we saw previously (push, pop, insert, and remove, and also the len function) have the same name of the corresponding functions of the Vector generic type.

In addition, both dynamic strings and vectors have the same implementation. Both are structures consisting of three fields:

- The address of the beginning of the heap-allocated buffer containing the data items

- The number of items that may be contained in the allocated buffer

- The number of items presently used in the allocated buffer

However, notice that for the strings, such "items" are bytes, not characters, like this code shows:

```rust
let mut s1 = "".to_string();
s1.push('e');
let mut s2 = "".to_string();
s2.push('è');
let mut s3 = "".to_string();
s3.push('€');
print!("{} {}; ", s1.capacity(), s1.len());
print!("{} {}; ", s2.capacity(), s2.len());
print!("{} {}", s3.capacity(), s3.len());
```

This may print: 8 1; 8 2; 8 3. That means that in all these cases the allocated buffer is eight bytes long. And the ASCII character e occupies just one byte in that buffer; the accented character è occupies two bytes; and the currency symbol € occupies three bytes. The number of bytes occupied by the characters is because of the UTF-8 standard, while the size of the buffers is dependent on the implementation of the Rust standard library. It has changed in previous versions of Rust, and it may change in future versions.

Let's see what happens when several characters are added to a dynamic string, one at a time:

```rust
let mut s1 = "".to_string();
for _ in 0..16 {
    println!("{:p} {} {}",
        s1.as_ptr(), s1.capacity(), s1.len());
    s1.push('a');
}
let s2 = "x".to_string();
s1.push('-');
println!("{:p}", s2.as_ptr());
println!("{:p} {} {}: {}",
    s1.as_ptr(), s1.capacity(), s1.len(), s1);
```

This, in a 64-bit system, may print:

```
0x1  0  0
0x55f7d528f9d0  8  1
0x55f7d528f9d0  8  2
0x55f7d528f9d0  8  3
0x55f7d528f9d0  8  4
0x55f7d528f9d0  8  5
0x55f7d528f9d0  8  6
0x55f7d528f9d0  8  7
0x55f7d528f9d0  8  8
0x55f7d528f9d0  16  9
0x55f7d528f9d0  16  10
0x55f7d528f9d0  16  11
0x55f7d528f9d0  16  12
0x55f7d528f9d0  16  13
0x55f7d528f9d0  16  14
0x55f7d528f9d0  16  15
0x55f7d528f9f0
0x55f7d528fa10  32  17: aaaaaaaaaaaaaaaa-
```

The as_ptr function (to be read "as pointer") returns the address of the heap-allocated buffer containing the characters of the string.

Notice that when the s1 string is empty, the capacity is zero, meaning that there are no allocated bytes. As no buffer is allocated, the address of such buffer is simply 1, which is an invalid memory address.

When one ASCII character is added to s1, an 8-byte buffer is allocated at an address represented by the hexadecimal number 55f7d528f9d0.

Adding seven other characters, no reallocations are required, because the allocated buffer is large enough.

When the ninth character is added, a reallocation is required, but, as the memory immediately following the buffer of s1 is still free, the buffer may simply be extended to 16 bytes. This avoids the overhead of allocating a new buffer, copying the eight used bytes, and deallocating the previous buffer.

This buffer extension may be long, as this program has no other allocations, so all the address space is available. So, just before adding the seventeenth character to the s1 string, the s2 variable is declared and initialized. It allocates a buffer containing only the letter x. That buffer will go just after the current buffer for the s1 string. So, when the buffer for the s1 string must be extended to 32 bytes, it has to be reallocated.

This can be seen by looking at the addresses printed by the program. Remember that 20 in hexadecimal is 32 in decimal. The buffer for s2 begins 32 bytes after the original position where the buffer for s1 begins. After the last push on s1, its buffer has been moved 32 bytes after the position where the buffer for s1 begins.

Creating Dynamic Strings

There are several ways to create an empty dynamic string.

```
let s1 = String::new();
let s2 = String::from("");
let s3 = "".to_string();
let s4 = "".to_owned();
let s5 = format!("");
print!("({}{}{}{}{})", s1, s2, s3, s4, s5);
```

This will print: ().

The new function of the String type is the basic constructor, similar to a *default constructor* in C++.

The from function of the String type is the converter constructor, similar to a *non-default constructor* in C++.

The functions to_string and to_owned are now interchangeable, but there are both because historically they were somewhat different.

The format macro is identical to the print macro, with the only difference that while the latter sends its result to the console, the former returns a String object containing the result.

Except for the new function, all the previous ways to create a dynamic string also can be used to convert a nonempty static string to a dynamic string. Here are some examples of such conversions:

```
let s = "a,";
let s1 = String::from(s);
let s2 = s.to_string();
let s3 = s.to_owned();
//let s4 = format! (s);
//let s5 = format!("a,{}");
let s6 = format!("{}", s);
print!("({}{}{}{})", s1, s2, s3, s6);
```

This will print: (a,a,a,a,).

Instead, the statements in the fifth and sixth lines would generate compilation errors.

For the fifth line, the error message `format argument must be a string literal` is printed. Indeed, the `format` macro, like the `print` and `println` macros, requires that the first argument is a literal.

For the sixth line, the error message `1 positional argument in format string,` `but no arguments were given` is printed. This is because the first argument of the `format` macro must contain as many placeholders as the successive arguments to the macro.

Converting Static Strings to Dynamic Strings

We have already seen how to convert a static string to a dynamic string, that is, to get an object of type `String` whose contents is equal to that of a given object of type `&str`. Is the reverse conversion possible, from a dynamic string to a static string?

Yes, with this code:

```
let s1: String = "abc".to_string();
let s2: &String = &s1;
let s3: &str = &s1;
println!("{} {} {}", s1, s2, s3);
```

It will print: abc abc abc.

In the first line, a dynamic string is declared and initialized.

In the second line, a reference to it is assigned to a variable whose type is that of reference to `String`.

In the third line, a reference to the dynamic string is assigned to a variable whose type is that of reference to str, that is, to a static string.

It is allowed to initialize a variable of type String with an expression of type &str, because the standard library defines such types in a way to allow an implicit conversion between them.

Notice that the two kinds of conversion are quite different.

A conversion from a static string to a dynamic string creates a distinct object, which allocates a distinct buffer and copies into it all the characters of the static string.

Whereas a conversion from a dynamic string to a static string creates a reference inside the dynamic string. No characters are copied. They are shared between the two strings.

Concatenating Strings

A dynamic string can be obtained also by concatenating two static strings, two dynamic strings, or a dynamic string and a static string. Here are some examples:

```
let ss1 = "He";
let ss2 = "llo ";
let ds1 = ss1.to_string();
let ds2 = ss2.to_string();
let ds3 = format!("{}{}", ss1, ss2);
print!("{}", ds3);
let ds3 = format!("{}{}", ss1, ds2);
print!("{}", ds3);
let ds3 = format!("{}{}", ds1, ss2);
print!("{}", ds3);
let ds3 = format!("{}{}", ds1, ds2);
print!("{}", ds3);
```

This will print: Hello Hello Hello Hello .

First, the two static strings ss1 and ss2 are declared. Then, they are converted to the dynamic strings ds1 and ds2. Then, the format macro is used four times to concatenate any combination of such strings: static-static, static-dynamic, dynamic-static, and dynamic-dynamic. The result is the same in all four cases.

Often, it is desired to have a loop that appends many strings to another string, which of course must be mutable. This is possible using the format macro, in the following way:

```
let vs = ["Hello", ", ", "world", "!"];
let mut result = String::new();
for s in vs {
    result = format!("{}{}", result, s);
}
print!("{}", result);
```

It will print: Hello, world!.

In each iteration, the previous result is concatenated with the new string piece, and the result becomes the new partial result.

Though, this is inefficient, because any iteration definitely destroys and reallocates the result string.

This is a better way:

```
let vs = ["Hello", ", ", "world", "!"];
let mut result = String::new();
for s in vs {
    result.push_str(s);
}
print!("{}", result);
```

The function push_str takes a static string and pushes all its characters to the end of the receiving string. It may be more efficient because, if the appended characters can be contained in the already allocated buffer, no reallocation is required.

To make the code even shorter, the function push_str can be replaced by the equivalent += operator, in this way:

```
let vs = ["Hello", ", ", "world", "!"];
let mut result = String::new();
for s in vs {
    result += s;
}
print!("{}", result);
```

It is a kind of syntactic sugar.

It's possible also to append dynamic strings or single characters:

```
let comma = ", ".to_string();
let world = "world".to_string();
let excl_point = '!';
let mut result = "Hello".to_string();
result += &comma;
result.push_str(&world);
result.push(excl_point);
print!("{}", result);
```

This program is equivalent to the previous ones.

Notice, at the fifth and sixth lines, that a dynamic string is passed as an argument of push_str and +=, respectively. However, such functions expect a static string, so our dynamic strings have to be converted to static strings beforehand. Such effect is obtained using the & operator.

At last, a single character is appended to the result string using push.

CHAPTER 15

Ranges and Slices

In this chapter, you will learn:

- How to use closed ranges and open-ended ranges, both right-exclusive and right-inclusive

- How to define and use slices of arrays, vectors, or other slices, using ranges

The Ranges

We already saw a way to write a `for` loop:

```
for i in 0..12 { println!("{}", i); }
```

But there is another possible way to write it:

```
let dozen = 0..12;
for i in dozen { println!("{}", i); }
```

This shows that the `0..12` clause is not a part of the `for` statement syntax, but it is an expression, whose value can be assigned to a variable; that value can be used in `for` statements. The type of such a value is named *range*.

Here is some more code using a range:

```
let range: std::ops::Range<usize> = 3..8;
println!("{:?}, {}, {}, {}",
    range, range.start, range.end, range.len());
for i in range { print!("{}, ", i); }
```

© Carlo Milanesi 2022
C. Milanesi, *Beginning Rust*, https://doi.org/10.1007/978-1-4842-7208-4_15

This will print:

```
3..8, 3, 8, 5
3, 4, 5, 6, 7,
```

In the first line, we see that any range is a concretization of the Range<T> generic type, where T must be an integer type able to represent both extremes of the range.

The second statement prints some values about the variable range. First, the variable itself is printed for debugging, obtaining 3..8; then the values of the two fields' start and end of range are printed, obtaining, respectively, 3 and 8. This shows that the type Range contains these two fields. Indeed, it does not contain anything else.

Then the len function is invoked, which simply evaluates the expression end - start, so it evaluates 8 - 3 and prints 5.

At last, that range is used in a for loop to scan the values from start *included* to end *excluded*. Notice that the iterated values are as many as the value returned by the invocation of len.

The parametric type T of the type Range<T> can be inferred by the two arguments:

```
let r1 = 3u8..12u8;
let r2 = 3u8..12;
let r3 = 3..12u8;
let r4 = 3..12;
let r5 = -3..12;
let r6 = 3..12 as i64;
print!(
    "{} {} {} {} {} {}",
    std::mem::size_of_val(&r1),
    std::mem::size_of_val(&r2),
    std::mem::size_of_val(&r3),
    std::mem::size_of_val(&r4),
    std::mem::size_of_val(&r5),
    std::mem::size_of_val(&r6));
```

This will print: 2 2 2 8 8 16.

The r1 variable has both extremes declared as u8, so they have that type, which occupies one byte, and the whole range occupies two bytes.

The r2 and r3 variables have one extreme declared as u8 and the other left unspecified. Therefore it is forced to be u8 too.

The r4 and r5 variables have both extremes of type unspecified, and there is no further constraint on such variables, so they get the default i32 type, which is used for the T parameters of the ranges.

The r6 variable has the second extreme of type i64 and the first extreme unconstrained, so T must be i64.

Notice that all the following statements are illegal:

```
let r1 = 3u8..12i8;
let r2: std::ops::Range<u32> = -3..12;
let r3: std::ops::Range<i32> = 3i16..12;
```

In the first statement, the two extremes have different types. (It is a mismatched types error.)

In the second statement, -3 is not a value of type u32. (It is a cannot apply unary operator `-` to type `u32` error.)

In the third statement, 3i16 is not a value of type i32. (It is a mismatched types error.)

Also the following statement is not allowed with default compiler settings, because it generate integer overflow:

```
let _r = 3u8..1200;
```

The range will use the first extreme to infer the type as Range<u8>, but when the second extreme is found to be larger than 255, the error literal out of range for `u8` is printed.

The following statements are allowed, even if they are probably nonsensical:

```
let _r1 = false .. true;
let _r2 = "hello" .. "world";
let _r3 = 4.2 .. 7.9;
```

Indeed, such absurd ranges cannot be used in a for loop.

Motivation for Slices

Let's assume you need to create a function that gets as argument an eight-number array, and that returns the smallest number in this array. For such a purpose, you could write this program:

```
fn min(arr: [i32; 8]) -> i32 {
    let mut minimum = arr[0];
    for i in 1..arr.len() {
        if arr[i] < minimum { minimum = arr[i]; }
    }
    minimum
}
print!("{}", min([23, 17, 12, 16, 15, 28, 17, 30]));
```

This program will correctly print: 12. However, such min function has some drawbacks:

1. It gets as argument a *copy* of the whole array, requiring a significant time to transfer it, and occupying a significant stack space and cache space.

2. It cannot receive the request to process just a portion of the array.

3. It can receive only eight-number arrays. If we would pass an array of seven or nine items, we would get a compilation error.

4. It cannot receive a vector as argument.

To overcome the first drawback, you can pass the array *by reference*, instead of *by value*, using the following code:

```
fn min(arr: &[i32; 8]) -> i32 {
    let mut minimum = arr[0];
    for i in 1..arr.len() {
        if arr[i] < minimum { minimum = arr[i]; }
    }
    minimum
}
print!("{}", min(&[23, 17, 12, 16, 15, 28, 17, 30]));
```

Two "&" characters have been added, one where the argument is declared, in the first line; and one where the function is invoked, in the last line. As we have already seen, it is not necessary to change the body of the function, as the arr reference is implicitly dereferenced.

To overcome the second drawback, you could add an argument to specify from which item to start processing, and another argument to specify how many arguments to process:

```rust
fn min(arr: &[i32; 8], start: usize, count: usize) -> i32 {
    // Let's assume 'start' is between 0 and 7,
    // and 'count' is between 1 and 8 - start.
    let mut minimum = arr[start];
    for i in start + 1..start + count {
        if arr[i] < minimum { minimum = arr[i]; }
    }
    minimum
}
print!("{}", min(&[23, 17, 12, 16, 15, 28, 17, 30], 3, 2));
```

This will print: 15. Indeed, it is specified to process two items starting from the one in position 3 (counting from 0). Therefore, only the two items having values 16 and 15 are processed.

However, two drawbacks remain.

Consider that our function needs to know only from which memory address to start processing, how many items to process, and which is the type of the items of the sequence. It is not required to know whether such sequence is a part of a larger sequence, and even less where such larger sequence starts and ends.

In addition, consider that any vector keeps its data in a heap-allocated array, so such a function could process it, once it knew where the items are to process.

The Slices

Considering all this, and to overcome all the cited drawbacks, the concept of *slice* has been introduced in the language. Its syntax is that of references:

```rust
fn min(arr: &[i32]) -> i32 {
    // Let's assume 'arr' is not empty.
    let mut minimum = arr[0];
```

```
    for i in 1..arr.len() {
        if arr[i] < minimum { minimum = arr[i]; }
    }
    minimum
}
print!("{}", min(&[23, 17, 12, 16, 15, 28, 17, 30]));
```

This program will also print 12, but it has the following single difference from the second program in the previous section: in the type of the argument, the "; 8" clause has disappeared. Now the type of the arr argument looks like a reference to an array, but without specifying the size of the array.

This kind of type is a *reference to a slice*, or *slice reference*. Its generic form is "&[T]," where T represents any type that can be contained in an array. Here, *slice* means *subsequence of items inside a sequence of items*. Such a larger sequence can be an array or a vector buffer. For this purpose, the implementation of a slice reference is a pair of values: the address of the first item of the sequence, and the number of items.

Notice that usually we have variables whose type is *slice reference*, but the use of a *slice* type, without considering a reference to it, is quite rare. A slice would have type "[T]," but such type cannot be passed as an argument to a function, because it has a size not defined at compilation time, and a requirement of the arguments of functions is that they have a compile-time defined size. Therefore, we can pass to a function only *references to slices*, not *slices*. Such objects are pairs of a pointer and a length, so their memory occupation is exactly twice that of normal references.

Using a slice reference is quite similar to using an array. The main implementation difference is that an invocation of the len function on an array can be optimized away, replacing it by the constant length defined by the type of the array, while an invocation of the len function on a reference to a slice is implemented as an access to the second field of such object.

Actually, in previous chapters we already saw something very similar to slices and to slice references: string buffers, and static strings.

We can build this table of similarities among the types str, &str, String, [u8], &[u8], and Vec<u8>.

Buffer	Reference to a Buffer	Handler of a Dynamically Allocated Buffer
Undefined-length sequence of bytes	(address of beginning, length in bytes)	(address of beginning, length in bytes, number of bytes used)
String buffer: str	Static string: &str	Dynamic string: String
Slice of bytes: [u8]	Reference to slice of bytes: &[u8]	Vector of bytes: Vec<u8>

There are three columns, one for each concept:

- The first column is for buffers, that is, sequences of bytes having a length not necessarily defined at compile time.

- The second column is for references to such buffers. They keep two fields: a memory address, and the current length in bytes of the referred buffer.

- The third column is for objects that can handle (i.e., to allocate or to deallocate) buffers. They keep three fields: the two needed to refer to the allocated buffer, and the number of items currently used in the buffer.

The types in the first column are those having undefined length. They are the *string buffers*, whose type is str, and the *slices* of unsigned 8-bit numbers, whose type is [u8].

The types in the second column are the references to the types of the first column. They are the *static strings*, whose type is &str, and the *references to slices* of unsigned 8-bit numbers, whose type is &[u8].

The types in the third column are those of the objects that can dynamically allocate buffers. They are the *dynamic strings*, whose type is String, and the *vectors* of unsigned 8-bit numbers, whose type is Vec<u8>.

Going back to the last example program, notice that the first argument in the invocation of the min function is the same of the previous program. A reference to an array is still passed as argument. In fact, such an array reference is implicitly converted into a slice reference, using the array address as slice address and the array length as slice length.

Therefore, the last statement of the program passes to the function a structure of two fields: the first is the memory address of the array item containing the number 23, and the second is the number 8.

Using slices, flexibility is much increased. Indeed, it's now possible to write:

```rust
fn min(arr: &[i32]) -> i32 {
    // Let's assume 'arr' is not empty.
    let mut minimum = arr[0];
    for i in 1..arr.len() {
        if arr[i] < minimum { minimum = arr[i]; }
    }
    minimum
}
print!("{} ", min(&[23, 17]));
print!("{}", min(&vec![55, 22, 33, 44]));
```

This will print: 17 22.

The first invocation passes only two arguments, and 17 is the lesser of them. So, the min function is not limited anymore to process 8-item arrays, but it can process arrays and slices having any nonnegative length.

The second invocation of min shows how our function can process data also belonging to a vector, with no need to copy them. The value passed to the function is a simple reference to a vector, but, because the function argument is of type "reference to slice," the argument becomes a reference to a slice representing the whole contents of the vector.

So, we have overcome all the drawbacks of the first solution except the second one, which is the need to separately specify which part of the sequence we want to process. Though, even this drawback can be overcome, as explained in the following section.

Slicing

Let's say we have an array or a vector, for example, the array [23, 17, 12, 16, 15, 2], and a function that gets a slice as argument, for example, the min function seen in the preceding code, and we want to use such a function to process just a portion of our array or vector. Let's say we want to find the minimum value among the third, fourth, and fifth items of that array.

What we need is a way to forge a slice as a portion of an array or vector, and so pass that slice to the min function, not necessarily the entire array or vector.

The syntax comes quite natural. To get the item of index 2 of an array arr or of a vector v, you'd write, respectively, arr[2] or v[2]. Well, to get all the items of index between 2 (included) and 5 (excluded) of such containers, you'd write, respectively, arr[2..5] or v[2..5].

Here is another use of our ranges!

So the program would be:

```
fn min(arr: &[i32]) -> i32 {
    // Let's assume 'arr' is not empty.
    let mut minimum = arr[0];
    for i in 1..arr.len() {
        if arr[i] < minimum { minimum = arr[i]; }
    }
    minimum
}
let arr = [23, 17, 12, 16, 15, 2];
let range = 2..5;
let slice_ref = &arr[range];
print!("{}", min(slice_ref));
```

This will print 12, which is the minimum among 12, 16, and 15. The last four lines can be merged into this one:

```
print!("{}", min(&[23, 17, 12, 16, 15, 2][2..5]));
```

The operation of taking a slice from an array or a vector is named *slicing*.

Notice that, like in the for loop, the upper extreme of the range is excluded from the generated slice. Indeed, specifying the range 2..5, the items included in the range are those in positions 2, 3, and 4, counting from zero.

The slicing operator can be applied to both arrays and vectors, but also to other slices:

```
let arr = [55, 22, 33, 44, 66, 7, 8];
let v = vec![55, 22, 33, 44, 66, 7, 8];
let sr1 = &arr[2..5];
let sr2 = &v[2..5];
print!("{:?} {:?} {:?} {:?}", sr1, sr2, &sr1[1..2], &sr1[1]);
```

This will print: [33, 44, 66] [33, 44, 66] [44] 44.

The sr1 variable is a reference to a slice, which refers to the third, fourth, and fifth items of the arr array.

The sr2 variable is a similar reference to a slice, but it refers to items in the v vector.

After having printed the items referred to by these slice references, a slice of the first slice is taken. It refers to the second item of that slice, which is the fourth item of the underlying array.

At last, the second item of sr1 is taken, by simple indexing.

Out-of-Range Slicing

In addition to normal slicing, one could do something even weirder:

```
let arr = [55, 22, 33, 44, 66];
let _r1 = 4..4; let _a1 = &arr[_r1];
let _r2 = 4..3; //let _a2 = &arr[_r2];
let _r3 = -3i32..2; //let _a3 = &arr[_r3];
let _r4 = 3..8; //let _a4 = &arr[_r4];
```

In this program, except for the first line, every line declares a range and then tries to use it to slice the array declared in the first line.

All the ranges are valid, but not all the slicing operations are valid, so some statements have been commented out.

The second line is perfectly valid. It gets a slice starting from position 4 and ending before position 4. So it is an empty slice, but empty slices are allowed.

The third line uses a backward slice that ends before starting. That is allowed by the compiler, but it causes a panic at runtime, like an out-of-range array access. The runtime error message, printed on the console, is slice index that starts at 4 but ends at 3. Try removing the comment symbol //, compile, and run to see this error, and then rewrite the comment symbol.

The fourth line uses a range whose extremes are of type i32. That causes a compilation error, because slicing, like sequence indexing, requires the usize type. The error message will be the type `[{integer}]` cannot be indexed by `std::ops::Range<i32>`. It means that our slice of integers, like any slice, cannot be indexed by a range whose extremes are of type i32.

The fifth line uses a range exceeding the size of the sequence. It can be compiled, but it causes a panic with the message `range end index 8 out of range for slice of length 5`.

Notice that all this has been shown when slicing an array, but it also holds for slicing vectors and for slicing slices.

Mutable Slicing

What does it mean to change the contents of a slice? A slice is a portion of another sequence, so changing its contents means changing the value of one or more items in the underlying sequence:

```
let mut arr = [11, 22, 33, 44];
{
    let sl_ref = &mut arr[1..3];
    print!("{:?}", sl_ref);
    sl_ref[1] = 0;
    print!(" {:?}", sl_ref);
}
print!(" {:?}", arr);
```

This will print: `[22, 33] [22, 0] [11, 22, 0, 44]`.

The `sl_ref` variable is an *immutable* reference to a *mutable* slice. Therefore, the reference cannot be changed, but its referred slice can be changed, and that means you can change the value of its items. And so it is done two lines below, by assigning zero to the second item of the slice, which is the third item of the underlying array.

To be able to get a reference to a mutable slice, the underlying sequence must be mutable. This requires the `mut` clause in the first line.

What does it mean to change a slice reference? A slice reference is a kind of reference, so changing it means to cause it to refer to another portion of sequence, that is, to another portion of the same sequence or to a portion of another sequence:

```
let arr = [11, 22, 33, 44];
{
    let mut sl_ref = &arr[1..3];
    print!("{:?}", sl_ref);
```

```
    sl_ref = &arr[0..1];
    print!(" {:?}", sl_ref);
}
print!(" {:?}", arr);
```

This will print: `[22, 33] [11] [11, 22, 33, 44]`.

In this program the `arr` variable is an immutable array, and indeed it will not be changed. The `sl_ref` variable is a *mutable* reference to an *immutable* slice. It is initialized to refer to the second and third items of the array, and then it is changed to refer to the first item of the array.

Open-Ended Ranges and Slicing

Sometimes it is desired to get all the items from the beginning of a sequence to a given position n, or all the items from a given position n to the end of a sequence.

It could be done in this way:

```
let arr = [11, 22, 33, 44];
let n = 2;
let sr1 = &arr[0..n];
let sr2 = &arr[n..arr.len()];
print!("{:?} {:?}", sr1, sr2);
```

This will print: `[11, 22] [33, 44]`.

But it is simpler to write it equivalently in this way:

```
let arr = [11, 22, 33, 44];
let n = 2;
let sr1 = &arr[..n];
let sr2 = &arr[n..];
print!("{:?} {:?}", sr1, sr2);
```

In the third line, the range has no lower limit; and in the fourth line, the range has no upper limit.

Actually, these ranges have distinct types:

```
let r1: std::ops::RangeFrom<i32> = 3..;
let r2: std::ops::RangeTo<i32> = ..12;
print!("{:?} {:?} {} {}", r1, r2,
    std::mem::size_of_val(&r1),
    std::mem::size_of_val(&r2));
```

This will print: `3.. ..12 4 4`. The `r1` variable is of type `RangeFrom`, meaning that it has a lower limit but not an upper limit. The `r2` variable is of type `RangeTo`, meaning that it has an upper limit but not a lower limit. Both occupy only four bytes, because they need to store only one `i32` object.

`RangeFrom` values may be used also to specify `for` loops.

```
for i in 3.. {
    if i * i > 40 { break; }
    print!("{} ", i);
}
```

This will print: `3 4 5 6`. The loop starts by assigning to `i` the value 3, and keeps incrementing it indefinitely, or until some other statement breaks the loop.

There is one last generic type of ranges:

```
let range: std::ops::RangeFull = ..;
let a1 = [11, 22, 33, 44];
let a2 = &a1[range];
print!("{} {:?} {:?}", std::mem::size_of_val(&range), a1, a2);
```

This will print: `0 [11, 22, 33, 44] [11, 22, 33, 44]`.

Any `RangeFull` stores no information, and so its size is zero. It is used to specify a range exactly as large as the underlying sequence.

Inclusive Ranges

All the types of range we saw in this chapter exclude the upper extreme for their values, and so they are named right-exclusive ranges.

Actually they are the most useful kinds of ranges. Though, sometimes a range is needed that includes the upper extreme. We have seen in Chapter 4 that in addition to the right-exclusive range operator (..), there is a right-inclusive range operator (..=). This can be used to create a right-inclusive range, which can be used for slicing too:

```
let arr = [11, 12, 13, 14, 15];
let r1: std::ops::RangeInclusive<usize> = 2..=3;
print!("{:?} ", &arr[r1]);
let r2: std::ops::RangeToInclusive<usize> = ..=2;
print!("{:?}", &arr[r2]);
```

This will print: [13, 14] [11, 12, 13].

The second line declares and initializes a variable of type RangeInclusive<usize>, which contains the extremes 2 and 3; but it means to also represent the upper extreme, so when it is used to slice the array, it extracts the values 13 and 14.

The fourth line declares and initializes a variable of type RangeToInclusive<usize>, which contains only the upper extreme 2; but it means to represent also such extreme, and when it is used to slice the array, it extracts the values 11, 12, and 13.

CHAPTER 16

Using Iterators

In this chapter, you will learn:

- How characters are stored in Rust strings, and why they do not allow direct access

- How to read string characters or string bytes using iterators

- How to extract items from vectors and arrays using iterators

- How to get references to items from vectors, arrays, and slices using nonmutating iterators

- How to modify items from vectors, arrays, and slices using mutating iterators

- A shorthand notation for using iterators in `for` loops

- How to use some iterator adapters: `filter`, `map`, and `enumerate`

- How to use some iterator consumers: `any`, `all`, `count`, `sum`, `min`, `max`, and `collect`

- The concepts of iterator chains and lazy processing

String Characters

We already saw that Rust has both static strings and dynamic strings, and that both types share the same character coding, which is UTF-8. Such coding uses sequences of one to six bytes to represent each Unicode character, so a string is not simply an array of characters, but it is an array of bytes that represents a sequence of characters.

But given that `s` is a string, what's the meaning of the expression `s[0]`? Is it the first character of `s` or the first byte of `s`?

© Carlo Milanesi 2022
C. Milanesi, *Beginning Rust*, https://doi.org/10.1007/978-1-4842-7208-4_16

Any of these choices could be surprising for someone, so in Rust such an expression is not allowed for strings. To get a byte from a string, it is necessary to first convert the string to a slice of bytes, like in this code:

```
let s = "abc012è€";
for i in 0..s.len() {
    println!("{}: {}", i, s.as_bytes()[i]);
}
```

It will print:

```
0: 97
1: 98
2: 99
3: 48
4: 49
5: 50
6: 195
7: 168
8: 226
9: 130
10: 172
```

The function as_bytes converts the string to which it is applied into a slice of immutable u8 numbers. Such conversion has zero runtime cost, because the representation of a string buffer is already that sequence of bytes.

The UTF-8 representation of any ASCII character is just the ASCII code of that character. And so, for the characters a, b, c, 0, 1, and 2, their ASCII value is printed.

The è character is represented by a pair of bytes, having values 195 and 168. And the € character is represented by a sequence of three bytes, having values 226, 130, and 172. Therefore, to get to a character in a given position in a string, it is necessary to scan all the previous characters.

This situation is similar to that of text files compared with fixed-record-length files. Using a fixed-record-length file, it is possible to read a record in any n position by *seeking* that position, without previously reading all the preceding lines. But using a variable-line-length file to read the nth line requires you to read all the preceding lines.

Scanning a String

Therefore, to process the characters of a string, it is necessary to scan them.

Let's assume that, given the string "€èe," we want to print the third character. First we must scan three bytes to get the first character, because the € character is represented by a sequence of three bytes; then we must scan two further bytes to get the second character, because the è character is represented by a sequence of two bytes; then we must scan one further byte to get the third character, because the e character is represented by a sequence of just one byte.

So, we need a way to get the next character of a string, given the current position, and to advance the current position, at the end of the read character.

In computer science, the objects that perform such behavior of extracting an item at the current position in a sequence, and then advance that position, are named *iterators* (or sometimes *cursors*). Therefore, we need a *string iterator*.

Here is a program that uses a string iterator:

```
fn print_nth_char(s: &str, mut n: u32) {
    let mut iter: std::str::Chars = s.chars();
    loop {
        let item: Option<char> = iter.next();
        match item {
            Some(c) => if n == 0 { print!("{}", c); break; },
            None => { break; },
        }
        n -= 1;
    }
}
print_nth_char("€èe", 0); // It prints: €
print_nth_char("€èe", 2); // It prints: e
```

This program first defines a function whose purpose is to receive a string s and a number n, and then to print the character of s at position n (counting from 0), if there is a character at such position, or else to do nothing. The last two lines of the program invoke such a function to print the first and the third character of €èe, and so the program prints €e.

The Rust standard library provides a string iterator type named Chars. Given a string s, you get an iterator over s by evaluating s.chars(), as is done in the second line of the preceding program.

Any iterator has the next function. Such a function returns the next item of the underlying sequence at the current position, and advances the current position.

Some sequences like the range 1.. do not have an end, but most sequences do have an end, like vectors, arrays, and slices. An iterator cannot return the next value when the end of the sequence has been reached. So when an iterator has reached such an end, it must be capable of communicating that there are no more items to return.

To consider the possibility of having finished the sequence, the next function of Rust iterators returns a value of Option<T> type. That value is None if the sequence has no more items.

Using the match statement, the Some case causes the processing of the next character of the string, and the None case causes the exit from the otherwise infinite loop.

If the function argument n was 0, the first character of the string must be printed, and so, at the first iteration of the loop, the value of the c variable would be printed, and the loop would be quit. For any other value of n, nothing is done with that character.

After the match statement, the n counter, which was mutable, is decremented so that, when it reaches 0, the required character to print is also reached.

Given a string, it is easy to print the numeric codes of its characters, as shown by this code:

```
fn print_codes(s: &str) {
    let mut iter = s.chars();
    loop {
        match iter.next() {
            Some(c) => { println!("{}: {}", c, c as u32); },
            None => { break; },
        }
    }
}
print_codes("€èe");
```

It will print:

```
€: 8364
è: 232
e: 101
```

For every character, the character itself is printed, along with its numeric code.

Using String Iterators in for Loops

The previous example was somewhat cumbersome, but it can undergo the following drastic syntactic simplification:

```
fn print_codes(s: &str) {
    for c in s.chars() {
        println!("{}: {}", c, c as u32);
    }
}
print_codes("€èe");
```

This program generates the same machine code as the previous one, but it is much clearer for a human reader.

It appears that the expression after the in keyword in a for loop can be an iterator.

But what exactly is an *iterator*? It is not a type, but, in a way, it is a type specification. An iterator is considered to be any expression that has a next method, with no arguments, returning an Option<T> value.

So far, in for loops, we used ranges. Well, all ranges with a starting limit are actually iterators, as they have the proper next function. Here is some code using ranges as iterators.

```
let _v1 = (0u32..10).next();
let _v2 = (5u32..).next();
// let _v3 = (..8u32).next(); // ILLEGAL: Missing start value
// let _v4 = (..).next(); // ILLEGAL: Missing start value
```

The first line is valid, as std::ops::Range<u32> is an iterator.

The second line is also valid, as std::ops::RangeFrom<u32> is an iterator.

The third and fourth lines wouldn't be legal, as std::ops::RangeTo<u32> and std::ops::RangeFull are not iterators.

It is also possible to iterate over the bytes of a string:

```
for byte in "€èe".bytes() {
    print!("{} ", byte);
}
```

It will print: 226 130 172 195 168 101. The first three numbers represent the
€ character; the next two numbers represent the è character; and the last byte, 101,
is the ASCII code of the e character.

This program can be broken down into the following code:

```
let string: &str = "€èe";
let string_it: std::str::Bytes = string.bytes();
for byte in string_it {
    print!("{} ", byte);
}
```

While the chars function, seen previously, returns a value whose type is
std::str::Chars, the bytes function, used here, returns a value whose type is
std::str::Bytes.

Both Chars and Bytes are string iterator types, but while the next function of Chars
returns the next character of the string, the next function of Bytes returns the next byte
of the string.

These string functions are both different from the as_bytes function, which returns a
slice reference on the bytes of the string.

The Rust Editions

The Rust language evolves in major versions named "editions". So far three editions of
Rust have been released: the 2015 Edition, the 2018 Edition, and the 2021 Edition. The
last one has been released on October 21st, 2021.

By default, the Rust compiler accepts code written according the 2015 edition. So
far all the code we wrote was accepted by all three editions of Rust. Though, since the
next section, and also in the ensuing chapters, some features supported only by the 2021
Edition will be used. Therefore, the compiler must be instructed to support such version
of the language.

Therefore, since now, the command to compile the example program must be this:

```
rustc --edition 2021 main.rs
```

Iterators over Vectors, Arrays, and Slices

In addition to iterating over strings, it is also quite typical to iterate over vectors, arrays, or slices. We have seen that strings have the `chars` function and the `bytes` function, which return two different string iterators types. Similarly, vectors, arrays, and slices have the `into_iter` function that returns an iterator over the sequence it is applied to. Here is some code that uses it:

```
let vec_iterator: std::vec::IntoIter<i32>
    = vec![10, 20, 30].into_iter();
for item in vec_iterator {
    let j: i32 = item;
    print!("{} ", j + 1);
}
```

It will print: `11 21 31`.

The `into_iter` function, when applied to a vector of `i32` items, returns an iterator of type `IntoIter<i32>`. Such iterator generates values taken from that vector.

That code can be simplified as this:

```
for item in vec![10, 20, 30].into_iter() {
    print!("{} ", item + 1);
}
```

Previously, we said that any type that implements the function `next` is said to be an iterator. Vectors do not implement the function `next`, so they are not iterators, although they implement the function `into_iter`, which returns an iterator. Any type that implements the function `into_iter` is said to be *iterable*.

In addition to vectors, arrays are also iterable, as shown in the following code:

```
let array_iterator: std::array::IntoIter<i32, 3_usize>
    = [10, 20, 30].into_iter();
for item in array_iterator {
    let j: i32 = item;
    print!("{} ", j + 1);
}
```

It will print: `11 21 31`.

The `into_iter` function, when applied to an array, generates an iterator over that array.

223

Similarly, slices are also iterable, as shown in the following code:

```
let slice_iterator: std::slice::Iter<i32>
    = [40, 50, 60][0..2].into_iter();
for item in slice_iterator {
    let j: &i32 = item;
    print!("{} ", *j + 1);
}
```

It will print: 41 51 . Only the two items contained in the slice are passed to the loop.

Notice that, when it is applied to a vector or to an array, the into_iter function returns an IntoIter iterator, which generates *values* taken from such sequences, as expected. Instead, when the into_iter function is applied to a slice, it returns an Iter iterator, which returns *references* to the items contained in the slice. The reason for this is that, in general, it may not be allowed to extract items from a slice.

Using the into_iter function on a vector or on an array, you get an iterator that *extracts* the items from the iterable object. By default, you cannot change such an item, because it is immutable even if the iterated object is mutable. Therefore, this code is illegal:

```
let mut v = vec![10, 20, 30];
for item in v.into_iter() {
    item += 1; // ILLEGAL: item is not mutable
    print!("{} ", item);
}
```

It generates the compilation error cannot assign twice to immutable variable `item`.

If we want to change such items, we can do that by decorating the declaration of the loop variable with the mut clause, in this way:

```
let v = vec![10, 20, 30];
for mut item in v.into_iter() {
    item += 1;
    print!("{} ", item);
}
```

It will print: 11 21 31 .

This code does not change the original vector, because the increment in the third line acts on a value that has been *extracted* from the vector.

Iterators Generating References

The examples in the previous sections used iterators that extracted values from the iterated objects, with those being strings, string slices, vectors, or arrays.

Instead, we could prefer to operate on the items of an iterable object while keeping such items inside the object that contains them. So we want our loop variable to be a *reference* inside the iterable object. With vectors, we can do that using the iter function, available for all iterable types, as shown in this code:

```
let v = vec![10, 20, 30];
let vec_ref_iterator: std::slice::Iter<i32> = v.iter();
for item_ref in vec_ref_iterator {
    print!("{} ", *item_ref + 1);
}
```

It will print: 11 21 31.

The iter function, applied to an object of type Vec<i32>, returns an iterator that generates items whose type is &i32. More in general, the iter function returns an iterator that generates items whose type is a reference to the items contained in the iterable to which it is applied.

Arrays and slices also have a similar iter function, as shown here:

```
let array_ref_iterator: std::slice::Iter<i32>
    = [10, 20, 30].iter();
for item in array_ref_iterator {
    print!("{} ", *item + 1);
}
print!("; ");
let slice_ref_iterator: std::slice::Iter<i32>
    = [10, 20, 30][0..2].iter();
for item in slice_ref_iterator {
    print!("{} ", *item + 1);
}
```

It will print: 11 21 31 ; 11 21.

Actually, for slices, the iter function is equivalent to the into_iter function, as both return an iterator that generates references.

Iterations *without* Mutation

So far we used iterators over sequences only *to read* the items contained in such sequences, and this is quite typical.

When iterating over the characters of a string, it is unreasonable to try to change such characters, as the new characters may be represented by a different number of bytes than the existing characters. For example, if an è character is replaced by an e character, two bytes would be replaced by just one byte. Therefore, the Rust standard library has no way to change a string character by character using a character string iterator.

In addition, when iterating over the bytes of a string, it is unsafe to try to change such bytes, as the new bytes may result in a sequence that is not a valid UTF-8 string. Therefore, the Rust standard library has no way to change a string byte by byte using a byte string iterator.

As we have seen, with the iterator obtained using the `into_iter` or the `iter` functions on a vector, an array or a slice, you are not allowed to change the items inside such sequences, even if such sequences are mutable.

However, in a mutable vector, array, or slice, you can change a single item by accessing it using its index. An iterator is just another tool to access the items of a sequence. So it is reasonable to desire changing the items of a sequence using an iterator. Such kinds of iterators are shown in the next section.

Iterations *with* Mutation

So, there is the need to change the values of a sequence using an iterator, though, to such end, a mutable iterator is of no help. In fact, a mutable iterator is an object that can be made to iterate over another sequence, not an object that can be used to mutate the sequence that it iterates over.

A possible use of a mutable iterator is this:

```
let slice1 = &[3, 4, 5];
let slice2 = &[7, 8];
let mut iterator = slice1.iter();
for item_ref in iterator {
    print!("{} ", *item_ref);
}
```

```
print!("; ");
iterator = slice2.iter();
for item_ref in iterator {
    print!("{} ", *item_ref);
}
```

It will print: 3 4 5 ; 7 8.

The mutable variable `iterator` first refers to the sequence `slice1` and then to the sequence `slice2`. If you remove the `mut` clause in the third line, you will get the compilation error `cannot assign twice to immutable variable \`iterator\``.

An iterator of type `Iter` is similar to a reference, in that a mutable reference is not the same concept of a reference to a mutable object.

So if you want to change the values in a sequence through an iterator over such a sequence, you cannot use a normal (mutable or immutable) iterator.

For such a purpose, you need another type of iterator, a *mutating* iterator, which, of course must be initialized over a mutable sequence, like this code shows:

```
let mut v = vec![3, 4, 5];
let iterator: std::slice::IterMut<i32> = v.iter_mut();
for mut_item_ref in iterator {
    *mut_item_ref += 1;
}
print!("{:?}", v);
```

It will print: [4, 5, 6].

The `iter_mut` function returns an object of type `IterMut<i32>`.

Think of the purpose of the `iter` function as "get an iterator that generates references to items to read," and the purpose of the `iter_mut` function as "get an iterator that generates references to items to read or to write."

Notice that the `v` variable has been declared as mutable. As the purpose of the `iter_mut` function is to allow changes to the iterated object, such object must be mutable. If you remove the `mut` clause in the first line, you get the compilation error `cannot borrow \`v\` as mutable, as it is not declared as mutable`.

We have seen the use of the `iter_mut` function applied to a vector. Similar functions exist for arrays and slices.

Shorthand for Using Iterators in Loops

When using for loops, there is a more compact syntax for using iterators.

Instead of writing:

```
for item in vec![10, 20, 30].into_iter() {
        print!("{} ", item + 1);
}
```

you can write, equivalently:

```
for item in vec![10, 20, 30] {
    print!("{} ", item + 1);
}
```

In this code, the call to into_iter has been removed. If a value that implements the into_iter function is passed to a for statement, such function is implicitly invoked.

Similarly, instead of writing:

```
for item in vec![10, 20, 30].iter() {
    print!("{} ", *item + 1);
}
```

you can write equivalently:

```
for item in &vec![10, 20, 30] {
    print!("{} ", *item + 1);
}
```

In this code, the call to iter has been removed, and an "&" sign has been added. If a reference to a value that implements the iter function is passed to a for statement, such function is implicitly invoked.

Similarly, instead of writing:

```
for item in vec![10, 20, 30].iter_mut() {
    *item += 1; print!("{} ", item);
}
```

you can write equivalently:

```
for item in &mut vec![10, 20, 30] {
    *item += 1; print!("{} ", item);
}
```

In this code, the call to iter_mut has been removed, and an "&mut" clause has been added. If a reference to a mutable value that implements the iter_mut function is passed to a for statement, such function is implicitly invoked.

Iterator Generators

So far we have encountered five functions that get a sequence and return an iterator: chars, bytes, into_iter, iter, and iter_mut. Functions that can be applied to a value that is not an iterator, but that return an iterator are named *iterator generators*, because they transform a noniterator into an iterator.

An Iterator Adapter: filter

Let's see some other uses of iterators.

Here is a problem that can be solved using iterators: Given an array of numbers, how can I print all the negative numbers of such an array?

A possible solution is this:

```
let arr = [66, -8, 43, 19, 0, -31];
for n in arr.into_iter() {
    if n < 0 { print!("{} ", n); }
}
```

It will print: -8 -31 .

But another possible solution is this:

```
let arr = [66, -8, 43, 19, 0, -31];
for n in arr.into_iter().filter(|x_ref| *x_ref < 0) {
    print!("{} ", n);
}
```

The `filter` function is in the standard library. It is to be applied to an iterator, and it takes a closure as argument. As its name suggests, the purpose of this function is *filtering* the iterated sequence, that is, to discard the items that do not satisfy the criterion implemented by the closure, and let pass only the items that satisfy such criterion.

The `filter` function gets an item at a time from the iterator, and invokes the closure once for every item, passing to the closure a reference to the current item. In our example, the reference to the current item, which is an integer number, is assigned to the `x_ref` closure argument.

The closure must return a Boolean that indicates whether the item is accepted (`true`) or rejected (`false`) by the filtering. The rejected items are destroyed, while the accepted ones are passed to the surrounding expression.

In fact, the `filter` function returns an iterator that (when its `next` function is invoked) produces just the items for which the closure returned `true`.

As we were interested in accepting only the negative numbers, the condition inside the closure is `*x_ref < 0`, because we want to compare with zero the item, not its reference.

We said that the `filter` function returns an iterator. Therefore we can use it inside a `for` loop, where we used to use iterators.

Because the `filter` function gets an iterator and returns an iterator, it can be seen that it *transforms* an iterator into another iterator. Such iterator *transformers* are usually named ***iterator adapters***. The term *adapter* recalls that of electrical connectors: if a plug does not fit a socket, you use an adapter.

The map Iterator Adapter

Here is another problem that can be solved using iterators: Given an array of numbers, how can you print the double of each number of that array?

You can do it in this way:

```
let arr = [66, -8, 43, 19, 0, -31];
for n in arr.into_iter() {
    print!("{} ", n * 2);
}
```

It will print: `132 -16 86 38 0 -62`.

But you can also do it in this way:

```
let arr = [66, -8, 43, 19, 0, -31];
for n in arr.into_iter().map(|x| x * 2) {
    print!("{} ", n);
}
```

The map function is another iterator adapter in the standard library. Its purpose is to *transform* the values produced by an iterator into other values. Differing from the filter function, the value returned by the closure can be of any type. Such value represents the transformed value.

Actually, the map function returns a newly created iterator that produces all the items returned by the closure received as an argument.

While the filter adapter removes some items of the iterated sequence, and it keeps the others unchanged, the map adapter does not remove any items, but it transforms them.

Another difference between them is that while filter passes a reference as the argument of its closure, map passes a value.

The enumerate Iterator Adapter

In most programming languages, to iterate over a sequence you increment an integer counter and then access the items of the sequence using that counter, in this way:

```
let arr = ['a', 'b', 'c'];
for index in 0..arr.len() {
    print!("{} {}, ", index, arr[index]);
}
```

It will print: 0 a, 1 b, 2 c, .

Using an iterator over the sequence, it is possible to avoid using the integer counter, with this code:

```
let arr = ['a', 'b', 'c'];
for ch in arr.into_iter() {
    print!("{}, ", ch);
}
```

It will print: `a, b, c, .`

But if you also need a counter, you could go back to the old technique, or you could add another variable and increment it explicitly, in this way:

```
let arr = ['a', 'b', 'c'];
let mut index = 0;
for ch in arr.into_iter() {
    print!("{} {}, ", index, ch);
    index += 1;
}
```

But there is this other possibility:

```
let arr = ['a', 'b', 'c'];
for (index, ch) in arr.into_iter().enumerate() {
    print!("{} {}, ", index, ch);
}
```

In the second line, the loop variable is actually a tuple of two variables: the `index` variable, having type `usize`; and the `ch` variable, having type `char`. At the first iteration, the `index` variable gets the value `0`, while the `ch` value gets as value the first character of the array. At every iteration, both `index` and `ch` receive new values.

This works because the `enumerate` function takes an iterator and returns another iterator. At each iteration, this returned iterator returns a value of type `(usize, char)`. This tuple has a counter as its first field, and as its second field the same item received from the first iterator.

An Iterator Consumer: any

Given a string, how can you determine if it contains a given character?

You could do it in this way:

```
let s = "Hello, world!";
let ch = 'R';
let mut contains = false;
```

```
for c in s.chars() {
    if c == ch {
        contains = true;
    }
}
print!("\"{}\" {} '{}'.",
    s,
    if contains {
        "contains"
    } else {
        "does not contain"
    },
    ch);
```

It will print: "Hello, world!" does not contain 'R'.

It does so because character comparison is case sensitive. But if you replace the uppercase R in the second line with a lowercase r, it will print: "Hello, world!" contains 'r'.

You could do it equivalently in this way:

```
let s = "Hello, world!";
let ch = 'R';
print!("\"{}\" {} '{}'.",
    s,
    if s.chars().any(|c| c == ch) {
        "contains"
    } else {
        "does not contain"
    },
    ch);
```

Here, the contains variable and the loop that possibly sets it to true have been removed; and the only other use of such a variable has been replaced by the expression s.chars().any(|c| c == ch).

As the only purpose of the contains variable was to indicate if the s string contained the ch character, the expression that replaces it must also have the same value.

We know that the s.chars() expression is evaluated to an iterator over the characters of the s string. Then the any function, which is in the standard library, is applied to such iterator. Its purpose is to determine if a Boolean function (a.k.a. *predicate*) is true for any item produced by the iterator.

The any function receives a closure as an argument. It applies that closure to every item received from the iterator, and it returns true as soon as the closure returns true on an item, or returns false if the closure returns false for all the items.

Therefore, such a function tells us if *any* item satisfies the condition specified by the closure.

You can also use the any function to determine if an array contains any negative number, as this code shows:

```
print!("{} ",
    [45, 8, 2, 6].into_iter().any(|n| n < 0));
print!("{} ",
    [45, 8, -2, 6].into_iter().any(|n| n < 0));
```

It will print: false true.

To clarify, you can annotate the closures with types:

```
print!("{} ", [45, 8, 2, 6].into_iter()
    .any(|n: i32| -> bool { n < 0 }));
print!("{} ", [45, 8, -2, 6].into_iter()
    .any(|n: i32| -> bool { n < 0 }));
```

Notice that while the iterator adapters seen previously returned iterators, the any function is applied to an iterator, but it returns a Boolean, not an iterator.

Every function that is applied to an iterator but does not return an iterator is called *iterator consumer*, because it gets data from an iterator but does not put them into another iterator, so it *consumes* data instead of *adapting* data.

The all Iterator Consumer

With the any function, you can determine if *at least* one iterated item satisfies a condition. And how can you determine if *all* iterated items satisfy a condition?

You can use the all iterator consumer. For example, to determine if all the numbers in an array are positive, you can write:

```
print!("{} ", [45, 8, 2, 6].into_iter()
    .all(|n: i32| -> bool { n > 0 }));
print!("{} ", [45, 8, -2, 6].into_iter()
    .all(|n: i32| -> bool { n > 0 }));
```

It will print: `true false`.

Notice that while the any function means a repeated application of the OR logical operator, the `all` function means a repeated application of the AND logical operator.

Notice also that, following the rules of logic, if the any function is applied to an iterator that does not return any item, the any function returns `false`, whichever is its closure. Similarly, the `all` function returns `true` when applied to an empty iterator, whichever is its closure.

The count Iterator Consumer

Given an iterator, how do you know how many items it will produce?

Well, if you have a vector, an array, or a slice, you would best use the `len` function of such objects, as it is the simplest and fastest way to get their lengths. But if you want to know how many characters there are in a string, you must scan it all, because the number of chars comprising a string is not stored anywhere, unless you did it.

So you need to use the simplest iterator consumer: `count`.

```
let s = "€èe";
print!("{} {}", s.chars().count(), s.len());
```

It will print: `3  6`, meaning that this string contains three characters represented by six bytes.

The `count` iterator consumer does not get any arguments, and it always returns a `usize` value.

The sum Iterator Consumer

If, instead of counting the iterated items, you want to add them up, it is almost as simple:

```
print!("{}", [45, 8, -2, 6].into_iter().sum::<i32>());
```

It will print: 57. Also, the sum iterator consumer does not get arguments. Yet, it requires a type parameter in angle brackets. It is the type of the returned number. Here, it is required, because otherwise the compiler could not infer such a type. But in other cases, like the following one, it is optional:

```
let s: i32 = [45, 8, -2, 6].into_iter().sum();
print!("{}", s);
```

Here, the value returned by sum is assigned to a variable having type i32, so it must return a value of such type.

It is also possible to add the items of an empty sequence:

```
let s: u32 = [0; 0].into_iter().sum();
print!("{}", s);
```

It will print: 0.

Notice that while the count function was applicable to any iterator, the sum function is applicable only to iterators that produce addable items. The statement [3.4]. into_iter().sum::<f64>(); is valid, while the statement [true].into_iter(). sum::<bool>(); is illegal, because it is not allowed to sum Booleans.

The min and max Iterator Consumers

If an iterator produces values that can be compared with one another, it is possible to get the minimum or the maximum of those values. But there is a problem: the empty sequences. If our iterator produces no items, we can count them, and this count is zero; we can add them up, and their sum is zero; but we cannot compute the maximum or the minimum of them. Therefore, the min and the max iterator consumers produce an Option value, which is Some number if they are applied to a nonempty sequence of numbers, but it is None if it is applied to an empty sequence:

```
let arr = [45, 8, -2, 6];
match arr.into_iter().min() {
    Some(n) => print!("{} ", n),
    _ => (),
}
```

```
match arr.into_iter().max() {
    Some(n) => print!("{} ", n),
    _ => (),
}
match [0; 0].into_iter().min() {
    Some(n) => print!("{} ", n),
    _ => print!("---"),
}
```

It will print: -2 45 ---.

The min and max consumers can also be applied to iterators that produce nonnumeric objects, provided they are comparable. For example, strings are comparable, so we can write this:

```
let arr = ["hello", "brave", "new", "world"];
match arr.into_iter().min() {
    Some(n) => print!("{} ", n),
    _ => (),
}
match arr.into_iter().max() {
    Some(n) => print!("{} ", n),
    _ => (),
}
```

It will print: brave world. Those two words are, respectively, the first and last of the array in alphabetical order.

The collect Consumer

The any, all, count, sum, min, and max iterator consumers return simple information regarding a possibly long sequence of items.

But we could wish to put all the consumed items into a vector. Here is a way to do it:

```
let arr = [36, 1, 15, 9, 4];
let v = arr.into_iter().collect::<Vec<i32>>();
print!("{:?}", v);
```

It will print: [36, 1, 15, 9, 4].

The collect function has created a new Vec<i32> object, and it has pushed into it all the items received from the iterator.

The collect function can be used to put items into various kinds of variable size collections, like vectors, linked lists, hashtables (but excluding arrays). Therefore, it is a generic function, parameterized by the type of destination collection. The expression it.collect::<Vec<i32>>() means that the numbers generated by the it iterator will be collected into a vector.

If the context does not allow inferring either the type of collection (Vec) or the type of the contained items (i32), we must specify both of them, like in the expression Vec<i32>. Though, in the previous example, the type of the items could be inferred to be i32, so we can write the following code:

```
let arr = [36, 1, 15, 9, 4];
let v = arr.into_iter().collect::<Vec<_>>();
print!("{:?}", v);
```

In this code, the type i32 has been replaced by the don't-care symbol _.

But if even the type of the resulting collection can be inferred, then it can be omitted from the parameterization of collect. So, this program is equivalent to the previous one:

```
let arr = [36, 1, 15, 9, 4];
let v: Vec<_> = arr.into_iter().collect();
print!("{:?}", v);
```

In addition, even string characters can be collected into a string or into a vector:

```
let s = "Hello";
println!("{:?}", s.chars().collect::<String>());
println!("{:?}", s.chars().collect::<Vec<char>>());
```

It will print:

```
"Hello"
['H', 'e', 'l', 'l', 'o']
```

The second and third statements apply the chars function to a string, obtaining an iterator producing characters. But the second statement collects those characters into a String object, while the third statement collects them into a vector of characters.

You can also handle the bytes of strings, in two ways:

```
let s = "Hello";
println!("{:?}", s.bytes().collect::<Vec<u8>>());
println!("{:?}", s.as_bytes().iter().collect::<Vec<&u8>>());
```

It will print:

```
[72, 101, 108, 108, 111]
[72, 101, 108, 108, 111]
```

The second statement uses the `bytes` function to obtain an iterator producing bytes. Then those bytes, which are the representation of the characters, are collected into a vector.

The third statement uses the `as_bytes` function to see the string as a slice of bytes. Next, the `iter` function is used to obtain an iterator over such slice, producing references to bytes. Then, such references to bytes are collected into a vector. When a vector of references is printed for debugging, the referenced objects are actually printed.

Notice that the `collect` function cannot be used to put the iterated items into a static string, an array, or a slice, because it needs to allocate the needed space at runtime, and such sequences cannot allocate heap memory.

Iterator Chains

Assume you have an array of numbers, and you want to create a vector containing only the positive numbers of such an array, multiplied by two.

You could write it without using iterators, in this way:

```
let arr = [66, -8, 43, 19, 0, -31];
let mut v = vec![];
for i in 0..arr.len() {
    if arr[i] > 0 { v.push(arr[i] * 2); }
}
print!("{:?}", v);
```

It will print: [132, 86, 38].

Or, equivalently, you could use an iterator generator, without using iterator adapters or iterator consumers:

```
let arr = [66, -8, 43, 19, 0, -31];
let mut v = vec![];
for n in arr.into_iter() {
    if n > 0 { v.push(n * 2); }
}
print!("{:?}", v);
```

Or, equivalently, you could use an iterator generator and two iterator adapters, without using iterator consumers:

```
let arr = [66, -8, 43, 19, 0, -31];
let mut v = vec![];
for n in arr
    .into_iter()
    .filter(|x| *x > 0)
    .map(|x| x * 2)
{
    v.push(n);
}
print!("{:?}", v);
```

Or, equivalently, you could use an iterator generator, two iterator adapters, and an iterator consumer:

```
let arr = [66, -8, 43, 19, 0, -31];
let v = arr
    .into_iter()
    .filter(|x| *x > 0)
    .map(|x| x * 2)
    .collect::<Vec<_>>();
print!("{:?}", v);
```

This last version shows a programming pattern that is typical of functional languages: *the iterator chain*.

From a sequence, an iterator is created; then zero or more iterator adapters are chained; and then an iterator consumer closes the chain.

Such chains begin with an iterator or an iterator generator, they proceed with zero or more iterator adapters, and they end with an iterator consumer.

We saw several iterator generators: `chars`, `bytes`, `into_iter`, `iter`, and `iter_mut`; and we saw ranges, which are iterators with no need to be created by a generator.

We saw several iterator adapters: `filter`, `map`, and `enumerate`.

And we saw several iterator consumers: `any`, `all`, `count`, `sum`, `min`, `max`, and `collect`.

The standard library contains many more such functions.

Iterators Are "Lazy"

Now, let's see an example that helps us to understand the mechanism behind the behavior of iterators. It is the previous code example, with some debug print statements added:

```
let v = [66, -8, 43, 19, 0, -31]
    .into_iter()
    .filter(|x| { print!("F{} ", x); *x > 0 })
    .map(|x| { print!("M{} ", x); x * 2 })
    .collect::<Vec<_>>();
print!("{:?}", v);
```

It will print: `F66 M66 F-8 F43 M43 F19 M19 F0 F-31 [132, 86, 38]`.

The runtime operations are the following ones.

The invocation of `into_iter` prepares a temporary iterator, but it does not access the array. Let's name "I" the iterator returned by `into_iter`.

The invocation of `filter` on "I" prepares another temporary iterator, but it does not manage data. Let's name "F" the iterator returned by `filter`.

The invocation of `map` on "F" prepares another temporary iterator, but it does not manage data. Let's name "M" the iterator returned by `map`.

The invocation of `collect` on "M" asks "M" for an item; "M" asks "F" for an item; "F" asks "I" for an item. Then "I" takes the number 66 from the array and passes it to "F", which prints it, checks whether it is positive, and passes it to "M", which prints it, doubles it, and passes it to `collect`, which then pushes it into the vector.

Then, `collect`, because it has just received `Some` item and not `None`, asks "M" for another item, and the trip is repeated until the number -8 arrives to "F", which rejects it as nonpositive. Indeed, -8 is not printed by "M". At this point, "F," because before it has just received `Some` item and has rejected it, asks "I" for another item.

The algorithm proceeds in this way until the array is finished. When "I" cannot find other items in the array, it sends a None to "F" to indicate there are no more items. When "F" receives a None, it sends it to "M", which sends it to collect, which stops asking items, and the whole statement is finished.

If this whole expression except for the collect invocation is in the header of a for loop, we have this code:

```
let mut v = vec![];
for item in [66, -8, 43, 19, 0, -31]
    .into_iter()
    .filter(|x| { print!("F{} ", x); *x > 0 })
    .map(|x| { print!("M{} ", x); x * 2 }) {
    v.push(item);
}
print!("{:?}", v);
```

This code is equivalent: the same mechanism is activated, and it prints the same output.

But let's omit both the for loop and any iterator consumer.

```
[66, -8, 43, 19, 0, -31]
    .into_iter()
    .filter(|x| { print!("F{} ", x); *x > 0 })
    .map(|x| { print!("M{} ", x); x * 2 });
```

This program prints nothing, because it does nothing. Even the compiler reports the warning: unused `Map` that must be used, and then the note: iterators are lazy and do nothing unless consumed.

In computer science, to be *lazy* means trying to do some processing as late as possible. Iterator adapters are lazy, as they process data only when another function asks them for an item: it can be another iterator adapter, or an iterator consumer, or a for loop, which acts as a consumer. If there is no data sink, there is no data access.

CHAPTER 17

Input/Output and Error Handling

In this chapter, you will learn:

- How to get the arguments from the command line used to launch the program

- How to return a status code to the operating system when exiting the program

- How to get and set the process environment variables

- Techniques and best practices to handle runtime errors

- How to read from the console keyboard and how to write to the console screen

- How primitive types are converted to string

- How to convert a string to a primitive type

- How to read or write a binary file

- How to read a text file, a line at a time

Command-Line Arguments

The most basic form of input of a program is through the command line. This program reads such input:

243

© Carlo Milanesi 2022
C. Milanesi, *Beginning Rust*, https://doi.org/10.1007/978-1-4842-7208-4_17

```
let command_line: std::env::Args = std::env::args();
for argument in command_line {
    print!("[{}]", argument);
}
```

If this program is compiled to create a file named, say, `main`, and that file is launched writing the following command line in Unix-like shell:

```
./main    first     second
```

it will print: `[./main][first][second]`, even if there are several spaces between the input words.

Instead, using the command prompt of Microsoft Windows (cmd.exe) you should type:

```
main    first     second
```

The `args` standard library function returns an iterator over the command-line arguments. Such an iterator has type `Args`, and it produces `String` values. The first value produced is the program name, with the path used to reach it. The others are the program arguments.

Any blank is usually removed; to keep blanks, you have to enclose arguments in quotation marks, which will be removed. If you launch `./main " first argument"` `"second argument "`, it will print: `[./main][ first argument][second argument ]`.

This program can be abbreviated to this:

```
for a in std::env::args() {
    print!("[{}]", a);
}
```

Process Return Code

The most basic form of output of a program is its return code, shown in this code:

```
std::process::exit(107);
```

This program will terminate immediately when it invokes the `exit` function, and it will return to the launching process the number 107.

If this program is launched from a console of Unix, Linux, or MacOS, and afterward you write the command echo $?, you will get 107 printed on the console. The corresponding Windows command is echo %errorlevel%.

Environment Variables

Another form of input/output is through environment variables:

```
for var in std::env::vars() {
    println!("[{}]=[{}]", var.0, var.1);
}
```

This program will print one line for every environment variable. However, to read or write a specific environment variable, this code is better:

```
print!("[{:?}]", std::env::var("abcd"));
std::env::set_var("abcd", "This is the value");
print!(" [{:?}]", std::env::var("abcd"));
```

It will print: [Err(NotPresent)] [Ok("This is the value")]. First, probably, the abcd environment variable is not yet defined, so the invocation of the var function returns the Err variant of a Result value. The specific kind of error is the enum NotPresent. Then, such an environment variable is set for the current process, by invoking the set_var function. And so, it is found at the next try to get it, and its string value is returned inside an Ok variant.

A similar program is this one:

```
print!("{}",
    if std::env::var("abcd").is_ok() {
        "Already defined"
    } else {
        "Undefined"
    });
std::env::set_var("abcd", "This is the value");
print!(", {}", match std::env::var("abcd") {
    Ok(value) => value,
    Err(err) => format!("Still undefined: {}", err),
});
```

245

It will print: `Undefined, This is the value.`

Reading from the Console

For command-line oriented programs, a typical way to get input is to read a line from the keyboard until the user presses Enter. Such input may be redirected to read from a file or from the output of another process. Here is a program that performs such input:

```
let mut line = String::new();
println!("{:?}", std::io::stdin().read_line(&mut line));
println!("[{}]", line);
```

As this program starts, it waits for your input from the keyboard, until you press some keys and then Enter. If, for example, you type `Hello` and then press Enter, it will print:

```
Ok(6)
[Hello
]
```

The `stdin` function returns a handle to the standard input stream of the current process. On that handle, the `read_line` function can be applied. It waits for an end-of-line or an end-of-file character from the standard input stream, and then it tries to read all the characters present in the input buffer. The read may fail, because another thread may be reading the standard input at the same time.

If that read is successful, the characters read are appended to the string contained in the `line` variable. That variable is received as argument by reference to a mutable object. The `read_line` function returns an `Ok` result object, whose data is the number of bytes read. Notice that such number is 6, because in addition to the five bytes of the string `Hello`, there is the end-of-line control character. In fact, when the `line` variable is printed, the terminating closed bracket is printed in a separate line, because the end-of-line character is printed too.

If the `read_line` function cannot read characters from the standard input stream, it returns an `Err` result object, and it does not change the value of the `line` variable.

Let's see what happens when several lines are read from the standard input stream:

```
let mut text = format!("First: ");
let inp = std::io::stdin();
```

```
inp.read_line(&mut text).unwrap();
text.push_str("Second: ");
inp.read_line(&mut text).unwrap();
println!("{}: {} bytes", text, text.len());
```

If when you start this program, you type eè€, then hit Enter, then type Hello, and then you hit Enter again, it will print:

```
First: eè€
Second: Hello
: 28 bytes
```

If your keyboard does not allow you to type those characters, try to type any non-ASCII character.

First, notice that the string printed in the last line spans three lines, as it contains two end-of-line characters. In addition, it contains the 7-byte ASCII string "First: ", and the 8-byte ASCII string "Second: ". Also Hello is an ASCII string, and it contains 5 bytes. As we saw in another chapter, the eè€ string contains 6 bytes, so we have $7 + 6 + 1 + 8 + 5 + 1 = 28$ bytes.

Second, let's see how the contents of the text variable are built up. Notice that the read_line function appends the typed line to the object specified by its argument, instead of overwriting it. The text variable is initialized to contain "First:". In the third line, the first typed line is appended to those contents. Then, in the fourth line, the literal string "Second:" is appended to it. Finally, in the fifth line, the second typed line is appended.

Third, notice that when the read_line function reads the input buffer, it clears it, as the original buffer contents are not read again when the function is invoked for the second time.

Fourth, notice that after every invocation of read_line, there is an invocation of unwrap, but its return value is ignored. Such invocation could be omitted, as shown in this code:

```
let mut text = format!("First: ");
let inp = std::io::stdin();
inp.read_line(&mut text);
text.push_str("Second: ");
inp.read_line(&mut text);
println!("{}: {} bytes", text, text.len());
```

However, when this program is compiled, the compiler emits, for both invocations of read_line, the warning unused `Result` that must be used. It means that read_line returns a value of type Result, and that value is ignored. The generic type Result is meant to distinguish between two cases: a success (the Ok variant) and a failure (the Err variant). In this code, such distinction between success and failure is lost, because the return values are not used in any way. In general, it is a bad practice to ignore a return value of type Result, because such a type could represent a runtime error, and the program logic does not take into account such a kind of error. The compiler just warns about this bad practice.

This practice is surely dangerous in production code, but it is not appropriate in debug code either, as it hides the errors that you are looking for.

Therefore, in debug code, it is appropriate to always write at least an unwrap() clause. Such clause ensures that the program will proceed only if the previous call was successful. In case of failure of the previous call, the unwrap call will panic. This is usually good when debugging, because in this way we find where the function fails unexpectedly.

But in production code, matters are not so simple.

Proper Runtime Error Handling

Real-world software often happens to make invocations of functions that return a Result type value. Let's call such functions *fallible*. A fallible function normally returns an Ok, but in exceptional cases it returns an Err.

In C++, Java, and other object-oriented languages, the standard error handling technique is based on the so-called *exceptions*, and on the throw, try, and catch keywords. In Rust, there are no such things; all error-handling is based on the Result type, its functions, and the match statement, or on the *panic* concept that we have already seen in Chapter 5.

Assume, as it is typical, that you are writing a function f, which, to accomplish its task, has to invoke several fallible functions, f1, f2, f3, and f4. If no function fails, the behavior is this: the argument of f is passed to f1, the value returned by f1 is passed to f2, the value returned by f2 is passed to f3, the value returned by f3 is passed to f4, and the value returned by f4 is returned by f.

The implementation of f can just be this:

```
fn f(x: i32) -> i32 {
    f4(f3(f2(f1(x))))
}
```

But now consider that such functions f1, f2, f3, and f4 are fallible. Each of them returns an error message if it fails, or a result if it is successful. If any one of such functions fails, its error message should be immediately returned by the f function as its error message. If a function is successful, its result should be passed on as shown in the previous code.

As further requirements, let's assume that f1 fails if its argument is 1, f2 fails if its argument is 2, f3 fails if its argument is 3, and f4 fails if its argument is 4. Otherwise, all of them return the argument received. So, the calls f(1), f(2), f(3) and f(4) should fail, and, for any other integer n, f(n) should return n.

One possibility to implement these requirements is to write this code:

```
fn f1(x: i32) -> Result<i32, String> {
    if x == 1 {
        Err(format!("Err. 1"))
    } else {
        Ok(x)
    }
}
fn f2(x: i32) -> Result<i32, String> {
    if x == 2 {
        Err(format!("Err. 2"))
    } else {
        Ok(x)
    }
}
fn f3(x: i32) -> Result<i32, String> {
    if x == 3 {
        Err(format!("Err. 3"))
    } else {
        Ok(x)
    }
}
```

```
fn f4(x: i32) -> Result<i32, String> {
    if x == 4 {
        Err(format!("Err. 4"))
    } else {
        Ok(x)
    }
}
fn f(x: i32) -> Result<i32, String> {
    match f1(x) {
        Ok(result) => {
            match f2(result) {
                Ok(result) => {
                    match f3(result) {
                        Ok(result) => f4(result),
                        Err(err_msg) => Err(err_msg),
                    }
                }
                Err(err_msg) => Err(err_msg),
            }
        }
        Err(err_msg) => Err(err_msg),
    }
}
match f(2) {
    Ok(y) => println!("{}", y),
    Err(e) => println!("Error: {}", e),
}
match f(4) {
    Ok(y) => println!("{}", y),
    Err(e) => println!("Error: {}", e),
}
match f(5) {
    Ok(y) => println!("{}", y),
    Err(e) => println!("Error: {}", e),
}
```

It will print:

```
Error: Err. 2
Error: Err. 4
5
```

It is quite obvious that such a pattern becomes unwieldy as the number of invocations increases, because the indentation level increases by two at every invocation added.

This code can be made linear by replacing the f function with the following one:

```
fn f(x: i32) -> Result<i32, String> {
    let result1 = f1(x);
    if result1.is_err() { return result1; }
    let result2 = f2(result1.unwrap());
    if result2.is_err() { return result2; }
    let result3 = f3(result2.unwrap());
    if result3.is_err() { return result3; }
    f4(result3.unwrap())
}
```

Every intermediate result is stored in a local variable, and then such variable is checked using the is_err function. In case of failure, that local variable is returned as the failure result of f; in case of success, the unwrap function is used to extract the actual result from the local variable.

This pattern is so typical that a language feature has been introduced into the language. Here is an equivalent version of the f function:

```
fn f(x: i32) -> Result<i32, String> {
    f4(f3(f2(f1(x)?)?)?)
}
```

The question mark is a special macro, which can be placed after an expression of type Result<T, E> or type Option<T>. In the first case, assuming the expression is represented by <expr>, the expression <expr>? is expanded as the following expression:

```
{
    let ex = <expr>;
    match ex {
        Ok(v) => v,
```

```
        Err(_) => return ex,
    }
}
```

This means that the expression is evaluated, and in case the result represents a success (Ok), the value inside it becomes the value of the whole expression; and in case the result represents a failure (Err), the containing function is exited returning such result.

Instead, if the type of <expr> is Option<T>, the expression <expr>? is expanded as the following expression:

```
{
    let ex = <expr>;
    match ex {
        Some(v) => v,
        None => return ex,
    }
}
```

In other words, the macro examines if its argument is Some or Ok, and in such cases it unwraps the argument; otherwise it returns the argument as a return value of the containing function.

Of course, this special macro can be used only inside a function with a proper return value type, like this code demonstrates:

```
fn f1(n: i32) -> Result<i64, String> {
    Ok(f2(n * 2)? as i64 * 3)
}
fn f2(n: i32) -> Result<i32, String> {
    if n >= 0 {
        Ok(n * 5)
    } else {
        Err("Negative argument".to_string())
    }
}
print!("{:?} ", f1(10));
```

```
print!("{:?} ", f1(7));
print!("{:?} ", f1(-1));
```

It will print: `Ok(300) Ok(210) Err("Negative argument")`.

The function `f1` is invoked three times, with arguments 10, 7, and -1. It invokes the function `f2`, passing the double of the argument it receives. So `f2` receives the values 20, 14, and -2. This function checks its argument, and fails if it is negative; otherwise it returns its argument multiplied by 5, encapsulated in an `Ok` variant. So, the values returned by the three calls to `f2` are `Ok(100)`, `Ok(70)`, and `Err("Negative argument".to_string())`.

So far, all the numbers are of type `i32`. The `f1` function uses the question mark macro to check whether the value returned by its call to `f2` is `Ok` or `Err`. In the second case, the error value is forwarded outside of the function. For such forward to be legal, the `f1` function must have a return value of type `Result`, with the `Err` variant containing a `String` value. This is required, because the question mark macro cannot change the type of the error variant.

In case the call to `f2` returned an `Ok` variant, the question mark macro strips the `Ok` casing and reveals the `i32` value inside it. That value can be converted to another type; here it is an `i64` type. Then the `f1` function multiplies that value by 3 and returns the successful result as an `Ok(i64)` variant. So the value that we got for the three calls to `f1` are `Ok(300i64)`, `Ok(210i64)`, and `Err("Negative argument".to_string())`, which are the printed values.

In general, the question mark macro can be used only in a function whose return value type has the form `Result<T1, E>` or `Option<T1>`. In the first case, it can be applied only to an expression whose type is `Result<T2, E>`, where T2 can be different from T1 but E must be the same; but, if the enclosing function return value type is `Option<T1>`, the question mark macro can be applied only to an expression whose type is `Option<T2>`.

So, the right pattern to build a robust error handling is the following one. Every function that contains an invocation to a fallible function should be a fallible function itself, or it should handle the `Result` value in a `match` statement, or by similar handling. In the first case, every invocation of a fallible function should be followed by a question mark to propagate the error condition. Even the `main` function (or the starting functions of a secondary thread) can be a fallible function, like this complete program (including the main function) shows:

```
fn main() -> Result<(), String> {
    fn incremented(n: i32) -> Result<i32, String> {
        if n < 0 { Err(format!("negative argument")) }
        else { Ok(n + 1) }
    }
    println!("{} ", incremented(4)?);
    println!("{} ", incremented(-3)?);
    println!("{} ", incremented(7)?);
    Ok(())
}
```

It will print:

```
5
Error: "negative argument"
```

In this program, the main function has a signature different than the usual one. Instead of having no return value type (that implies an empty tuple), it has the return value type Result<(), String>. Here, the success type must be an empty tuple, but the failure type can be any type that can be printed for debugging, including strings and all primitive types.

Inside the main function the increment fallible function is defined. It could have been defined just as well outside the main function.

The increment function fails if its argument is negative; otherwise it returns a number.

Then the main function contains three print statements, all invoking the increment function.

The first one succeeds, so the number 5 is printed.

The second one fails, so the string received from the increment function is returned as error from the main function. The Rust runtime support that invoked the main function, receives this error value and prints it on the console using debug formatting, preceded by the string "Error:". Of course, this kind of output is only for debugging purposes.

The last two statements are never executed.

Notice that this `main` function must end with the expression `Ok(())`, because its signature expects a `Result`.

Writing to the Console

We already wrote to the console in almost every program snippet we wrote, but we did that always using the `print` or `println` macros, which are implemented using standard library functions. However, you can also directly use library functions to print some text to the console. Here is an example of this:

```
use std::io::Write;
//ILLEGAL: std::io::stdout().write("Hi").unwrap();
//ILLEGAL: std::io::stdout().write(String::from("Hi")).unwrap();
std::io::stdout().write("Hello ".as_bytes()).unwrap();
std::io::stdout().write(String::from("world").as_bytes()).unwrap();
```

It will print: `Hello world`.

The `stdout` standard library function returns a handle to the standard output stream of the current process. The `write` function can be applied on that handle.

However, the `write` function cannot directly print static or dynamic strings, and of course neither numbers nor general composite objects.

The `write` function gets an argument of `&[u8]` type, which is a reference to a slice of bytes. Such bytes are printed to the console as a UTF-8 string. So, if you want to print a value that is not a slice of bytes in UTF-8 format, first you have to translate it to such a sequence of bytes.

To convert both a static string and a dynamic string to a reference to a slice of bytes, you can use the `as_bytes` function.

Finally, notice that the `write` function returns a `Result` type value, that is, it is a fallible function. If you are quite sure it is not going to fail, you'd best invoke the `unwrap` function on its return value.

Converting a Value to a String

If you want to print the textual representation of another kind of value, you can try to use the "to_string" function, defined for all primitive types. Here it is applied to an integer, a floating-point number, and a Boolean:

```
let int_str: String = 45.to_string();
let float_str: String = 4.5.to_string();
let bool_str: String = true.to_string();
print!("{} {} {}", int_str, float_str, bool_str);
```

It will print: `45 4.5 true`.

The `to_string` function allocates a String object, whose header is in the stack and whose contents are in the heap. Therefore, it is not very efficient.

Converting a String to a Value

When your program gets input from the console or from a text file, only strings are read. If you want to interpret such strings as numbers, you need to *parse* them. The Rust standard library contains functions to parse strings into numbers, as shown by this code:

```
println!("{:?}", "true".parse::<bool>());
println!("{:?}", "1.23e7".parse::<f32>());
println!("{:?}", "1.23y7".parse::<f32>());
```

It will print:

```
Ok(true)
Ok(12300000.0)
Err(ParseFloatError { kind: Invalid })
```

The `parse::<T>` function of strings returns a value of type `Result<T, E>`, where T is the type specified in the call, and E is a type that describes the kind of parse error.

The first call to the `parse` function specifies that the string must be parsed as a Boolean value. That conversion is successful, so the resulting value, encapsulated in an `Ok` enum variant, is printed.

The second call to the parse function specifies that the string must be parsed as a single-precision floating-point number. That conversion is successful, so the resulting number is printed.

The third call to the parse function cannot perform the conversion, so an Err variant is returned. Inside that variant it is specified that it is an error of parsing floating-point numbers, and that the kind of error is Invalid.

If you are sure that a string parsing is valid, you can use the unwrap function; and if you are sure that a string parsing is invalid, you can use the unwrap_err function, like in this code:

```
println!("{}", "true".parse::<bool>().unwrap());
println!("{}", "1.23e7".parse::<f32>().unwrap());
println!("{}", "1.23y7".parse::<f32>().unwrap_err());
```

It will print:

```
true
12300000
invalid float literal
```

File Input/Output

In addition to reading and writing to the console, in Rust it is also rather easy to read and write both binary and text sequential files. Here is a program that writes three characters into a new file:

```
use std::io::Write;
let mut file = std::fs::File::create("data.txt").unwrap();
file.write_all("eè€".as_bytes()).unwrap();
```

The second line invokes the create function to create a file named data.txt in the current folder of the file system. This function is fallible, and, if it is successful in creating that file, it returns a file handle to the file just created.

The last line invokes the write_all function to write some bytes in the newly create file. The saved bytes are the six bytes representing the string eè€.

Before, we saw the write function, which is quite similar to the write_all function. Actually, they are equivalent, when they write to a disk file or to the console. The difference appears when they write to a stream that can accept a limited number of bytes at a time, like a network connection. The `write` function makes just one attempt to output the buffer, and, if the call is at least partially successful, it returns how many bytes have been actually written, so that further calls can proceed later to output the remaining bytes. Instead, the `write_all` function keeps making attempts to output the buffer, until the whole buffer is output, or until an error happens. In case of success, it returns just an empty tuple.

Assuming that in the current directory there is the text file named `data.txt` you just created by running the previous program, you can read that file by running the following program:

```
use std::io::Read;
let mut file = std::fs::File::open("data.txt").unwrap();
let mut contents = String::new();
file.read_to_string(&mut contents).unwrap();
print!("{}", contents);
```

This program will print: eè€.

The second line invokes the `open` function to open an existing file named `data.txt` in the current folder. This function fails if the file does not exist, or if it is not accessible for whatever reason. If it succeeds, a file handle to such file is assigned to the `file` variable.

The fourth line invokes the `read_to_string` function on the `file` handle to read all the contents of that file and append them to a string variable, passed by reference to a mutable object.

The last line prints to the console the contents just read from the file.

So now, putting together the previous two programs, you should be able to copy a file into another one. But if a file is huge, it may be infeasible to load it all into a string before writing it. It is required to read and write a portion of the file at a time. However, it is inefficient to read and write small portions.

Here is a rather efficient program to copy a file:

```
use std::io::Read;
use std::io::Write;
let mut command_line: std::env::Args = std::env::args();
command_line.next().unwrap();
let source = command_line.next().unwrap();
```

```
let destination = command_line.next().unwrap();
let mut file_in = std::fs::File::open(source).unwrap();
let mut file_out = std::fs::File::create(destination).unwrap();
let mut buffer = [0u8; 4096];
loop {
    let nbytes = file_in.read(&mut buffer).unwrap();
    file_out.write_all(&buffer[..nbytes]).unwrap();
    if nbytes < buffer.len() { break; }
}
```

This program must be launched passing two command-line arguments. The first one is the path of the source file, and the second one is the path of the destination file.

The lines from the third to the sixth one assign to the source variable the contents of the first argument, and to the destination variable the contents of the second argument.

The next two lines open the two files. First the source file is opened, and the new handle is assigned to the file_in variable. Then the destination file is created (or truncated, if already existing), and the new handle is assigned to the file_out variable.

Then a 4096-byte buffer is allocated in the stack.

At last, a loop repeatedly reads a 4096-byte chunk from the source file and writes it to the output file. The number of bytes read is implicitly specified by the length of the buffer. But if the remaining portion of the file is not long enough, the read bytes do not fill the buffer.

So, we need the number of bytes read. Such value is put into the nbytes variable.

For a file larger than 4096 bytes, at the first iteration the number of bytes read will be 4096, so some other iterations will be required. For a very small file, one iteration will be enough.

In any case, the buffer must be written to the output file up to the number of bytes read. So, a slice of the buffer is taken from the beginning to the number of read bytes.

Then, if the number of bytes read was less than the length of the buffer, the loop is terminated, as the end of the input file has been reached. Otherwise the loop continues with other iterations.

Notice that there is no need to explicitly close the files. As soon as the file handles exit their scopes, the files are automatically closed, saving and releasing all internal temporary buffers. Differently from the corresponding type of the C++ standard library, fstream, which can be opened after being instantiated and then explicitly closed before being destroyed, so that in any instant can be in open or closed state, Rust File objects are necessarily opened when they are created, and they cannot be closed explicitly. So, when a File object exists, it is necessarily open. To anticipate the closing of a File object, you can add a pair of braces that encloses just the portion of code in which that file must remain open.

Processing Text Files

We saw how to sequentially read or write a file of arbitrary data, usually named *binary data*.

But when a file contains raw text, like a program source file, it is more convenient to process it a line at a time.

For example, if we want to compute how many lines there are in a text file, and how many of them are empty or contain only blanks, we can write this program:

```
let mut command_line = std::env::args();
command_line.next();
let pathname = command_line.next().unwrap();
let counts = count_lines(&pathname).unwrap();
println!("file: {}", pathname);
println!("n. of lines: {}", counts.0);
println!("n. of empty lines: {}", counts.1);

fn count_lines(pathname: &str)
-> Result<(u32, u32), std::io::Error> {
    use std::io::BufRead;
    let f = std::fs::File::open(pathname)?;
    let f = std::io::BufReader::new(f);
    let mut n_lines = 0;
    let mut n_empty_lines = 0;
    for line in f.lines() {
        n_lines += 1;
        if line?.trim().len() == 0 {
            n_empty_lines += 1;
        }
    }
    Ok((n_lines, n_empty_lines))
}
```

If this program, enclosed in the usual `main` function, is saved in a file named `countlines.rs` and then compiled, and it is run with the argument `countlines.rs`, it will print:

```
file: countlines.rs
n. of lines: 25
n. of empty lines: 1
```

In the first line, the invocation of `args` gets the command-line iterator and stores it into the `command_line` variable.

In the second line, the command-line argument at position zero is discarded.

In the third line, the command-line argument at position one is consumed and assigned to the `pathname` variable. If there is no such argument, the `next()` function call returns `None`, so the `unwrap()` function applied to it panics.

In the fourth line, the `count_lines` function, defined later, is invoked, passing to it a reference to the path name of the file to read. It is a fallible function. If it is successful, it returns a tuple of two values: the total number of lines counted in the read file, and the number of those lines that are empty or that contain only blanks. That pair is assigned to the `counts` variable.

The fifth, sixth, and seventh lines are print statements.

From the ninth line, there is the declaration of the `count_lines` function. It gets a string slice as an argument, and returns a `Result` that in case of success is a pair of `u32` numbers, and in case of failure is a standard I/O error.

The `open` function is invoked to get a handle for the file indicated by the path name received as an argument. The question mark following it means that if the `open` function fails, the `count_lines` function immediately returns the same error code returned by the `open` function.

The operations performed on a file are not buffered by default. That is optimal if you don't need buffering, or if you prefer to apply your own buffering. Text lines are usually much shorter than the optimal I/O buffer size, so, when reading a text file, it is more efficient to use a buffered input stream.

If you want to use a buffered stream, you can create a `BufReader` object from a *raw* file handle, like these lines from the preceding code do:

```
let f = std::fs::File::open(pathname)?;
let f = std::io::BufReader::new(f);
```

After having created a `BufReader` object, there is no more need to explicitly use the existing `File` object; so the newly created object can be assigned to another variable named `f`, so that it will shadow the preexisting variable.

Then, the two counters `n_lines` and `n_empty_lines` are declared and initialized.

Then, there is the loop over the file contents. The `BufReader` type provides the `lines` iterator generator. It returns an iterator over the lines contained in the file. Notice that Rust iterators are lazy; that is, there is never a memory structure containing all the lines, but every time the iterator is asked for a line, it asks the file buffered reader for a line, and then provides the obtained line. So, at each iteration, the `for`-loop puts the next line into the `line` variable and executes the loop block.

But any file read can fail, so `line` is not a simple string; its type is `Result<String, std::io::Error>`. Therefore, when it is used, `line` is followed by a question mark, to get its string value or to return the I/O error.

In the loop body, the `n_lines` counter is incremented by one at any line, while the `n_empty_lines` counter is incremented by one only when the line has zero length, after having removed from it any leading or trailing blanks by invoking `trim`.

The last statement returns a successful value: `Ok`. The data of such value are the two counters.

CHAPTER 18

Data Encapsulation

In this chapter, you will learn:

- Why the dot notation for calling a function is more convenient than the functional notation

- How to use the `impl` and `self` keywords to declare functions that can be invoked using the dot notation

- How to encapsulate function declarations in modules, selecting which functions declared in a module should be accessible from other modules

- How to create a hierarchy of modules, and how to access any function in such hierarchy

- How to define type aliases

The Need for Methods

We already saw that there are two possible notations to invoke a function: `f(x, y)` and `x.f(y)`. The first one is the *functional* notation, and the second one is the *dot notation*. Previously, we invoked some functions of the standard library using the functional notation, like `String::new()` or `std::fs::File::open("data.txt")`, and other functions using the dot notation, like `"abcd".len()` or `vec![0u8; 0].push(7u8)`. The dot notation is similar to the notation used to access the fields of tuples, tuple-structs, and structs.

Not every function can be invoked using the dot notation. For example, the `String::new` and `File::open` functions can only be invoked using the functional notation.

© Carlo Milanesi 2022

C. Milanesi, *Beginning Rust*, https://doi.org/10.1007/978-1-4842-7208-4_18

However, any function that may be invoked using the dot notation may also be invoked using the functional notation. Here is an example:

```
print!("{} {}",
    "abcd".to_string(),
    std::string::ToString::to_string("abcd"));
```

It will print: abcd abcd. First, the to_string function is invoked using the dot notation and then using the functional notation.

Here is another example:

```
print!("{} {}",
    [1, 2, 3].len(),
    <[i32]>::len(&[1, 2, 3]));
```

It will print: 3 3.

And yet another example:

```
let mut v1 = vec![0u8; 0];
let mut v2 = vec![0u8; 0];
v1.push(7);
Vec::push(&mut v2, 7);
print!("{:?} {:?}", v1, v2);
```

It will print: [7] [7]. First, two empty mutable vectors are created. Then, the byte 7 is pushed onto them using two different notations.

The dot notation is typical of the object-oriented programming paradigm, and this is not by chance. Such notation is possible in Rust, because Rust, in some way, supports such paradigm.

The gist of object-oriented programming is having a data type, traditionally named *class*, which, in addition to containing data, has some specific behavior, implemented as functions associated to such type. Such associated functions are traditionally named *methods*. Considering a method call like a.f(b, c), we see that this method f is a function that has a privileged argument, a, and two normal arguments b and c. The privileged argument a is an instance of the type to which this method is associated. Such argument is considered the *current object* of the associated type, therefore it is usually simply called *this* or *self*.

When the dot notation is transformed into the functional notation, the current object becomes an additional first argument. In this example, it would become f(a, b, c). Though, the current object must be decorated by the possibly required dereference symbol (&) or mutation keyword (mut), or both, like in f(&mut a, b, c). Such decorations are implicit, using the dot notation.

In addition, there is a scoping issue. In an application, there may be several functions having the same name. For example, the standard library contains several functions named to_string, len, and push. Using the dot notation, the proper method is automatically chosen, because it is the only one having that name among those associated with the type of the current object. Instead, using the functional notation, the scope of the function must be written explicitly. In the preceding examples, the to_string function is in the std::string::ToString scope, the len function is in the <[i32]> scope, and the push function is in the Vec scope. If you omit the scope specifier in the first example, writing simply to_string("abcd"), you get the compilation error: cannot find function `to_string` in this scope.

The dot notation and the underlying object-oriented programming paradigm appear to be so good in simplifying code, that you may wish to use them often, and in particular for the functions you declare. To that purpose, a specific syntax is required to declare methods.

Method Declarations

Let's see how to implement the basics of object-oriented programming in Rust, by declaring methods for a user-defined datatype.

First, let's define a type and a function that accesses objects of such type using the known functional notation:

```
struct Person {
    personal_names: String,
    family_names: String,
}
fn naming(p: Person) -> String {
    format!("{} {}",
        p.personal_names,
        p.family_names)
}
```

```
let person = Person {
    personal_names: "John".to_string(),
    family_names: "Doe".to_string(),
};
print!("{}", naming(person));
```

It will print: John Doe.

First, there is the declaration of the Person struct, and then the declaration of the naming function, which receives an instance of such type by value. Then, an instance of the Person type is created, and it is passed to an invocation of the naming function.

Now, assume that in the last line we would like to use the dot notation. We could try to replace the last line with this line:

```
print!("{}", person.naming());
```

Though, we would get the compilation error: no method named `naming` found for struct `Person` in the current scope.

To obtain the desired result, we must use the following method declaration syntax:

```
struct Person {
    personal_names: String,
    family_names: String,
}
impl Person {
    fn naming(self) -> String {
        format!("{} {}",
            self.personal_names,
            self.family_names)
    }
}
let person = Person {
    personal_names: "John".to_string(),
    family_names: "Doe".to_string(),
};
print!("{}", person.naming());
```

Here, the declaration of the naming function has been inserted into a block preceded by the clause impl Person. The impl keyword is shorthand for *implementation*. In Rust, the impl block is a construct designed to encapsulate the methods associated to the type specified just after the impl keyword.

A noticeable aspect of the impl feature is that, differing from most object-oriented languages, in Rust the data and the methods are separated in distinct blocks.

Notice also that the declaration of the naming function has changed. In the argument list, instead of p: Person, there is the self keyword. It is a special argument that represents the current object, on which the method will be applied. This method is declared for the Person type, so here the type of self is implicitly Person. You can specify such type explicitly, like in this line:

```
fn naming(self: Person) -> String {
```

In the body of the function, the two occurrences of p have been replaced by self, which represents the method argument, and so also the current object.

After such definition, it is possible to use the dot notation, in the expression person. naming(). It is still possible also to use the functional notation, in this equivalent expression: Person::naming(person).

Object-oriented languages are traditionally classified as pure and hybrid:

- In a pure object-oriented language, like Smalltalk or Ruby, every function is associated to a class, and there is no type that cannot have methods.

- In a hybrid object-oriented language, like C++ and Python, there are functions not associated to any class, and only the types defined as classes (or structs) can have methods.

According to this classification, Rust is intermediate between these two categories. For Rust, there are functions not associated to any class, like in hybrid languages, but methods can be added to any Rust type having a name, even to primitive types.

Let's see some examples:

```
struct Person (String, u32);

#[allow(dead_code)]
enum Visibility { Visible, Hidden, Collapsed }
```

```
impl Person {
    fn age(&self) -> u32 {
        self.1
    }
}

impl Visibility {
    fn is_not_visible(&self) -> bool {
        match self {
            Visibility::Visible => false,
            _ => true,
        }
    }
}

print!("{} ", Person ("John".to_string(), 30).age());
print!("{}", Visibility::Collapsed.is_not_visible());
```

It will print: 30 true.

First, two types have been defined, a tuple-struct and an enum.

Then, the age method has been declared for the tuple-struct, and the is_not_ visible method has been declared for the enum.

Then, such types are instantiated, and their methods are invoked on such instances.

There are some types without a name, like tuples and closures, and they cannot have methods.

Primitive types and types imported from the standard library or from third-party libraries can have methods, too. For example, we have already seen the expression "abcd".to_string(). Though, the syntax that we have seen for declaring methods is valid only for types defined in your own code. In a future chapter we will see how to add methods to primitive types or to types declared in external libraries.

The self and Self Keywords

The Rust self keyword is similar to the this keyword of C++, C#, Java, or to the self keyword of other languages. However, Rust has some differences with such languages:

- The `self` special argument is not implied in the declaration of the method. If you need it, you must specify it in the signature.

- `self` is not implied when accessing the current object. If you are accessing a field or a method of that object, you must specify `self` before the name of the field or of the method.

- `self` is not a pointer or reference. It receives the current object argument by value. If you need an immutable reference, you should write `&self` in the signature. If you need a mutable reference, you should write `&mut self` in the signature.

The type of the `self` expression is implicitly the type specified just after the `impl` keyword. Though, to avoid repeating such name, Rust has another keyword: `Self`. Remember that Rust is case sensitive, so `self` and `Self` are two different keywords. `Self` represents the type of `self`.

Here is an example that shows some other Rust features regarding methods:

```rust
struct Person {
    personal_names: String,
    family_names: String,
}
impl Person {
    fn new() -> Self {
        Self {
            personal_names: String::new(),
            family_names: String::new(),
        }
    }
    fn naming(&self) -> String {
        format!("{} {}",
            self.personal_names,
            self.family_names)
    }
}
```

```
impl Person {
    fn set_personal_names(&mut self, new_name: String) {
        self.personal_names = new_name;
    }
}
let mut person = Person::new();
print!("[{}] ", person.naming());
person.personal_names = "John".to_string();
person.family_names = "Doe".to_string();
print!("[{}] ", person.naming());
person.set_personal_names("Jane".to_string());
print!("[{}]", person.naming());
```

It will print: [ ] [John Doe] [Jane Doe].

First of all, notice that there are two impl blocks, both for the Person type. The first block declares the new and naming functions, and the second block declares the set_personal_names functions. So, it is possible to define several functions in a block, but it is also possible to split the set of functions declarations into several blocks.

In this case, there was no point in having two impl blocks, but in more complex applications it may be useful to be able to add functions to a type in several parts of the code base.

Then, notice that the new function has no arguments, not even the self argument. A function declared in an impl block, but without a self argument, is actually not a method but an *associated function*. An associated function cannot access an instance of the type to which it is associated, because there is no such current object for it. Keeping it inside an impl block is just an encapsulation choice; it means that this function is considered to be strictly related to the currently implemented type, so it is available only in such scope.

Rust associated functions correspond to static or class methods in C++, C#, Java, and Python, while Rust methods correspond to instance methods in such languages. Though, Rust has no notion of static data members. This concept, present in many other object-oriented languages, is that of a variable present in a single instance in the entire program, but declared inside the scope of a class, and therefore accessible with no further specification only from the class methods or the instance methods of that class. Rust does not allow declaring a variables inside impl blocks (except the local variables of methods), and it does not allow marking as static the members of a type.

A typical use of associated functions is for constructing new instances of the implemented type. Actually, in Rust you can also create any object without calling any method, though you can also encapsulate such creation in an associated function, like the new method in the example.

In C++, C#, and Java, there is the new keyword, and there is the rule that constructors must have the same name of the class. In Rust there are no such features, but there is the convention to name new a method that has no arguments and that returns an instance of type Self. Such method plays the role of default constructor.

The second method shown in the preceding example is naming. Notice that it receives self by immutable reference, to avoid getting it by value. That method corresponds to a const method in C++, because it receives the current object, but it cannot mutate it.

The third method shown in the example is set_personal_names. It needs to change the current object, so it receives the argument &mut self. That method corresponds to a non-const method in C++, because it receives the current object, and it can mutate it.

The mod and the pub Keywords

Those who already know object-oriented programming will find it strange that so far the words private or public have never been mentioned. This is because the concepts of privacy are handled only by the Rust module system. Rust modules are similar to namespaces in other languages.

When a program is very small, all the code can easily be put into just one source file, and in just one module. But, when you have to manage a large code base, there is the need to split the code into several source files, and into several modules too.

Here is an example of a module declared and used in a single source file:

```
mod routines {
    fn f() -> u32 { g() }
    fn g() -> u32 { 123 }
}
print!("{}", f());
```

This program first uses the **mod** keyword to declare a module named `routines`, containing two function declarations, and then it tries to invoke one of those functions.

If you compile it, though, you get the error: `cannot find function ``f`` in this scope`. This happens because the f function is declared inside a block, and that block defines a distinct scope. Such scope is not automatically accessed from outside it. So, the previous code is actually similar to this:

```
{
    fn f() -> u32 { g() }
    fn g() -> u32 { 123 }
}
print!("{}", f());
```

While identifiers defined in an anonymous block can never be accessed from outside such a block, identifiers defined in a module can be accessed from outside that module, as shown by the following program:

```
mod routines {
    pub fn f() -> u32 { g() }
    fn g() -> u32 { 123 }
}
print!("{}", routines::f());
```

This program will be compiled, and it will print: 123.

There are two changes, with respect to the previous program:

- The declaration of the f function is preceded by the **pub** keyword.

- The invocation of the f function is preceded by the scope specification `routines::`.

Every identifier declared in a module is accessible to every part of that module. Before this section, we always used only the anonymous global module. This explains why we had little problem accessing identifiers declared by our program.

Though, by default, every identifier declared in a module is not accessible (i.e., it is private) to other modules. To let other modules access an identifier, a module must prefix its declaration with the `pub` keyword, which is shorthand for *public*. We needed to allow the last line of the program to access the f function, so we had to make that function public. Instead, the g function is accessed only from inside the module, so it can remain private. There is no way to specify that an identifier is private; it is just the default.

The f function is public, and so it can be accessed by any module. However, when accessed from other modules, its scope path must be specified, as we did in the last statement.

A module can be declared inside another module, like in this example program, in which the main function is explicitly written:

```
fn f() {
    print!("f ");
    g();
    m::f();
    m::m::f();
}
fn g() { print!("g "); }
mod m {
    pub fn f() {
        print!("1.f ");
        g();
        m::f();
        super::g();
    }
    fn g() { print!("1.g "); }
    pub mod m {
        pub fn f() {
            print!("2.f ");
            g();
            super::g();
            super::super::g();
            crate::g();
        }
        fn g() { print!("2.g "); }
    }
}
```

```
fn main() {
    f();
}
```

It will print: `f g 1.f 1.g 2.f 2.g 1.g g g g 2.f 2.g 1.g g g`.

In the global module of this program, there are the declarations of an `f` function, a `g` function, an `m` module, and the `main` function.

In the `m` module there are declarations of an `f` function, a `g` function, and an `m` module. Of course, such functions and such a module are different from those declared in the global module. To name them in an unambiguous way, we can use the specifications: `m::f`, `m::g`, and `m::m`.

In the `m::m` module there are declarations of an `f` function and a `g` function. To name them in an unambiguous way, we can use the specifications: `m::m::f`, and `m::m::g`.

The `main` function calls the `f` function at the same level, so such function does not need to be marked as public to be accessible.

The `f` function calls the `g` function at the same level, so such function does not need to be marked as public to be accessible.

Then, the `f` function calls the `m::f` function in a nested module, so the function needs to be marked as public to be accessible. The `m` module is at the same level of the `f` function, so it does not need to be marked as public.

Then, the `f` function calls the `m::m::f` function in a doubly nested module, so the function and also the `m::m` module that contains it need to be marked as public.

In the `m::m::f` function, we want to call three functions named `g`:

- The one at the same nesting level, which we name `m::m::g`, can be called simply with the expression `g()`.

- The one up one level, which we name `m::g`, can be called with the expression `super::g()`; the **super** Rust keyword means to move up the hierarchy by one level.

- The one up two levels, which we name simply `g`, can be called with the expression `super::super::g()`. Alternatively, we can use an absolute pathname, starting from the top global module, using the expression `crate::g()`; the **crate** Rust keyword is a reference to the global module.

Notice that every statement can access any identifier declared in any containing module. The `pub` keyword is needed only to access identifiers declared in inner modules.

We already saw such nested notation in expressions like `std::fs::File::open("data.txt")`. This expression means that we want to access the `std` global module, the `fs` public module declared inside it, the public `File` type declared inside it, and the public `open` associated function declared for this type.

The type Keyword

Now, let's see another feature of Rust that allows you to decouple design choices from code.

Say you want to write a portion of code that now uses the `f32` type, but in the future it could use the `f64` type or some other type. If you intersperse your code with the `f32` keyword, when you want to switch to the `f64` type you should search and replace all those occurrences, and that is time-consuming and error-prone.

A possible solution is to encapsulate your code in a generic function having such numeric type as parametric type. Though, if that code is just a portion of a function or, conversely, if it spans several functions, that solution is inconvenient.

This situation is similar to the use of literals. It is well known that instead of writing *magic* literals inside your code, it is better to define named constants, and use those constants inside your code. In this way the purpose of your code becomes clearer, and when you want to change the value of a constant, you change only one line.

Similarly, instead of writing:

```
fn f1(x: f32) -> f32 { x }
fn f2(x: f32) -> f32 { x }
let a: f32 = 2.3;
let b: f32 = 3.4;
print!("{} {}", f1(a), f2(b));
```

it is better to write:

```
type Number = f32;
fn f1(x: Number) -> Number { x }
fn f2(x: Number) -> Number { x }
let a: Number = 2.3;
```

```
let b: Number = 3.4;
print!("{} {}", f1(a), f2(b));
```

Both source programs generate the same executable program, which will print: 2.3 3.4. But the second one begins with an additional statement. The type keyword introduces a *type alias*. It simply means that whenever the word Number is used as a type, it means the f32 type. Indeed, in the rest of the program every one of the six occurrences of the word f32 has been replaced by the Number word, which has just the same meaning.

The corresponding construct in C language is that using the typedef keyword.

Such constructs do not introduce a distinct type; they introduce just a new name for the same type. This implies that the following code is valid:

```
type Number = f32;
let a: Number = 2.3;
let _b: f32 = a;
```

The _b variable is of f32 type, and it is initialized by the value of the a variable, so a must also be of f32 type. But a is declared to be of the Number type, so Number and f32 must be the same type.

Using the type construct has at least two advantages:

- The purpose of a type may become clearer if you use a meaningful name instead of a primitive type.

- If, in the previous program, you later decide to use the f64 type everywhere instead of the f32 type, you need to change only one occurrence instead of six occurrences.

CHAPTER 19

Using Traits

In this chapter, you will learn:

- How traits can avoid incomprehensible compiler error messages when invoking generic functions

- How the bounding of a generic parameter can be monolithic, or it can be broken up into several traits

- What little you can do with an unbounded generic parameter

- How traits create a scope for the functions they contain

- How to create traits containing multiple methods

- How to bound generic parameters to multiple traits

- How to use trait inheritance

- How to use traits to add methods to external types

- How to implement the standard traits `Display` and `Debug`

- Why generic traits may be useful, and how to declare them

- How to use associated types to simplify the use of traits having unspecified types

- The implementation of iterators

The Need for Traits

Let's say we need a function to compute the mathematical fourth root, named *quartic root*. Exploiting the `sqrt` standard library method, which computes the square root of the number to which it is applied, we could write:

© Carlo Milanesi 2022
C. Milanesi, *Beginning Rust*, https://doi.org/10.1007/978-1-4842-7208-4_19

```
fn quartic_root(x: f64) -> f64 { x.sqrt().sqrt() }
let qr = quartic_root(100f64);
print!("{} {}", qr * qr * qr * qr, qr);
```

It will print: 100.00000000000003 3.1622776601683795.

But we also could need a function to compute the quartic root of 32-bit floating-point numbers, without casting them to the f64 type. Exploiting the fact that f32 also has a sqrt method, we could write:

```
fn quartic_root_f64(x: f64) -> f64 { x.sqrt().sqrt() }
fn quartic_root_f32(x: f32) -> f32 { x.sqrt().sqrt() }
print!("{} {}",
    quartic_root_f64(100f64),
    quartic_root_f32(100f32));
```

It will print: 3.1622776601683795 3.1622777.

But instead of writing similar functions differing only in the types of their arguments and variables, we could try to write a generic function, like this one:

```
fn quartic_root<Number>(x: Number) -> Number {
    x.sqrt().sqrt() // ILLEGAL: no sqrt method for Number
}
print!("{} {}",
    quartic_root(100f64),
    quartic_root(100f32));
```

Yet this code is illegal, generating the compilation error: no method named `sqrt` found for type parameter `Number` in the current scope. It means that in the expression x.sqrt(), where the expression x is of the Number generic type, such type doesn't have the sqrt method. Actually, the type Number has just been defined, so it has pretty much no methods.

In this aspect, Rust differs from C++. In this latter language, we can write the following code, in which a function template is corresponding to our generic function:

```
#include <iostream>
#include <cmath>
template <typename Number>
```

```
Number quartic_root(Number x) {
    return sqrt(sqrt(x));
}
int main() {
    std::cout << quartic_root((float)100)
        << " " << quartic_root((double)100);
}
```

Even in C++ code, the Number generic type has no methods when the compiler first encounters the invocation of sqrt, so the compiler cannot know if such statement is allowed. But when the two invocations of the quartic_root function are encountered, the compiler generates the two concrete functions quartic_root<float> and quartic_root<double>. This kind of code generation is called *generic function instantiation*, or *function monomorphization*. The latter is the term used in Rust documentation. Such instantiations check that, for the float and for the double concrete types, there is a sqrt function that is applicable to them.

The drawback of the C++ solution appears when there is a programming error, like this one:

```
#include <iostream>
#include <cmath>
template <typename Number>
Number quartic_root(Number x) {
    return sqrt(sqrt(x));
}
int main() {
    std::cout << quartic_root("Hello");
}
```

Here the C++ compiler tries to instantiate the quartic_root function for the const char* type, which is the type of the expression "Hello". For this operation, the compiler needs to generate, inside that function, the invocation of the function whose signature is sqrt(const char*). Failing that, it tries to generate the implicit conversion from the type const char* to the type double. However, none of these operations are possible, so the compiler emits a compilation error.

The drawback is that typically the `quartic_root` function declaration is written by one developer (or developer organization), and the invocation of that function is written by another developer (or developer organization). The developer who invokes the function passing a string instead of a number would like to get an error message like `in the invocation of quartic_root, you cannot pass a string`. Instead, in C++, you necessarily get an error message like `no matching function for call to 'sqrt'`, or an error message like `cannot convert 'const char*' to 'double'`, both referring to the code inside the `quartic_root` generic function.

The C++ message is somewhat obscure if you don't know how `quartic_root` is implemented.

And this is a very simple example. In real-world C++ code, error messages for type errors in generic function invocation tend to be very obscure, because they talk about variables, functions, and types that belong to the implementation of the library, not to its interface. To understand them, it is not enough to know the API well; it is necessary to know the whole library implementation.

Traits to the Rescue

The Rust solution to the problem of wrong invocations of a generic function is to first define an abstract *capability* that should be satisfied by the types of the arguments of the function; if the function is invoked with an argument whose type satisfies such capability, it is guaranteed that the function can be monomorphized with that type; if the function is invoked with an argument whose type does not satisfy such capability, the error message explains why the call is wrong.

Such capability is named ***trait***, and it is essentially a set of method signatures. A type is said *to satisfy* or *to implement* a trait, if it declares the body of all the methods specified by that trait.

The resulting Rust code is more complicated than the C++ code, but it creates much clearer error messages for more complex cases, like those of real-world software. Here it is:

```
trait HasSquareRoot { // trait declaration
    fn sq_root(self) -> Self;
}
impl HasSquareRoot for f32 { // an implementation of the trait
    fn sq_root(self) -> Self { self.sqrt() }
}
```

```
impl HasSquareRoot for f64 { // another implementation
    fn sq_root(self) -> Self { self.sqrt() }
}
// function that depends on the Number parameter,
// that must implement the HasSquareRoot trait
fn quartic_root<Number>(x: Number) -> Number
where Number: HasSquareRoot {
    x.sq_root().sq_root()
}
// Here that function if instantiated twice, in both cases
// using types that implement the HasSquareRoot trait
print!("{} {}",
    quartic_root(100f64),
    quartic_root(100f32));
```

It will print: 3.1622776601683795 3.1622777.

The first statement uses the trait keyword to declare a trait named HasSquareRoot, containing the signature of a method named sq_root. The meaning of this trait is that the sq_root method can be invoked on every type that implements the HasSquareRoot trait.

But which types are implementing the HasSquareRoot trait? Well, none do, because we just defined that trait, and any trait is not implemented by any type, except the ones that have been declared to implement it.

So, the next two statements in the preceding example, those beginning with the impl keyword, make the f32 and f64 types implement that trait. In other words, with these impl statements, the capability to invoke the sq_root method is given to the f32 and f64 types.

In Chapter 18, we saw how the impl keyword, followed by the name of a type, was used to declare associated functions and methods for the specified type.

Here we see another syntax for impl statements. After the impl keyword, there is the name of a trait, the for keyword, and then the name of a type. These impl statements mean that the HasSquareRoot trait is implemented here for the specified types by the specified code. The signatures of the methods contained in the impl statements must be the same as the signature contained in the previous trait statement; but they also have a body, because they are implementations of such signatures. Speaking in C++ terms, they are *definitions* of the previous function *declarations*.

In the example, because of the first three statements, we have a new trait and two existing types that now implement such trait.

The fourth statement is the declaration of the `quartic_root` generic method, parameterized by the `Number` generic type. However, such a declaration has a new portion: at the end of the signature, there is the clause `where Number: HasSquareRoot`. That clause is named *trait bound*, and it is a part of the signature of the method. It means that the `Number` generic type must implement the `HasSquareRoot` trait.

The signature of a method is a kind of contract between the code that invokes that method and the code in the body of that method, so its `where` clause is part of that contract.

For the code that invokes the method, such `where` clause means: *when invoking this method, you must ensure that the type you pass for the* `Number` *type parameter implements the* `HasSquareRoot` *trait.*

For example, the `100f32` and `100f64` expressions are of the `f32` and `f64` types, respectively, and now both such types implement the `HasSquareRoot` trait, so they are valid arguments. But if you replace the argument in the last line of the program with `true`, then the type of that expression, that is `bool`, does not implement the `HasSquareRoot` trait, so you are violating the contract. Indeed, you would get the compilation error: `the trait bound `bool: HasSquareRoot` is not satisfied`.

Trying to compute the quartic root of a Boolean is nonsensical, but even if you replace the argument in the last line of the program with `81i32`, you get a compilation error. Its message is `the trait bound `i32: HasSquareRoot` is not satisfied`. This is because the `HasSquareRoot` trait has not been implemented for the `i32` type, regardless of the reasonableness of the operation. If you think that such a trait is worthwhile for some types, you can implement it for them.

For the code in the body of the method that implements the trait, the contract signed by the trait bound is seen as: *when this method is invoked, the type passed in place of the* `Number` *type parameter is ensured to implement the* `HasSquareRoot` *trait, so you can use every method belonging to such trait.*

For example, in the body of the method, the `x.sq_root()` expression is valid, because the `x` expression is of the `Number` generic type. That type is declared to implement the `HasSquareRoot` trait, and that trait contains the `sq_root` method. So such method is available to the `x` variable.

The value returned by the x.sq_root() expression is of type Self, which means the Number type. So, the second invocation of sq_root() is again applied to a value of a type that implements the HasSquareRoot trait, so even it is valid.

But now let's consider the abs method, which returns the absolute value of a number. It is applicable to any numeric type that allows negative values, including f64 and f32. For example, the value of (-3.4f64).abs() is 3.4. If you replace the body of the generic method quartic_root with x.abs(), you get the compilation error: no method named `abs` found for type parameter `Number` in the current scope. It means that the x expression, which is of the Number generic type, is not able to invoke the abs method. In fact, inside the method body, it is not known that x will be an f64 or an f32; it is just a Number, and all that a Number is able to do is what is contained in the HasSquareRoot trait, which is the sq_root method.

Generic Functions with No Parameter Bounds

In the declaration of a generic function, if there is no where clause, or if a type parameter is not cited in the where clause, no trait is associated to that type, so you can do very little with an object of that generic type. Actually, all you can do is in this code:

```
fn f<T>(a: T) -> T { a }
fn g<T>(a: T) -> T {
    let b: T = a;
    let mut c = b;
    c = f(c);
    c
}
fn h<T>(a: &T) -> &T { a }
```

With a value of an unbounded type parameter T, like in this example, you can only:

- Pass it as function argument, by value (as in the declarations of f and of g) or by reference (as in the declaration of h)

- Return it from a function, by value (as in the declarations of f and of g) or by reference (as in the declaration of h)

- Declare, initialize, or assign a local variable (as in the body of g)

Instead, even the rather trivial following code causes compilation errors:

```
fn g(a: i32) { }
fn f<T>(a: T) -> bool {
    g(a);
    a == a
}
```

The third line is illegal (`mismatched types`), because the g function requires a value having i32 type, while a could have any type. And the fourth line is illegal (`binary operation `==` cannot be applied to type `T``), because the T type could be unable to be compared for equality.

Therefore, trait bounds on the type parameters of generic functions are almost always needed.

A very rare case of an important generic standard library function that does not need trait bounds is used in this program:

```
let mut a = 'A';
let mut b = 'B';
print!("{}, {}; ", a, b);
std::mem::swap(&mut a, &mut b);
print!("{}, {}", a, b);
```

It will print: A, B; B, A.

The swap generic function can exchange the values of any two objects having the same type. Its signature is: fn swap<T>(x: &mut T, y: &mut T).

Scope of Traits

Our trait contained a method named sq_root, to make it clear it was not the same thing as the sqrt standard library method. The two implementations of the sq_root method *use* the standard library sqrt methods, but they are distinct methods. However, we could also name our methods sqrt, obtaining this equivalent program:

```
fn sqrt() {}
trait HasSquareRoot {
    fn sqrt(self) -> Self;
}
```

```
impl HasSquareRoot for f32 {
    fn sqrt(self) -> Self { self.sqrt() }
}
impl HasSquareRoot for f64 {
    fn sqrt(self) -> Self { self.sqrt() }
}
fn quartic_root<Number>(x: Number) -> Number
where Number: HasSquareRoot {
    x.sqrt().sqrt()
}
sqrt();
print!("{} {}",
    quartic_root(100f64),
    quartic_root(100f32));
```

Notice that in this program the identifier sqrt appears nine times. Though, there are four distinct meanings of that identifier:

- self.sqrt(), used at the end of the sixth line, refers to a method declared in the standard library for the f32 type. It computes the square root of a value having f32 type, and returns a value having f32 type.

- self.sqrt(), used at the end of the ninth line, refers to a method declared in the standard library for the f64 type. It computes the square root of a value having f64 type, and returns a value having f64 type.

- fn sqrt(self) -> Self is a method of the HasSquareRoot trait; all the types that implement that trait must have a method with that same signature. Its signature is declared in the third line, it is implemented in the sixth and ninth lines, and it is invoked twice in the thirteenth line. So, these five occurrences are related.

- fn sqrt(), declared in the first line and invoked in the fifteenth line, is a local function outside the HasSquareRoot trait. It has nothing to do with this trait and with numbers in general. By the way, it does nothing.

You know Rust does not allow two functions with the same name in the same scope. Nevertheless the preceding code is valid; that means that these nine occurrences of sqrt are referring to four different scopes.

Traits with Multiple Methods

If in the previous example we replaced the expressions 100f64 and 100f32 with -100f64 and -100f32, the program would print NaN NaN. The NaN text means *Not a Number*, and it is a standard result of the attempt to compute the square root of a negative floating-point number.

Let's assume we need a method that computes the quartic root of the absolute value of floating-point numbers. We could choose to check if the argument is negative, and in such case use its opposite, or we could choose to use the abs method of the standard library to compute the absolute value.

In the second case, our Number generic type also needs the abs method. So we can write this program:

```
// Removed the standalone sqrt function.
trait HasSqrtAndAbs { // Trait renamed.
    fn sqrt(self) -> Self;
    fn abs(self) -> Self; // Added this function signature.
}
impl HasSqrtAndAbs for f32 { // Trait renamed.
    fn sqrt(self) -> Self { self.sqrt() }
    fn abs(self) -> Self { self.abs() } // Implemented.
}
impl HasSqrtAndAbs for f64 { // Trait renamed.
    fn sqrt(self) -> Self { self.sqrt() }
    fn abs(self) -> Self { self.abs() } // Implemented.
}
fn abs_quartic_root<Number>(x: Number) -> Number // Function renamed.
where Number: HasSqrtAndAbs { // Trait renamed.
    x.abs().sqrt().sqrt() // Added call to abs method.
}
```

```
print!("{} {}",
    // Function renamed, and argument become negative.
    abs_quartic_root(-100f64),
    // Function renamed, and argument become negative.
    abs_quartic_root(-100f32));
```

It will print: `3.1622776601683795 3.1622777`.

The changes with respect to the previous program are the following ones.

First, the useless standalone `sqrt` function has been removed.

Next, in the trait declaration, the signature of an `abs` method has been added.

Then, such `abs` method has been implemented for the `f32` and `f64` types. Such implementations invoke the `abs` method of the `f32` and `f64` types, respectively.

Next, the four occurrences of the trait name have been changed to `HasSqrtAndAbs`, to clarify the new purpose of the trait.

Then, in the generic method, the `abs` method is applied to the `x` argument, just before the two invocations of `sqrt`.

Next, the three occurrences of the name of the generic function have been changed to `abs_quartic_root`, to clarify the new purpose of the function.

Then, the arguments of the two invocations of `abs_quartic_root` have become negative.

In this way you can easily add method invocations (like that of `abs`) to your generic function definitions (like that in the body of `abs_quartic_root`).

Generic Parameters with Multiple Bounds

Having a trait containing several method signatures may have a drawback.

Let's consider the block that implements the trait for the `f64` type. If in that block you omit the implementation of the `abs` method, you get the compilation error: `not all trait items implemented, missing: `abs``. On the other hand, if you add to that block the implementation of another method named, say, `exp`, you get the compilation error: `method `exp` is not a member of trait `HasSqrtAndAbs``. Therefore, every `impl` block used to implement a trait must have the same signatures of the trait it is implementing: not one more, not one less, not one different.

Sometimes, a few functions are strictly coupled, and so, every time one of them is needed, all of them should be implemented anyway. But what if in some generic functions you want to use a type that has a sqrt function, but not an abs function, or conversely? You are forced to implement even the functions you don't need.

To avoid this, you can declare a new trait, obtaining the following equivalent program:

```
trait HasSquareRoot {
    fn sqrt(self) -> Self;
}
impl HasSquareRoot for f32 {
    fn sqrt(self) -> Self { self.sqrt() }
}
impl HasSquareRoot for f64 {
    fn sqrt(self) -> Self { self.sqrt() }
}
trait HasAbsoluteValue {
    fn abs(self) -> Self;
}
impl HasAbsoluteValue for f32 {
    fn abs(self) -> Self { self.abs() }
}
impl HasAbsoluteValue for f64 {
    fn abs(self) -> Self { self.abs() }
}
fn abs_quartic_root<Number>(x: Number) -> Number
where Number: HasSquareRoot + HasAbsoluteValue {
    x.abs().sqrt().sqrt()
}
print!("{} {}",
    abs_quartic_root(-100f64),
    abs_quartic_root(-100f32));
```

Here, the HasSquareRoot trait is the original one, but the new HasAbsoluteValue trait has been declared, and it has been implemented for the types f32 and f64.

Moreover, the where clause of the declaration of the abs_quartic_root method has one more trait bound for the Number type parameter: in addition to the HasSquareRoot trait, the HasAbsoluteValue trait has been added. The two traits are separated by a *plus* symbol.

This trait bound adds the capabilities of both traits to the capabilities of Number. In this way, you can pick the traits you need for your generic type.

Trait Inheritance

In the previous sections we have seen that if a generic type parameter needs several methods, we can bound that parameter on a single trait having several methods, or we can bound that parameter on several traits, each having one method.

In addition, hybrid solutions are possible. For example, if our parameter needs seven methods, we can bound it to three traits, one implementing one method, one implementing two methods, and one implementing the remaining four methods.

Now assume that your code, or some third-party code, already defines some traits, and you need all of them. You can specify several trait bounds, like in the previous section, but you can also combine them into a new trait, using a Rust feature named *trait inheritance*.

Differing from most object-oriented languages, Rust data types do not support inheritance. This is by design, as data type inheritance is considered harmful, though Rust supports trait inheritance. Here is a modification of the example from the previous section, resulting in an equivalent program:

```rust
trait HasSquareRoot {
    fn sqrt(self) -> Self;
}
impl HasSquareRoot for f32 {
    fn sqrt(self) -> Self { self.sqrt() }
}
impl HasSquareRoot for f64 {
    fn sqrt(self) -> Self { self.sqrt() }
}
trait HasAbsoluteValue {
    fn abs(self) -> Self;
}
```

```
impl HasAbsoluteValue for f32 {
    fn abs(self) -> Self { self.abs() }
}
impl HasAbsoluteValue for f64 {
    fn abs(self) -> Self { self.abs() }
}
trait HasSqrtAndAbs: HasSquareRoot + HasAbsoluteValue { }
impl HasSqrtAndAbs for f32 {}
impl HasSqrtAndAbs for f64 {}
fn abs_quartic_root<Number>(x: Number) -> Number
where Number: HasSqrtAndAbs {
    x.abs().sqrt().sqrt()
}
print!("{} {}",
    abs_quartic_root(-100f64),
    abs_quartic_root(-100f32));
```

Three lines have been added just before the declaration of the abs_quartic_root function.

The first one declares the new trait HasSqrtAndAbs. This trait is defined to have all the signatures of the HasSquareRoot trait, plus all the signatures of the HasAbsoluteValue trait, plus a list of other signatures, that in this case is empty.

The second and third lines are the implementations of this trait for the f32 and f64 types, respectively. These implementation statements are required, and they must declare all the methods not yet implemented. However, all the inherited methods have already been implemented, and no other signature has been declared, so these blocks are empty.

Then, for the abs_quartic_root function, the Number parameter is bound to the HasSqrtAndAbs trait.

Adding Methods to External Types

In Chapter 18, we have seen that an impl statement can be used to add methods directly to a type. In this chapter we have seen that an impl statement can be used to add methods to a trait for a type. So a type can have two kinds of methods: those associated through a trait, and those associated without specifying a trait. These last methods are said to be *inherent implementations*, as they do not pass through a trait.

In Chapter 18 it was also said that it is possible to add method declarations even to primitive types, and to types imported from the standard library or from third-party libraries. Let's name the data types not declared inside the current program or library *external types*. So, we may want to add methods to external types. For example, assume you have a function that returns the number of characters in a string:

```
fn length(s: &str) -> usize { s.chars().count() }
let s = "€èe";
print!("{} {}", s.len(), length(s));
```

It will print: 6 3.

Now we try to declare a method equivalent to such function, to allow the dot notation for it:

```
impl str { // ILLEGAL: Inherent implementation for str type
    fn length(&self) -> usize { self.chars().count() }
}
let s = "€èe";
print!("{} {}", s.len(), s.length());
```

However, when compiling this code, it will generate this compilation error: `only a single inherent implementation marked with `#[lang = "str"]` is allowed for the `str` primitive`. It means that for the str primitive type, only the Rust language itself is allowed to define methods using an inherent implementation. You will get this error every time you try to declare an inherent implementation for a primitive type.

You will also get an error if you try to declare an inherent implementation for a type declared in the standard library or in a third-party library. For example, if you compile this expression: `impl Vec<i32> { }`, you will get the error message: `cannot define inherent `impl` for a type outside of the crate where the type is defined`.

The reason for these errors is that, to avoid changing the behavior of external types in surprising ways, Rust does not allow inherent implementations for external types.

Though, you can still associate methods to an external type, as long as you associate such methods through a trait. You can implement the length method using the following code:

```
trait HasLength {
    fn length(&self) -> usize;
}
impl HasLength for str {
    fn length(&self) -> usize { self.chars().count() }
}
let s = "€èe";
print!("{} {}", s.len(), s.length());
```

We have defined a trait named HasLength, containing the signature of the desired method, and then we have implemented that trait for the desired type. This is the standard technique for implementing a method for an external type.

The name of the trait (HasLength) is arbitrary. Usually, if a trait contains only one method, the name of the trait is the name of that method put into Pascal-case. Following this convention, it had to be named Length.

Standard Traits: Display and Debug

We saw from the first chapters of this book that when using the print, println, and format macros, you can use the "{}" placeholder only for the types that support it. For the other types you should use the "{:?}" placeholder, which is meant for debugging purposes, though even the debugging placeholder may be unsupported.

But how come some types support the "{}" placeholder, some types support the "{:?}" placeholder, and others don't? And how could you make your own type support those placeholders?

Actually, whenever the "{}" placeholder is found, those macros use the fmt method specified by the std::fmt::Display standard library trait, and whenever the "{:?}" placeholder is found, those macros use the fmt method specified by the std::fmt::Debug standard library trait. All the primitive types implement those traits, and if you do it for your types, you can obtain the same results. Here is an example that shows how to support the "{}" placeholder for a user-defined type:

```
struct Complex {
    re: f64,
    im: f64,
}
```

```
impl std::fmt::Display for Complex {
    fn fmt(&self, f: &mut std::fmt::Formatter) -> std::fmt::Result {
        write!(
            f,
            "{} {} {}i",
            self.re,
            if self.im >= 0. { '+' } else { '-' },
            self.im.abs()
        )
    }
}
let c1 = Complex { re: -2.3, im: 0. };
let c2 = Complex { re: -2.1, im: -5.2 };
let c3 = Complex { re: -2.2, im: 5.2 };
print!("{}, {}, {}", c1, c2, c3);
```

It will print: -2.3 + 0i, -2.1 - 5.2i, -2.2 + 5.2i.

First, the Complex type is declared. Then, the standard Display trait is implemented for our type. Such implementation uses the write macro that is similar to the format macro, except for this:

- It has an additional first argument, having Formatter type. Such argument is received as argument by the fmt method.

- Its return value type is Result<(), std::fmt::Error>. In case of success, the resulting string is written to the received Formatter object.

The Debug trait is identical to the Display trait, but they are distinct. So to support the "{:?}" placeholder for a user-defined type, it is enough to repeat the preceding implementation, replacing the word Display with the word Debug.

In the standard library, there are many other traits, and there are many implementations of them for the primitive types.

Generic Traits

In Chapter 10, we saw generic functions, generic structs, and generic enums. Well, even a trait can be parameterized by one or more types. Let's see a case in which it can be useful.

Assume there is no library containing an exponentiation function, that is, a function to raise a given number to a given power. We have only the exp exponential method, with no arguments, and the ln natural logarithm method, with no arguments. We can implement the exponentiation function using them, with this code:

```
fn exponentiate(base: f64, exponent: f64) -> f64 {
    (base.ln() * exponent).exp()
}
print!("{}", exponentiate(2.5, 3.2));
```

It will print: 18.767569280959872.

This implementation requires that the type of both the base and the exponent is f64.

If we would also like to support the f32 type, or other types, without adding as many similar implementations, we could make it generic. We can do that as long as we take into consideration that the implementation of exponentiate must handle objects that support the natural logarithm, the multiplication, and the exponential functions. So, we can write:

```
trait HasLnExpMultiply {
    fn ln(self) -> Self;
    fn exp(self) -> Self;
    fn multiply(self, other: Self) -> Self;
}

impl HasLnExpMultiply for f64 {
    fn ln(self) -> Self { self.ln() }
    fn exp(self) -> Self { self.exp() }
    fn multiply(self, other: Self) -> Self { self * other }
}
```

```
impl HasLnExpMultiply for f32 {
    fn ln(self) -> Self { self.ln() }
    fn exp(self) -> Self { self.exp() }
    fn multiply(self, other: Self) -> Self { self * other }
}

fn exponentiate<Number>(base: Number, exponent: Number) -> Number
where Number: HasLnExpMultiply
{
    (base.ln().multiply(exponent)).exp()
}
print!("{} {}", exponentiate(2.5, 3.2), exponentiate(2.5f32, 3.2));
```

It will print: 18.767569280959872 18.767574.

This solution allows different types for the arguments of exponentiate, as long as the two arguments and the return value have the same type.

Yet, we could desire to have different types for the two arguments. For example we want to call: exponentiate(2.5, 3).

Here is the code that does it:

```
trait HasLnExp {
    fn ln(self) -> Self;
    fn exp(self) -> Self;
}
impl HasLnExp for f64 {
    fn ln(self) -> Self { self.ln() }
    fn exp(self) -> Self { self.exp() }
}
impl HasLnExp for f32 {
    fn ln(self) -> Self { self.ln() }
    fn exp(self) -> Self { self.exp() }
}
trait HasMultiply<Rhs> {
    fn multiply(self, rhs: Rhs) -> Self;
}
```

```
impl<Rhs> HasMultiply<Rhs> for f64 where Rhs: Into<Self> {
    fn multiply(self, rhs: Rhs) -> Self { self * rhs.into() }
}
impl<Rhs> HasMultiply<Rhs> for f32 where Rhs: Into<Self> {
    fn multiply(self, rhs: Rhs) -> Self { self * rhs.into() }
}
fn exponentiate<Base, Exponent>(
    base: Base, exponent: Exponent) -> Base
where Base: HasLnExp + HasMultiply<Exponent>
{
    (base.ln().multiply(exponent)).exp()
}
println!("{}", exponentiate(2.5f32, 3i16));
println!("{}", exponentiate(2.5f64, 3i16));
println!("{}", exponentiate(2.5f32, 3f32));
println!("{}", exponentiate(2.5f64, 3f32));
println!("{}", exponentiate(2.5f64, 3f64));
```

It will print:

```
15.625001
15.625000000000002
15.625001
15.625000000000002
15.625000000000002
```

Let's examine this solution.

To have arguments with possibly distinct types, the exponentiate function must have two type parameters, one for the base and one for the exponent. Let's name such type parameters Base and Exponent, respectively. Let's assume that it is reasonable that the return value has the same type of the base, and so its type is Base too.

Let's accurately examine the capabilities required to be supported by the body of the exponentiate function.

First, there is base.ln(), so Base must be able to compute a natural logarithm of itself, returning a Base.

Then, there is .multiply(exponent), so Base must be able to be multiplied by an Exponent, returning a Base.

Then, there is .exp(), so Base must be able to compute an exponential of itself, returning a Base.

We have seen that Base must support both ln and exp. This is specified by this code:

```
trait HasLnExp {
    fn ln(self) -> Self;
    fn exp(self) -> Self;
}
```

We want to support the types f32 and f64 for Base, so we need this implementation for f64, and a similar one for f32:

```
impl HasLnExp for f64 {
    fn ln(self) -> Self { self.ln() }
    fn exp(self) -> Self { self.exp() }
}
```

Then, we need to support multiplication between Base and Exponent. For that, a normal impl statement is not enough, as it implements a trait just for one type. We need a generic trait, whose type parameter is the right-hand side (Rhs, for short) of the multiplication. Here it is:

```
trait HasMultiply<Rhs> {
    fn multiply(self, rhs: Rhs) -> Self;
}
```

This declaration means that any type, to satisfy the HasMultiply capability regarding the Rhs type, must implement the multiply method, whose arguments are itself (that is the left-hand side of the multiplication) and a value having type Rhs. Such function must return a value having the same type of the left-hand side.

So we need the following implementation of this trait for f64, and a similar one for f32:

```
impl<Rhs> HasMultiply<Rhs> for f64 where Rhs: Into<Self> {
    fn multiply(self, rhs: Rhs) -> Self { self * rhs.into() }
}
```

They are generic implementations, as the Rhs parameter type appears in angular brackets just after the impl keyword, and also just after the HasMultiply trait name.

In the following where clause, the Rhs parameter type is bound to satisfy the Into<Self> trait. Into is a generic trait declared in the Rust standard library. It means that any type that implements it declares a generic function named into. Such function is a type converter without precision loss. So, this clause bounds the right-hand side of the multiplication to be able to convert itself to the Self type, without losing precision.

Actually, in the two bodies of the multiply functions, there are calls to the into method. The parameter type bounds allow such calls.

Such calls to into are needed, because in Rust two numbers can be multiplied with the multiplication operator ("*") only if they are of the same type. So the right-hand side is converted to the type of the left-hand side just before the actual multiplication.

After all these trait declarations and implementations, we can declare our doubly generic exponentiation function:

```
fn exponentiate<Base, Exponent>(
    base: Base, exponent: Exponent) -> Base
where Base: HasLnExp + HasMultiply<Exponent>
{
    (base.ln().multiply(exponent)).exp()
}
```

Here the interesting line is the one containing the where clause.

The Base type must support the logarithm and the exponential methods (HasLnExp), and it must also support the multiplication (HasMultiply) by a value having type Exponent.

Finally, we can call this function in several ways.

Notice that the types of the base can only be f64 and f32, because only for them the traits have been implemented. Instead, the types of the exponent are actually generic, as long as they can be converted without precision loss to the type of the base. For example, the type i32 wouldn't be allowed with a base having type f32, but it would be allowed with f64.

Using Associated Types

Sometimes generic traits are not quite convenient to use. Let's consider the following problem.

Suppose, as is shown in the following code snippet, that we would like to write a generic function named get_name, which takes as arguments a generic dictionary and a numeric search key, and returns the name associated to that key, if it is found in that dictionary, or None if that key is not found:

```
trait Dictionary<Key> {
    fn get(&self, key: Key) -> Option<String>;
}
fn get_name<D>(dict: &D, id: u32) -> Option<String>
where
    D: Dictionary<u32>
{
    dict.get(id)
}
```

To accomplish such function, a generic method named get is invoked on the dictionary. That method is declared as part of the Dictionary trait, so the D type parameter must be bounded to such trait. But that trait allows us to perform searches using different types of keys, so the trait is also generic, having the type of the search key as the Key type parameter. In the get_name function signature, the trait bound specifies the u32 type as the value of the trait type parameter, because that type will be the one used to search the collection.

Here is a complete valid program that uses that architecture:

```
trait Dictionary<Key> {
    fn get(&self, key: Key) -> Option<String>;
}
struct Record {
    id: u32,
    name: String,
}
struct RecordSet {
    data: Vec<Record>,
}
impl Dictionary<u32> for RecordSet {
    fn get(&self, key: u32) -> Option<String> {
        for record in self.data.iter() {
```

```
            if record.id == key {
                return Some(String::from(&record.name));
            }
        }
        None
    }
}
fn get_name<D>(dict: &D, id: u32) -> Option<String>
where
    D: Dictionary<u32>,
{
    dict.get(id)
}
let names = RecordSet {
    data: vec![
        Record { id: 34, name: "John".to_string() },
        Record { id: 49, name: "Jane".to_string() },
    ],
};
print!("{:?}, {:?}",
    get_name(&names, 48), get_name(&names, 49));
```

It will print: None, Some("Jane").

After the declaration of the Dictionary generic trait, two structs are declared: Record, representing a data item identified by a unique number; and RecordSet, representing a collection of items having Record type.

Then, the trait is implemented for this collection type. There are two possible ways to implement a generic trait: to keep it generic, by writing something like impl<T> Dictionary<T> for RecordSet; or to monomorphize it, by writing something like impl Dictionary<u32> for RecordSet. Here the second way has been chosen, because the following implementation of the get method had to be specific not only for the RecordSet collection type, but also for the u32 search key type.

After the declaration of the get_name function, a collection object containing two items is constructed, and it is assigned to the names variable. At last, the get_name function is invoked twice; the key 48 is not found, but the key 49 is found.

This solution works, but is has some drawbacks.

One is this. The needed implementation of the `Dictionary` trait had to be specific for the search key type u32, so it had to specify it as type parameter value; but in the where clause of the get_name function declaration, such a type was specified again as a type parameter value. It seems a useless repetition, and a future type change requires a double edit.

The second drawback can be seen by considering this more complex program:

```
trait Dictionary<Key, Count> {
    fn get(&self, key: Key) -> Option<String>;
    fn count(&self, key: Key) -> Count;
}
struct Record {
    id: u32,
    name: String,
}
struct RecordSet {
    data: Vec<Record>,
}
impl Dictionary<u32, usize> for RecordSet {
    fn get(&self, key: u32) -> Option<String> {
        for record in self.data.iter() {
            if record.id == key {
                return Some(String::from(&record.name));
            }
        }
        None
    }
    fn count(&self, key: u32) -> usize {
        let mut c = 0;
        for record in self.data.iter() {
            if record.id == key {
                c += 1;
            }
        }
        c
    }
}
```

```
fn get_name<D>(dict: &D, id: u32) -> Option<String>
where
    D: Dictionary<u32, usize>
{
    dict.get(id)
}
let names = RecordSet {
    data: vec![
        Record { id: 34, name: "John".to_string() },
        Record { id: 49, name: "Jane".to_string() },
    ],
};
print!(
    "{}, {}; {:?}, {:?}",
    names.count(48),
    names.count(49),
    get_name(&names, 48),
    get_name(&names, 49));
```

It will print: 0, 1; None, Some("Jane").

Here the Dictionary generic trait has a new function signature, and a new type parameter, needed by such function. Of course, the implementation of such trait for the RecordSet type must also implement the new function.

What is not so obvious is that the signature of the get_name generic function must also specify a type for the new generic parameter bound. Instead of being Dictionary<u32>, it is Dictionary<u32, usize>. Well, this function does not use that usize type at all, so this information is useless here, but it is required.

Actually, the following workflow is typical:

- A generic trait is written, like Dictionary.

- A few implementations for such trait are written, with those implementations that may specify some or all the generic parameters for that trait, like impl Dictionary<u32, usize> for RecordSet, which specifies both generic parameters.

- Many generic functions are written, with such functions that bound one of their generic parameters to that trait, like `fn get_name<D>...` `where D: Dictionary<u32, usize>`.

With the preceding syntax, all those generic functions are forced to depend on every generic parameter type, even those that they are not interested in.

A better solution for those cases is allowed by a feature of traits that we have not yet seen. Actually any trait is not only a set of functions; it may also contain type aliases, like in this trait declaration:

```
trait Dictionary {
    type Key;
    type Count;
    fn get(&self, key: Self::Key) -> Option<String>;
    fn count(&self, key: Self::Key) -> Self::Count;
}
```

This trait declares the name of two type aliases, without specifying which are such types. Such declarations are named *associated types*.

When implementing a trait, in addition to specifying all the associated functions and all methods, all the type aliases must be specified also, like in this implementation snippet:

```
// Incomplete code, do not compile it.
impl Dictionary for RecordSet {
    type Key = u32;
    type Count = usize;
    fn get(&self, key: Self::Key) -> Option<String> { ... }
    fn count(&self, key: Self::Key) -> Self::Count { ... }
}
```

So, using type aliases for the trait, it is possible to write the following program, which is equivalent to the previous one:

```
trait Dictionary { //1
    type Key; //2
    type Count; //3
    fn get(&self, key: Self::Key) -> Option<String>; //4
    fn count(&self, key: Self::Key) -> Self::Count; //5
}
```

```
struct Record {
    id: u32,
    name: String,
}
struct RecordSet {
    data: Vec<Record>,
}
impl Dictionary for RecordSet { //6
    type Key = u32; //7
    type Count = usize; //8
    fn get(&self, key: Self::Key) -> Option<String> { //9
        for record in self.data.iter() {
            if record.id == key {
                return Some(String::from(&record.name));
            }
        }
        None
    }
    fn count(&self, key: Self::Key) -> Self::Count { //10
        let mut c = 0;
        for record in self.data.iter() {
            if record.id == key {
                c += 1;
            }
        }
        c
    }
}
fn get_name<D>(
    dict: &D,
    id: <D as Dictionary>::Key, //11
) -> Option<String>
where
    D: Dictionary, //12
```

```
{
    dict.get(id)
}
let names = RecordSet {
    data: vec![
        Record { id: 34, name: "John".to_string() },
        Record { id: 49, name: "Jane".to_string() },
    ],
};
print!(
    "{}, {}; {:?}, {:?}",
    names.count(48),
    names.count(49),
    get_name(&names, 48),
    get_name(&names, 49));
```

The lines changed with respect to the previous version are marked by a "//" marker.

First (at markers 1, 2, and 3), the Dictionary trait is no more generic. Its two generic parameters have become associated types.

As a consequence, every use of the Key and Count type parameters inside the trait declaration (at markers 4 and 5) had to be prefixed by Self::.

Of course, the implementation had to be changed too. It is no more generic (at marker 6), and it had to specify values for the associated types (at markers 7 and 8). Then, optionally, the concrete type u32 can and should be made generic, replacing it with an associated type (at markers 9 and 10).

The advantages of all these changes appear in the signature of the get_name function. First (at marker 11), instead of specifying a concrete type, a reference to the associated type Key is specified; and then (at marker 12), there is no more need to specify type parameters for the Dictionary trait, because it is no longer generic.

Let more deeply examine the type specification at marker 11. Here, we want to refer to the type name Key, declared at marker 2 and specified at marker 7. That type name definition was inside a trait block and inside an implementation block, so a scope specification is needed. We want to access the Dictionary trait, when it is used to bound the D type parameter, as it is specified at marker 12. To specify such a scope, the syntax is <type1 as type2>, which in this case is not to be read as *type1 converted to type2*, but as *type1 restricted to type2*.

You can better understand all this if you consider that a data type is in essence the set of operations you can apply on such data. Bounding (or restricting) a type means considering only some of the operations available for that type. So the expression `D as Dictionary` means *get all the features of the* D *type, and consider only those that come from the* Dictionary *trait.* Actually, the D type could be bounded to several traits, and several of them could have a Key type name. The type expression `<D as Dictionary>::Key` means *the* Key *type defined for the* D *type when implementing the* Dictionary *trait.*

Summarizing, we have seen that, to abstract the specification of a type in a trait declaration, there are two possible techniques: adding a generic parameter, or adding an associated type. The former technique allows us to keep such genericity even after the trait has been implemented for a type, but it requires us to specify all the traits needed by the usage of such type parameter; the latter forces to specify a concrete type for that associated type when the trait is implemented, but it makes the code simpler afterward.

The Iterator Standard Trait

In Chapter 18, we said that Rust defines the *iterator* concept as any object that has a next function.

Actually, iterators are defined by the Rust standard library, not by the Rust language. An iterator is just every type that implements the Iterator standard library trait. This trait contains the next function, so every iterator must have that function.

You can think of the Iterator standard library trait as defined in this way:

```
trait Iterator {
    type Item;
    fn next(&mut self) -> Option<Self::Item>;
}
```

That definition forces any concrete iterator to define:

- A type for Item that represents the type of the generated items

- A function body for next that returns the next item, if possible, or None, if there are no more items to generate

Let's see how the following problem can be solved by implementing an iterator.

You can write a function that, given a *range*, returns its third item, if it has at least three items; or nothing, if it has not enough items:

```
fn get_third(r: std::ops::Range<u32>) -> Option<u32> {
    if r.len() >= 3 {
        Some(r.start + 2)
    } else {
        None
    }
}
print!("{:?}, {:?}", get_third(10..12), get_third(20..29));
```

It will print: None, Some(22).

You can also write a function that, given a *slice*, returns its third item, if it has at least three items; or nothing, if it has not enough items.

```
fn get_third(s: &[f64]) -> Option<f64> {
    if s.len() >= 3 {
        Some(s[2])
    } else {
        None
    }
}
print!("{:?}, {:?}",
    get_third(&[3.1, 3.2]),
    get_third(&[4.1, 4.2, 4.3, 4.4]));
```

It will print: None, Some(4.3).

These two programs are quite similar. So it should be possible to write a generic function that, given an iterator, returns its third produced item, if it can produce at least three items; or nothing, if it cannot produce enough items. Then, you can apply this function to replace the two previous programs, because a range is just an iterator, and a slice can be iterated over.

This problem is solved by this code:

```
fn get_third<Iter>(mut iterator: Iter) -> Option<Iter::Item>
where
    Iter: Iterator,
{
    iterator.next();
    iterator.next();
    iterator.next()
}
print!(
    "{:?}, {:?}, {:?}, {:?}",
    get_third(10..12),
    get_third(20..29),
    get_third([3.1, 3.2].iter()),
    get_third([4.1, 4.2, 4.3, 4.4].iter()));
```

It will print: `None, Some(22), None, Some(4.3)`.

The `get_third` function gets any mutable iterator as an argument, and so it is a generic function parameterized by the type of such iterator. By getting an iterator type, it is allowed to access its `Item` associated type, and its `next` method. So, we can declare that the value returned by our function has the same type as the value returned by the iterator, which is `Option<Iter::Item>`, which, inside the iterator implementation, is `Option<Self::Item>`.

This example was useful to demonstrate how to write a function that gets an iterator as an argument. Yet, actually there is no need for this specific function, as the standard library already contains a function even more generic than that: the `nth` iterator consumer. The following program is equivalent to the previous one:

```
print!(
    "{:?}, {:?}, {:?}, {:?}",
    (10..12).nth(2),
    (20..29).nth(2),
    ([3.1, 3.2].iter()).nth(2),
    ([4.1, 4.2, 4.3, 4.4].iter()).nth(2));
```

CHAPTER 20

Object-Oriented Programming

In this chapter, you will learn:

- How to implement destructors, that is, methods to run when an object is deallocated

- How to implement operator overloading, that is, methods that allow use of Rust operators with user-defined types

- How to implement infallible or fallible type converters

- Why Rust does not use data inheritance and how to do without it

- What are static dispatch and dynamic dispatch, how they are implemented, and when to use them

Peculiarities of Rust Object-Orientation

In previous chapters, we have already seen that Rust supports some concepts of object-oriented programming, like methods, privacy, and trait inheritance.

In this chapter–addressed mainly to those who already know the object-oriented paradigm–for any concept of object-oriented programming, the corresponding Rust idiom will be introduced.

© Carlo Milanesi 2022
C. Milanesi, *Beginning Rust*, https://doi.org/10.1007/978-1-4842-7208-4_20

Destructors

We already saw that types can have constructors. Well, they also have *destructors*. For a type, a destructor is that method that is automatically invoked on an object of that type, when that object is deallocated.

Let's see the purpose of destructors. If an object can reserve some system resources, like file handles or database connections, such resources should be automatically released when that object is destroyed, to avoid a bug named *resource leak*. Here is an example, in which actual reservation, use, and release of resources are replaced by prints on the console:

```rust
struct CommunicationChannel {
    address: String,
    port: u16,
}
impl Drop for CommunicationChannel {
    fn drop(&mut self) {
        println!("Closing port {}:{}", self.address, self.port);
    }
}
impl CommunicationChannel {
fn create(address: &str, port: u16) -> CommunicationChannel
    {
    println!("Opening port {}:{}", address, port);
        CommunicationChannel {
            address: address.to_string(),
            port: port,
        }
    }
    fn send(&self, msg: &str) {
        println!("Sent to {}:{} the message '{}'",
            self.address, self.port, msg);
    }
}
```

```
let channel_a = CommunicationChannel::create("usb4", 879);
channel_a.send("Message 1");
{
    let channel_b = CommunicationChannel::create("eth1", 12000);
    channel_b.send("Message 2");
}
channel_a.send("Message 3");
```

This program will print:

```
Opening port usb4:879
Sent to usb4:879 the message 'Message 1'
Opening port eth1:12000
Sent to eth1:12000 the message 'Message 2'
Closing port eth1:12000
Sent to usb4:879 the message 'Message 3'
Closing port usb4:879
```

The second statement implements the trait **Drop** for the newly declared type CommunicationChannel. Such trait, defined by the Rust language, has the peculiar property that its only method, named **drop**, is automatically invoked exactly when the object is deallocated, and therefore it is a *destructor*. In general, to create a destructor for a type, it is enough to implement the Drop trait for such type. You can implement the Drop trait only for the types declared inside your program, because that trait is not declared by your own code.

The third statement of the previous program is a block that defines two methods for our struct: the create constructor and the send operation.

At last, there is the application code, which uses the CommunicationChannel type. A communication channel is created, and such creation prints the first line of output. A message is sent, and that operation prints the second line. Then there is a nested block, in which another communication channel is created, printing the third line, and a message is sent through such channel, printing the fourth line.

So far, there is nothing new. But now, the nested block ends. That causes the channel_b variable to be destroyed, so its drop method is invoked, and that prints the fifth line.

Now, after the nested block has ended, another message is sent to the channel_a variable, causing it to print the last-but-one line. At last, the channel_a variable is destroyed, and that prints the last line.

As it will be seen in Chapter 22, in Rust, memory is already released by the language, and therefore there is no need to invoke functions similar to the free function of C language, or to the delete operator of C++ language. But other resources are not automatically released. Therefore destructors are most useful to release resources like file handles, communication handles, GUI windows, graphical resources, and synchronization primitives. If you use a library to handle such resources, that library should already contain a proper implementation of the Drop trait for any of its types that handle a resource.

Another use of destructors is to better understand how memory is managed, like this code shows:

```rust
struct S ( i32 );
impl Drop for S {
    fn drop(&mut self) {
        println!("Dropped {}", self.0);
    }
}
let _a = S (1);
let _b = S (2);
let _c = S (3);
{
    let _d = S (4);
    let _e = S (5);
    let _f = S (6);
    println!("INNER");
}
println!("OUTER");
```

It will print:

```
INNER
Dropped 6
Dropped 5
Dropped 4
```

```
OUTER
Dropped 3
Dropped 2
Dropped 1
```

Notice that objects are destroyed in exactly the opposite order than their declaration order, and just when they get out of their block.

This program is similar to the previous one, but its variables have been replaced by variable placeholders:

```
struct S ( i32 );
impl Drop for S {
    fn drop(&mut self) {
        println!("Dropped {}", self.0);
    }
}
let _ = S (1);
let _ = S (2);
let _ = S (3);
{
    let _ = S (4);
    let _ = S (5);
    let _ = S (6);
    println!("INNER");
}
println!("OUTER");
```

It will print:

```
Dropped 1
Dropped 2
Dropped 3
Dropped 4
Dropped 5
Dropped 6
INNER
OUTER
```

Variable placeholders do not allocate objects lasting for the entire block; they allocate temporary objects. Temporary objects are destroyed at the end of their statements, that is, when a semicolon in encountered. Therefore, all the objects are dropped in the same statement in which they are allocated.

This program is equivalent to the following one:

```
struct S ( i32 );
impl Drop for S {
    fn drop(&mut self) {
        println!("Dropped {}", self.0);
    }
}
S (1); S (2); S (3);
{
    S (4); S (5); S (6);
    println!("INNER");
}
println!("OUTER");
```

Operator Overloading

In many object-oriented languages, it is possible to redefine the language operators for the user-defined types. Also Rust allows us to redefine most of its operators. Though, differing from C++, some operators are not redefinable.

A typical use of operator overloading is for creating new numeric types not defined by the language, like the *complex* numbers of higher mathematics. Here, some features of these types of numbers will be implemented using stepwise refinement. The first draft is the following program:

```
struct Complex {
    re: f64,
    im: f64,
}

fn add_complex(lhs: Complex, rhs: Complex) -> Complex {
    Complex { re: lhs.re + rhs.re, im: lhs.im + rhs.im }
}
```

```
let z1 = Complex { re: 3.8, im: -2.1 };
let z2 = Complex { re: -1.5, im: 8.6 };
let z3 = add_complex(z1, z2);
print!("{} + {}i", z3.re, z3.im);
```

It will print: `2.3 + 6.5i`.

Complex numbers are actually a pair of real numbers: one item of the couple is named *real part, re* for short, and the other item is named *imaginary part, im* for short. The addition between any two complex numbers is defined to be a number whose real part is the sum of the real parts of the addends, and whose imaginary part is the sum of the imaginary parts of the addends. The words `lhs` and `rhs` stand, respectively, for *left-hand side* and *right-hand side* for the addition operation.

Now we want to replace the expression `add_complex(z1, z2)` with the expression `z1 + z2`. In Rust, the expression `a + b` is just syntax sugar for the call `a.add(b)`, where add is a function belonging to the `Add` trait, declared in the standard library. Here is the declaration of that trait:

```
trait Add<Rhs = Self> {
    type Output;
    fn add(self, rhs: Rhs) -> Self::Output;
}
```

Let's explain it. When you add two numbers, there may be three distinct types around: the type of the first addend, the type of the second addend, and the type of the result. They may be the same type, as is reasonable when we add two real numbers or two complex numbers, but in general there may be cases in which you want to write the expression `c = a + b`, where a, b, and c have three different types.

The first addend, that is, the left-hand side of the operation, is the current object, or `self`. Its type is `Self`.

The type of the second addend, that is, the right-hand side of the operation, is specified using a type parameter named `Rhs` (for right-hand side). Usually, when we monomorphize a generic function or a generic type, we must specify all its generic parameters. So, as we want to implement an addition of a `Complex` object with another `Complex` object, we should implement the `Add<Complex>` trait.

Though, Rust allows us to specify a default value for generic parameters. In the preceding definition, the default value for the `Rhs` generic parameter is `Self`. So, if we are implementing the `Add` trait, without specifying a generic parameter, it means that we are actually implementing the Add<Self> trait. And in particular, if we are implementing the Add trait for the Complex type, it means that we are implementing the Add<Complex> trait for the Complex type.

The type of the operation result is specified as the Output associated type. Such type alias is used as the return value type of the add method.

So, in our code, it is enough to implement the Add trait for the Complex type, with Self implicitly specified as the Rhs generic parameter, and again Self explicitly specified as the Output associated type. It is what this program does:

```
struct Complex {
    re: f64,
    im: f64,
}

impl std::ops::Add for Complex {
    type Output = Self;
    fn add(self, rhs: Self) -> Self {
        Self { re: self.re + rhs.re, im: self.im + rhs.im }
    }
}

let z1 = Complex { re: 3.8, im: -2.1 };
let z2 = Complex { re: -1.5, im: 8.6 };
use std::ops::Add;
let z3 = z1.add(z2);
print!("{} + {}i", z3.re, z3.im);
```

You can obtain an equivalent program if you replace the last-but-two and last-but-one statements with this statement:

```
let z3 = z1 + z2;
```

So, we got our operator overloaded. Now, to make a somewhat more realistic example, let's encapsulate the Complex type in a module. There are two possibilities: to let any user freely access the fields re and im, with no data hiding; or to make those fields private, forcing the use of public functions to access them. For the Complex type, there is no invariant to keep, so we can keep the fields public, like in this complete example.

Notice that, in the following examples in this section, the `complex` module is outside of the `main` function:

```
mod complex {
    pub struct Complex {
        pub re: f64,
        pub im: f64,
    }

    impl std::ops::Add for Complex {
        type Output = Self;
        fn add(self, rhs: Self) -> Self {
            Self { re: self.re + rhs.re, im: self.im + rhs.im }
        }
    }
}

fn main () {
    use complex::Complex;
    let z1 = Complex { re: 3.8, im: -2.1 };
    let z2 = Complex { re: -1.5, im: 8.6 };
    let z3 = z1 + z2;
    print!("{} + {}i", z3.re, z3.im);
}
```

Here, we see the `Complex` type has been encapsulated in the `complex` module, so it would have become implicitly private, were it not for the `pub` keyword in the second line. Its two fields also would have become implicitly private, were it not for their `pub` keyword.

Then, the `use` directive is specified to avoid having to explicitly write `complex::Complex` every time that type name is to be specified.

Notice that the trait implementation has no `pub` keywords (and they are even forbidden there), because the implementations of a trait are implicitly public as long as that trait is accessible.

Now, let's apply data hiding, making private the fields of Complex, with this code:

```
mod complex {
    pub struct Complex {
        re: f64,
        im: f64,
    }

    impl Complex {
        pub fn from_re_im(re: f64, im: f64) -> Self {
            Self { re, im }
        }
        pub fn re(&self) -> &f64 { &self.re }
        pub fn im(&self) -> &f64 { &self.im }
    }
    impl std::ops::Add for Complex {
        type Output = Self;
        fn add(self, rhs: Self) -> Self::Output {
            Self { re: self.re + rhs.re, im: self.im + rhs.im }
        }
    }
}

fn main() {
    use complex::Complex;
    let z1 = Complex::from_re_im(3.8, -2.1);
    let z2 = Complex::from_re_im(-1.5, 8.6);
    let z3 = z1 + z2;
    print!("{} + {}i", z3.re(), z3.im());
}
```

Notice that the structure itself has remained public, but its fields are private now, so we need some additional functions to access them: the constructor from_re_im, and the getter methods re and im. They must be marked as public.

At last, let's consider the case that we want to generalize our type to use other numeric types for its components: not only f64, but also f32 or even some user-defined numeric type. We must declare a generic type Complex<Num> with Num, a type that can be added to another Num object, returning a Num value. Here is the code:

```
mod complex {
    pub struct Complex<Num> {
        re: Num,
        im: Num,
    }

    impl<Num> Complex<Num> {
            pub fn from_re_im(re: Num, im: Num) -> Self {
            Self { re, im }
        }
        pub fn re(&self) -> &Num { &self.re }
        pub fn im(&self) -> &Num { &self.im }
    }

    impl<Num> std::ops::Add for Complex<Num>
    where Num: std::ops::Add<Output = Num> {
        type Output = Self;
        fn add(self, rhs: Self) -> Self::Output {
            Self { re: self.re + rhs.re, im: self.im + rhs.im }
        }
    }
}

fn main() {
    use complex::Complex;
    let z1 = Complex::from_re_im(3.8, -2.1);
    let z2 = Complex::from_re_im(-1.5, 8.6);
    let z3 = z1 + z2;
    print!("{} + {}i", z3.re(), z3.im());
}
```

Notice the following changes, with respect to the previous version:

- The six occurrences of f64 have been replaced by Num.

- The two occurrences of impl have been replaced by impl<Num>.

- The three occurrences of Complex in the complex module have been replaced by Complex<Num>.

- In the implementation of the Add trait, a type parameter bound has been added: where Num: std::ops::Add<Output = Num>. It means that to implement this trait, we require knowing how to add an object of type Num with an object of type Num (implicitly specified), generating a result of type Num.

We have seen how to overload only the addition operator, though many other Rust operators can be overloaded. Each of them has its own trait, with its own method. The main ones are listed in the following table:

Operator	Trait	Method
+ (addition)	Add	add
- (subtraction)	Sub	sub
- (unary negation)	Neg	neg
* (multiplication)	Mul	mul
/ (division)	Div	div
% (remainder)	Rem	rem
+= (addition assignment)	AddAssign	add_assign
-= (subtraction assignment)	SubAssign	sub_assign
*= (multiplication assignment)	MulAssign	mul_assign
/= (division assignment)	DivAssign	div_assign
%= (remainder assignment)	RemAssign	rem_assign

Other operators that can be overloaded are the bit-twiddling operators: !, &, |, ^, <<, >>, &=, |=, ^=, <<=, >>=.

The Index trait and the IndexMut trait allow us to define the indexing operations with square brackets, for immutable objects and mutable objects, respectively.

The function call itself also can be overloaded, to implement smart pointers, using three traits: Fn, which takes the argument by immutable reference; FnMut, which takes the argument by mutable reference; and FnOnce, which takes the argument by value.

Rust does not allow redefining the following operators: =, ==, != , <, <=, >, >=. Actually, the behavior of such operators can be changed too, but using different mechanisms.

Infallible Type Converters

In many object-oriented languages, it is possible to declare type converters. Let's see an example that shows the need of such converters.

Using primitive types, we can write:

```
let ln = 1_f64 / 3_f64;
let sn = ln as f32;
print!("{}", sn);
```

It will print: 0.33333334. This is possible because the as keyword allows converting between primitive types. Though, if we define custom types:

```
struct LargeNumber (f64);
struct SmallNumber (f32);
let ln = LargeNumber (1. / 3.);
let sn = ln as SmallNumber;
print!("{}", sn.0);
```

This generates the compilation error: non-primitive cast: `LargeNumber` as `SmallNumber`. This is caused by the use of the as keyword to convert between nonprimitive types. This notation is not allowed, and anyway the compiler doesn't know how to perform such a conversion.

To allow conversions between arbitrary types, Rust provides four different techniques, which make use of the standard library traits Into, From, TryInto, and TryFrom. Let's see an example of the first one:

```
struct LargeNumber (f64);
struct SmallNumber (f32);

impl Into<SmallNumber> for LargeNumber {
    fn into(self) -> SmallNumber {
        SmallNumber (self.0 as f32)
    }
}

let ln = LargeNumber (1. / 3.);
let sn: SmallNumber = ln.into();
print!("{}", sn.0);
```

It will print: 0.33333334. In the last-but-one line, the into method is applied to the value of the ln variable, and it returns the conversion of that value into a value assigned to the sn variable. Notice that the type of the value returned by into must be inferred from the context.

To be able to write this statement, the previous impl statement is required. It implements the generic Into trait for the LargeNumber type, which is the source type of the conversion. Such implementation monomorphizes the implementation for the SmallNumber type, which is the destination of the conversion.

Here, both the source type and the destination type are user-defined types. This solution can also be applied if the source type *or* the destination type is an external type, that is, a primitive type or a type defined in another crate. However, it is not allowed to convert from an external type to an external type.

This solution works, but it has the drawback of requiring us to call the into function in a context in which the destination type can be inferred.

The other allowed solution uses the From standard library trait, as this example shows:

```
struct LargeNumber (f64);
struct SmallNumber (f32);

impl From<LargeNumber> for SmallNumber {
    fn from(source: LargeNumber) -> Self {
        Self (source.0 as f32)
    }
}
```

```
let ln = LargeNumber (1. / 3.);
let sn = SmallNumber::from(ln);
print!("{}", sn.0);
```

Here, in the last-but-one statement, the function `from`, associated with the `SmallNumber` type is called to convert its argument `ln`. Type inference is not required, because the destination type is specified anyway.

To be able to write this statement, the previous `impl` statement implements the generic `From` trait for the `SmallNumber` type, which is the destination type of the conversion. Such implementation monomorphizes the implementation for the `LargeNumber` type, which is the source of the conversion. Notice that the source and destination types have been swapped, with respect to the implementation of `Into`.

Also this solution allows that the source or destination type is external, but not both.

The `From` solution has an additional advantage, with respect to the `Into` solution. In the previous example, try to replace the last-but-one statement with this one:

```
let sn: SmallNumber = ln.into();
```

You will get a valid, equivalent program. Actually, when you implement the `From` trait, a default implementation of the `Into` trait is implicitly declared. Therefore, it is recommended to implement only the `From` trait, and then freely use the `from` or `into` functions. You should implement the `Into` trait only when, for some reason, you require that the `From` trait is not implemented, or when you are not satisfied by the default implementation of `Into`.

These solutions have a possible drawback, though. They are not fallible. Whenever a conversion of such kind is called, it must always return a value. But, in some cases you may want a conversion to succeed for some values and fail for some other values.

Fallible Type Converters

To support fallible type conversions, the standard library declares the `TryInto` and the `TryFrom` traits are available. Let's see an example using the last one:

```
struct LargeNumber (f64);
struct SmallNumber (f32);
```

```
impl TryFrom<LargeNumber> for SmallNumber {
    type Error = String;
    fn try_from(source: LargeNumber) -> Result<Self, Self::Error> {
        if source.0.abs() > f32::MAX as f64 {
            Err("too large number".to_string())
        }
        else if source.0 != 0.
        && source.0.abs() < f32::MIN_POSITIVE as f64 {
            Err("too small number".to_string())
        }
        else {
            let result = source.0 as f32;
            if result as f64 == source.0 {
                Ok(Self (result))
            }
            else {
                Err("precision loss".to_string())
            }
        }
    }
}

fn show_result(n: Result<SmallNumber, String>) {
    match n {
        Ok(x) => println!("Converted to {}", x.0),
        Err(msg) => println!("Conversion error: {}", msg),
    }
}

let ln = LargeNumber (1.5);
show_result(SmallNumber::try_from(ln));
let ln = LargeNumber (1. / 3.);
show_result(SmallNumber::try_from(ln));
let ln = LargeNumber (1e50);
show_result(SmallNumber::try_from(ln));
let ln = LargeNumber (1e-50);
show_result(SmallNumber::try_from(ln));
```

It will print:

```
Converted to 1.5
Conversion error: precision loss
Conversion error: too large number
Conversion error: too small number
```

In the last eight lines, four objects of type LargeNumber are created, all named ln. For each of them, the try_from function is called; the result of that conversion attempt is passed to the show_result function, which prints a result message.

The first variable contains the 64-bit number 1.5, which can be translated to a 32-bit number without loss of precision. Therefore, it is converted successfully.

The second variable contains the 64-bit number obtained dividing one by three. That number cannot be represented exactly in a binary representation; therefore it is represented in an approximate way. However, a 64-bit representation has more significant digits than a 32-bit representation, so the two approximate representations are different. So, the conversion fails with the error message: precision loss.

The third variable contains a 64-bit number larger than the maximum value that can be represented by a 32-bit number. So, the conversion fails with an error message: too large number.

The fourth variable contains a 64-bit number that is nearer to zero than the minimum positive value that can be represented by a 32-bit number. So, the conversion fails with an error message: too small number.

To get such behavior, the try_from method, instead of returning a value of type Self, returns a value of type Result<Self, Self::Error>. In case that routine succeeds in the conversion, an Ok variant is returned. In case it fails, an Err variant is returned. The type of that error must be specified as the Error associated type of the trait implementation. In our example, such error type was String.

Composition Instead of Inheritance

At the beginning of the object-oriented programming era, inheritance appeared as a panacea, a technique that could be applied to any problem. In fact, there are three kinds of inheritance: data inheritance, method implementation inheritance, and method interface inheritance. As years went by, it was realized that data inheritance created more problems than it solved, so Rust does not support it. In place of data inheritance, Rust uses composition.

Let's consider an example. Assume we already have a type representing a text to draw on the graphical screen, and we want to create a type representing a text surrounded by a rectangle. For simplicity, instead of drawing the text, we will print it on the console; and instead of drawing the rectangle, we will surround the text in brackets. Here is our code:

```rust
struct Text { characters: String }
impl Text {
    fn from(text: &str) -> Text {
        Text { characters: text.to_string() }
    }
    fn draw(&self) {
        print!("{}", self.characters);
    }
}
let greeting = Text::from("Hello");
greeting.draw();
struct BoxedText {
    text: Text,
    first: char,
    last: char,
}
impl BoxedText {
    fn with_text_and_borders(
        text: &str, first: char, last: char)
        -> BoxedText
    {
        BoxedText {
            text: Text::from(text),
            first: first,
            last: last,
        }
    }
```

```
    fn draw(&self) {
        print!("{}", self.first);
        self.text.draw();
        print!("{}", self.last);
    }
}
let boxed_greeting =
    BoxedText::with_text_and_borders("Hi", '[', ']');
print!(", ");
boxed_greeting.draw();
```

It will print: `Hello, [Hi]`.

The first statement defines a struct representing a text, characterized only by the string that contains its characters.

The second statement defines two methods for this struct: `from`, which is a constructor; and `draw`, which prints the string contained in the object. So, we can create a Text object, and we can draw it using such a method.

Now assume that you want to capitalize on this struct and its associated methods to create a text enclosed in a box, represented by a struct named `BoxedText`. That is what inheritance usually is touted for.

In Rust, instead of using inheritance, you create a `BoxedText` struct that *contains* an object of Text type and some additional fields. In this case, there are two fields representing the character to print before and after the base text.

Then, you declare the implementation of the methods you want to encapsulate in the `BoxedText` type, that is, to apply to objects of `BoxedText` type. They are a constructor, named `with_text_and_borders`, and a function to draw the current object, named `draw`.

The constructor gets all the information it needs and initializes a new object with that information. In particular, the field having type Text is initialized by invoking the `Text::from` constructor.

The method to draw the current object has the same signature as the similar method associated with Text objects, but this is just a coincidence, due to the fact that such methods do similar things. They could have different names, different argument types, or different return value types. The body of this `draw` method, though, contains an invocation of the `draw` method of Text.

Finally, an object having type `BoxedText` is created, and its method `draw` is invoked, having as a result that the string `[Hi]` is printed.

In this program, reuse happens in the following places:

- The first field of struct BoxedText is text: Text. It reuses that data structure.

- The constructor of BoxedText contains the expression Text::from(text). It reuses the constructor of the Text type.

- The body of the draw method of the BoxedText type contains the statement self.text.draw();. It reuses the draw method associated with the Text type.

Static Dispatch

In the previous section, we have seen how to define the Text and BoxedText types so that the latter reuses some data and code written for the former.

Now assume you need to write a function capable of drawing several kinds of text objects. In particular, if it receives as an argument an object of Text type, it should invoke the draw method associated with the Text type; while, if it receives as argument an object of BoxedText type, it should invoke the draw method associated to the BoxedText type.

If Rust were a dynamically typed language, this function would be:

```
fn draw_text(txt) {
    txt.draw();
}
```

Of course, this is not allowed in Rust, because the type of the txt argument must be specified explicitly.

Rust allows two nonequivalent solutions for this problem. One is this:

```
trait Draw {
    fn draw(&self);
}
struct Text { characters: String }
impl Text {
    fn from(text: &str) -> Text {
        Text { characters: text.to_string() }
    }
}
```

```rust
impl Draw for Text {
    fn draw(&self) {
        print!("{}", self.characters);
    }
}
struct BoxedText {
    text: Text,
    first: char,
    last: char,
}
impl BoxedText {
    fn with_text_and_borders(
        text: &str, first: char, last: char)
        -> BoxedText
    {
        BoxedText {
            text: Text::from(text),
            first: first,
            last: last,
        }
    }
}
impl Draw for BoxedText {
    fn draw(&self) {
        print!("{}", self.first);
        self.text.draw();
        print!("{}", self.last);
    }
}
let greeting = Text::from("Hello");
let boxed_greeting =
    BoxedText::with_text_and_borders("Hi", '[', ']');
// SOLUTION 1 //
fn draw_text<T>(txt: T) where T: Draw {
    txt.draw();
}
```

```
draw_text(greeting);
print!(", ");
draw_text(boxed_greeting);
```

It will print: `Hello, [Hi]`.

The last three lines are the ones that print the resulting text. The `draw_text(greeting)` statement receives an object having type `Text` and prints `Hello`; and the `draw_text(boxed_greeting)` statement receives an object having type `BoxedText` and prints `[Hi]`. Such a generic function is defined just before. These last six lines are the first solution to the problem. The preceding part of the program is in common with the second solution.

But let's start to examine this program from the beginning.

First, the `Draw` trait is declared, as the capability of an object to be drawn.

Then the `Text` and `BoxedText` types are declared, with their associated methods, similarly to the example of the previous section. Though, only the two constructors `Text::from` and `BoxedText::with_text_and_borders` are kept as inherent implementations; the two `draw` functions, instead, now are implementations of the `Draw` trait.

Regarding the previous example, we said that the two `draw` methods had the same signature by coincidence, and they could have different signatures just as well. In this last example, instead, this equality is no more a coincidence; such functions are now used to implement the `Draw` trait, so they must have the same signature of the function declared in such trait.

After having declared the two types, their associated functions, and their implementations of the `Draw` trait, the two variables `greeting` and `boxed_greeting` are created and initialized, one for each of those types.

Then there is the first solution. The `draw_text` generic function receives an argument of `T` type, where `T` is any type that implements the `Draw` trait. Because of this, it is allowed to invoke the `draw` function on that argument.

So, whenever the compiler encounters an invocation of the `draw_text` function, it determines the type of the argument, and checks if such type implements the `Draw` trait. In case that trait is not implemented, a compilation error is generated. Otherwise, a monomorphized version of the `draw_text` function is generated. In this concrete function, the `T` type is replaced by the type of the argument, and the invocation of the `draw` generic method in the body of the function is replaced by an invocation of the implementation of `draw` for the type of the argument.

This technique is named ***static dispatch***. In programming language theory, *dispatch* means choosing which function to invoke when there are several functions with the same name. In this program there are two functions named draw, so a dispatch is required to choose between them. In this program, this choice is performed by the compiler, at compile time, so this dispatch is *static*.

Dynamic Dispatch

The previous program can be changed a little, by replacing the last seven lines with the following ones:

```
// SOLUTION 1/bis //
fn draw_text<T>(txt: &T) where T: Draw {
    txt.draw();
}
draw_text(&greeting);
print!(", ");
draw_text(&boxed_greeting);
```

This version has substantially the same behavior of the previous version. Now, the draw function receives its argument by reference, and so an "&" character has been added in its signature, and other "&" characters have been added at the two invocations of this function.

This solution is still a case of static dispatch. So, we see that static dispatch can work both with pass-by-value and with pass-by-reference.

The previous program can be changed further, by replacing the last seven lines with the following ones:

```
// SOLUTION 2 //
fn draw_text(txt: &dyn Draw) {
    txt.draw();
}
draw_text(&greeting);
print!(", ");
draw_text(&boxed_greeting);
```

Also this program has the same external behavior as before, but it uses another kind of technique. Now only the draw_text signature has been changed. The T generic parameter and the where clause have been removed, and the argument has type &dyn Draw instead of &T.

Here, the new **dyn** keyword is used. It means that this type is not a usual reference, but it is something new. It is a *dynamic-dispatch reference*. So now, instead of a generic function, we have a concrete function, which gets as argument a *dynamic-dispatch* reference. Though, the calls to this function haven't changed: one passes as argument a reference to a Text, and the other a reference to a BoxedText. So such references are automatically converted to dynamic-dispatch references.

Let's see the purpose of this dynamic-dispatch reference argument. When the draw_text method is called using the &greeting argument, the method receives a pointer to the greeting object, but it also receives some indication that the type of this object has implemented the Draw trait for the Text type. Instead, when the &boxed_greeting argument is used, the draw_text method, in addition to the pointer to the boxed_greeting object, receives some indication that the type of this object has implemented the Draw trait for the BoxedText type. Having such additional information, the draw_text method is able to invoke the appropriate draw method at runtime.

So, &dyn Draw is a kind of pointer capable of choosing the right draw method to invoke, according to the type of the referenced object. This is a kind of dispatch, but it happens at runtime, so it is a *dynamic dispatch*.

Dynamic dispatch is handled in C++ by using the virtual keyword, albeit with a slightly different mechanism.

Implementation of Dynamic-Dispatch References

Get back to the program showing the last solution to the dispatch problem, and replace the last seven lines (from the one starting with // SOLUTION) with the following code:

```
// PRINTING OBJECT SIZES
use std::mem::size_of_val;
print!("{} {} {}, {} {} {}, ",
    size_of_val(&greeting),
    size_of_val(&&greeting),
    size_of_val(&&&greeting),
```

```
        size_of_val(&boxed_greeting),
        size_of_val(&&boxed_greeting),
        size_of_val(&&&boxed_greeting));
fn draw_text(txt: &dyn Draw) {
    print!("{} {} {} ",
        size_of_val(txt),
        size_of_val(&txt),
        size_of_val(&&txt));
    txt.draw();
}
draw_text(&greeting);
print!(", ");
draw_text(&boxed_greeting);
```

The resulting program, in a 64-bit target, will print: `24 8 8, 32 8 8, 24 16 8`
`Hello, 32 16 8 [Hi]`.

Remember that the `size_of_val` standard library generic function gets a reference to an object of any type, and returns the size in bytes of that object.

First, the `greeting` variable is processed. Its type is `Text`, which contains only a `String` object. We already discovered that `String` objects occupy 24 bytes in the stack, plus a variable buffer in the heap. That buffer is not taken into account by the `size_of_val` function. The `size_of_val` function requires a reference, so the expression `size_of_val(greeting)` would be illegal.

The size of a reference to a `Text` is printed, and then the size of a reference to a reference to a `Text`. They are ordinary references, so they occupy 8 bytes.

Then, the `boxed_greeting` variable is processed in the same way. This struct contains a `Text` and two `char` objects. Each `char` occupies 4 bytes, and so it is 24 + 4 + 4 = 32 bytes. Its references are normal references too.

Then, near the end of the program, the expression `&greeting`, having type `&Text`, is passed as an argument to the `draw_text` function, where it is used to initialize the argument `txt`, having type `&dyn Draw`.

The `txt` argument is a kind of reference, so it is possible to evaluate the expression `size_of_val(txt)`. It will return the size of the referenced object. But which type has the object referenced to by an object of type `&dyn Draw`? Of course, it is not `Draw`, because `Draw` is not a type. Actually, this cannot be said at compile time. It depends on the object referenced at runtime by the expression used to initialize the `txt` argument. The first time that the `draw_text` function is invoked, the `txt` argument receives a reference to a Text object, so 24 is printed.

If you jump forward in the output, going after the comma, you see that the second time that the `draw_text` function is invoked, the `txt` argument receives a reference to a BoxedText object, so 32 is printed.

Going back to the invocation using `greeting`, we see that the value of the expression `size_of_val(&txt)` is 16. This may be surprising. This expression is the size of an object having type `&dyn Draw`, initialized by an object having type `&Text`. So we use a normal 8-byte reference to initialize a 16-byte dynamic-dispatch reference. Why is a dynamic-dispatch reference so large? The mechanism of dynamic dispatch lies in how it is initialized.

Actually any dynamic-dispatch reference has two fields. The first one is a copy of the reference used to initialize it, and the second one is a pointer used to choose the proper version of the `draw` function, or any other function needing dynamic dispatch. It is named `virtual table pointer`. This name comes from C++.

At last, the size of a reference to a dynamic-dispatch reference is printed. This is a normal reference, occupying eight bytes.

The same numbers are printed for the references to the `boxed_greeting` variable.

Static vs. Dynamic Dispatch

So you can use static or dynamic dispatch. Which should you use?

Like any instance of static-versus-dynamic dilemma, where *static* means *compile-time*, and *dynamic* means *runtime*, static requires a somewhat longer compilation time, and generates somewhat faster code; but if not enough information is available to the compiler, the dynamic solution is the only possible one.

Assume that, for the example programs shown before, there is the following requirement. The user is asked to enter a string. If that string is b, a boxed text should be printed; and for any other input, a nonboxed text should be printed.

Using the static dispatch, the final part of the program (replacing the lines from `// PRINTING OBJECT SIZES`) becomes:

```
// SOLUTION 1/ter //
fn draw_text<T>(txt: T) where T: Draw {
    txt.draw();
}
```

```
let mut input = String::new();
std::io::stdin().read_line(&mut input).unwrap();
let to_box = input.trim() == "b";
if to_box {
    draw_text(boxed_greeting);
} else {
    draw_text(greeting);
}
```

If you run it and then you press b and Enter, the text [Hi] will be printed. If instead you type nothing or any other text and then Enter, the text Hello will be printed.

Instead, using the dynamic dispatch, you have this equivalent code:

```
// SOLUTION 2/bis //
fn draw_text(txt: &dyn Draw) {
    txt.draw();
}
let mut input = String::new();
std::io::stdin().read_line(&mut input).unwrap();
let to_box = input.trim() == "b";
draw_text(if to_box { &boxed_greeting } else { &greeting });
```

The static dispatch forces you to write several function invocations, one for each type to use for the argument to pass to draw_text. Instead, the dynamic dispatch allows you to write just one call to draw_text, and let the dynamic dispatch mechanism perform the choice.

In addition, static dispatch uses generic functions, and this technique may create code bloat, so it may end up being slower.

CHAPTER 21

Standard Library Collections

In this chapter, you will learn:

- How to measure the time spent running portions of Rust code

- How performance reasons suggest which kind of collection to use

- Which is the best collection for various kinds of operations: sequential scan, insertion and removal of items at both ends, removal of the largest item, search by value, search by key, or scan in order

- Which collections in the Rust standard library correspond to the collections in the C++ standard library

Collections

Arrays, vectors, structs, tuple-structs, tuples, and enums are data types whose objects may contain several other objects. However, for structs, tuple-structs, tuples, and enums, for each contained object a specific clause must be specified both in the type declaration and in the object construction, so they are not usable to contain hundreds of objects. Instead, arrays and vectors are data types that may contain many objects, even if they are defined and instantiated with simple formulas. The objects of such kinds are named *collections*.

Arrays and vectors are optimal collections in many cases: they use memory efficiently, they are fast to scan, they use CPU caches efficiently, and they allow fast direct access through an integer offset (or index). Yet, for some operations, they are definitely inefficient, so in such cases it is appropriate to use other kinds of collections.

© Carlo Milanesi 2022
C. Milanesi, *Beginning Rust*, https://doi.org/10.1007/978-1-4842-7208-4_21

The Rust standard library provides various kinds of them: VecDeque<T>, LinkedList<T>, BinaryHeap<T>, BTreeSet<T>, BTreeMap<K,V>, HashSet<T>, and HashMap<K,V>.

Speaking of collections, arrays are a separate case, because they are entirely stack allocated, and they have a size defined at compile time. All the other collections, including vectors, contain a variable number of items; and they store a fixed-length header in the stack, while the data, if there is some, is allocated in the heap. We will name them *dynamically sized collections*.

Measuring Execution Time

Because the choice of a collection depends much on its performance, here we take a detour, where we see how we can measure with precision the time spent by different portions of Rust code.

Performance is important for all software developers. However, those who program in a high-level language typically reason about how many milliseconds or how many seconds are spent by a command, while those who program in a low-level language, like Rust, often reason about how many microseconds or even nanoseconds are spent by a single function.

In the Rust standard library, there are functions that can precisely measure the time elapsed between two source code points:

```
let start_time = std::time::Instant::now();
for i in 0..10_000 {
    println!("{}", i);
}
println!("{:?}", start_time.elapsed());
```

This program first will print all the integer numbers from 0 to 9999, and then it will print the time spent to print such numbers. A possible content of the last line is: 20.695631ms. It means that the time taken to run the loop has been a bit more than 20 milliseconds.

Such time depends mainly on the power of the computer used, on the operating system, and on the terminal emulator program. It depends little on the optimization level used by the Rust compiler, as most time is used by library code and operating system code.

However, some programs perform a lot of computations, and for such programs the level of optimizations performed by the compiler can dramatically affect the time to run a command.

At the beginning of the book, we saw that to compile a Rust program it was enough to write the `rustc` command, followed by the name of the source file, with no need for any other arguments. Yet, such a command does not activate the compiler optimizations, so it generates machine code that is good for debugging but not as efficient as it could be.

If you are interested in performance, you should activate the compiler optimizations. These are activated using the command-line option -O (it's an uppercase letter, not a zero). If that option is omitted, every optimization is disabled.

Therefore, in this chapter it is assumed that the examples are compiled by the following command line:

```
rustc -O main.rs
```

If you go back to the previous example, you will notice that first the `Instant` type has been included from the standard library. It represents time instants with a resolution smaller than a microsecond.

To measure a time, you should invoke the `now` function of the `Instant` type. Every invocation of `now` returns an object of type `Instant`, representing the current time instant. Then, the `elapsed` method of the `Instant` type returns an object of type `std::time::Duration`, which represents the time elapsed from the creation time of the Instant object to the current time. If a Duration is printed for debug (using the `{:?}` placeholder), the nearest unit of measurement is automatically chosen, and the symbol of such unit is output as suffix.

Performing Arbitrary Insertions and Removals

Now let's get back to the operations on the collections.

The following program is very efficient:

```
use std::time::Instant;
const SIZE: usize = 100_000_000;
let start_time = Instant::now();
let mut v = Vec::<usize>::with_capacity(SIZE);
let t1 = start_time.elapsed();
```

```
for i in 0..SIZE {
    v.push(i);
}
let t2 = start_time.elapsed();
for _ in 0..SIZE {
    v.pop();
}
let t3 = start_time.elapsed();
print!("{:?} {:?} {:?}", t1, t2 - t1, t3 - t2);
```

Remember to compile it specifying the -O option.

This program will print three numbers that depend on the computer, on the operating system, and possibly even on the version of the compiler.

A possible result is: 3.517µs 449.095194ms 61.93267ms.

That means that to create a vector that allocates room for one hundred million usize objects, which in a 64-bit system occupies 800 MB, few microseconds are spent; to put one hundred million values in such space, without ever allocating memory, less than half a second is spent; and to remove all such numbers, one at a time, proceeding from the last one, less than one tenth of a second is spent.

Instead, the following program is very *inefficient*:

```
use std::time::Instant;
const SIZE: usize = 100_000;
let start_time = Instant::now();
let mut v = Vec::<usize>::with_capacity(SIZE);
let t1 = start_time.elapsed();
for i in 0..SIZE {
    v.insert(0, i);
}
let t2 = start_time.elapsed();
for _ in 0..SIZE {
    v.remove(0);
}
let t3 = start_time.elapsed();
print!("{:?} {:?} {:?}", t1, t2 - t1, t3 - t2);
```

It could print: 6.663µs 1.151939082s 1.015383097s.

First of all, notice that this time only one hundred thousand items are processed, which is one thousandth of those processed by the previous example.

To create the 800KB-large vector, few microseconds are spent, but to insert one hundred thousand items from the beginning of the vector, more than one second is spent, and as much time is spent to remove them by proceeding from the first one. So, such an insertion operation appears to be more than two thousand times slower than that of the previous example, and such a deletion operation appears to be more than sixteen thousand times slower than that of the previous example.

The reason for such times is easy to explain.

To add an item at the end of a vector having enough capacity, all you need to do is to check that there is enough space, to copy the item into the vector buffer, and to increment the item count. That, for a `usize`, in the computer used to measure those times, takes less than five nanoseconds, including the time to move the iterator to the next item.

To remove an item from the end of a nonempty vector, all you need to do is to check that the vector is not empty, and to decrement the item count. That takes less than one nanosecond.

To insert an item at the beginning of a vector, first you need to shift by one place all the items already in the vector, to free the first place for the new item. At the start of the loop, the shift operation is fast, but as the item count grows, the time spent to insert an item at the beginning of the vector grows as much.

Similarly, to remove the first item, you must shift all the items but the first one, which will be overwritten by the second item.

Using the notation of the theory of computational complexity, we can say that the insertion and the removal of an item at the end of a vector have a O(K) complexity, which is *constant complexity*, while the insertion and the removal of an item at the beginning of a vector already containing N items have O(N) complexity, which is *linear complexity*.

If the insertions and removals are not really at the beginning, but in an intermediate position, the performance will be better, but still much slower than insertion and removal at the end.

Queues

If you need to insert and remove items only at the beginning of a vector, it is enough to redesign the vector in inverted order, so that such operations will be applied at the end.

Instead, if you need to insert items at one end of the sequence, and remove items at the other end, the vector type is not the optimal collection. Such use case is that of a First-In-First-Out queue. Here is an example of a queue implemented using a Vec, inserting items at the end and removing them from the beginning:

```rust
use std::time::Instant;
const SIZE: usize = 40_000;
let start_time = Instant::now();
let mut v = Vec::<usize>::new();
for i in 0..SIZE {
    v.push(i);
    v.push(SIZE + i);
    v.remove(0);
    v.push(SIZE * 2 + i);
    v.remove(0);
}
let t1 = start_time.elapsed();
while v.len() > 0 {
    v.remove(0);
}
let t2 = start_time.elapsed();
print!("{:?} {:?}", t1, t2 - t1);
```

It could print: 330.812316ms 163.214733ms.

The first timed code portion creates an empty vector, and then, for forty thousand times, it inserts three numbers at the end of the vector and it extracts two items from the beginning. The second code portion extracts from the beginning all the remaining items. The first portion spends about a third of a second, and the second portion about a sixth of a second. Actually, almost all the time is spent for the extractions, because insertions are extremely fast.

We could try, instead, to insert items at the beginning and extract them from the end:

```
use std::time::Instant;
const SIZE: usize = 40_000;
let start_time = Instant::now();
let mut v = Vec::<usize>::new();
for i in 0..SIZE {
    v.insert(0, i);
    v.insert(0, SIZE + i);
    v.pop();
    v.insert(0, SIZE * 2 + i);
    v.pop();
}
let t1 = start_time.elapsed();
while v.len() > 0 {
    v.pop();
}
let t2 = start_time.elapsed();
print!("{:?} {:?}", t1, t2 - t1);
```

It could print: `505.627254ms 211ns`.

Now the insertions are slow, and the removals spend virtually zero time. However, the sum of the two times hasn't improved at all.

Now, instead of the Vec type, let's use the VecDeque type:

```
use std::time::Instant;
const SIZE: usize = 40_000;
let start_time = Instant::now();
let mut vd = std::collections::VecDeque::<usize>::new();
for i in 0..SIZE {
    vd.push_back(i);
    vd.push_back(SIZE + i);
    vd.pop_front();
    vd.push_back(SIZE * 2 + i);
    vd.pop_front();
}
```

```
let t1 = start_time.elapsed();
while vd.len() > 0 {
    vd.pop_front();
}
let t2 = start_time.elapsed();
print!("{:?} {:?}", t1, t2 - t1);
```

It could print: 994.255µs 47.34µs.

The difference from the previous times is abysmal. Indeed, the whole program spends less than one millisecond, compared with around 500 milliseconds spent by the versions using a vector.

Notice that while the Vec type is automatically imported in the current namespace, the VecDeque type, like the types of the other collections, must be explicitly qualified.

The VecDeque name is shorthand for *vector-based double-ended queue.* Here, the *queue* word means: *sequential collection, into which items are inserted at one end and from which items are extracted at the other end.* The fact of being *double-ended* means that the items can be inserted at both ends and extracted from both ends, with no penalty. Finally, the fact of being vector-based means that it is implemented storing its items in a vector, and that its items can be accessed using an integer offset, similarly to arrays and vectors.

To insert or remove items at the end of a vector, you can use the simple words push and pop, without specifying the point of insertion or extraction; it is understood that such point is the end, which is the only point where such operations are mostly efficient. Instead, VecDeque collections handle both ends equally well; so, the recommended functions to insert items at the beginning and at the end are, respectively, push_front and push_back; and the recommended functions to remove items from the beginning and from the end are, respectively, pop_front and pop_back. The VecDeque type also supports the insert and remove functions, similarly to vectors, but such functions are not recommended because they can be inefficient.

Given that queues are so efficient, why shouldn't we always use them, instead of vectors?

The reason is that for the most frequent operations on vectors, which are iteration and direct access, vectors are faster by a constant factor. Here is a program that first adds forty thousand numbers to a VecDeque collection and to a Vec collection, and then computes the sum of the inserted items by scanning such collections:

```rust
use std::time::Instant;
const SIZE: usize = 40_000;
let mut v = Vec::<usize>::new();
let mut vd = std::collections::VecDeque::<usize>::new();
let start_time = Instant::now();
for i in 0..SIZE {
    v.push(i);
}
let t1 = start_time.elapsed();
for i in 0..SIZE {
    vd.push_back(i);
}
let mut count = 0;
let t2 = start_time.elapsed();
for i in v.iter() {
    count += i;
}
let t3 = start_time.elapsed();
for i in vd.iter() {
    count += i;
}
let t4 = start_time.elapsed();
print!("{} {:?} {:?} {:?} {:?}", count,
    t1, t2 - t1, t3 - t2, t4 - t3);
```

It could print: 1599960000 495.299µs 466.374µs 16.642µs 89.7µs.

The count is printed just to force the compiler to do the actual computation. Otherwise, the optimizer could skip it all.

The times mean that to insert each item at the end of a collection, the Vec and the VecDeque collection types have almost the same performance, but for scanning the whole collection, Vec is five as fast.

Linked Lists

For some applications, there is the need to frequently insert and remove items in intermediate positions. In such cases, both vectors and queues perform such operations inefficiently, so, if you have such a need, you can resort to another kind of collection, LinkedList. Though, there are really few cases in which the usage of a LinkedList is justified.

Binary Heaps

There can be another access use case for a collection, the so-called *priority queue*. It happens when only two functions are used: one to insert an item and one to extract it. But every item is inserted with a priority value, and the function to extract an item must get the item with the highest value among the items contained in the collection. Using vectors, you could start with the following program:

```
let data = vec![
    48, 18, 20, 35, 17, 13, 39, 12, 42, 33, 29, 27, 50, 16];
let mut v = Vec::<i32>::new();
fn add(v: &mut Vec<i32>, item: i32) {
    v.push(item);
}
fn extract(v: &mut Vec<i32>) -> i32 {
    v.pop().unwrap()
}
let mut i = 0;
loop {
    if i == data.len() { break; }
    add(&mut v, data[i]);
    i += 1;
    if i == data.len() { break; }
    add(&mut v, data[i]);
    i += 1;
    print!("{} ", extract(&mut v));
}
```

```
while ! v.is_empty() {
    print!("{} ", extract(&mut v));
}
```

It will print: `18 35 13 12 33 27 16 50 29 42 39 17 20 48`.

The `data` vector is used as an item provider. Its 14 objects are processed, two each iteration, in the seven iterations of the first loop. At each iteration, two items of the `data` vector are passed to the `add` function, which inserts them at the end of the `v` vector. Then, the last item is extracted from the `v` vector and printed. The last statement of the program repeatedly extracts and prints the last items of the vector, until the vector becomes empty.

The result is not the desired one, as the last inserted item will be always extracted, even if the collection contains an item bigger than it. For example, after having inserted the numbers 48 and 18, the first extracted number is 18, even though the number 48 is greater than it.

The correct result can be obtained by replacing the add function with the following one:

```
fn add(v: &mut Vec<i32>, item: i32) {
    v.push(item);
    v.sort();
}
```

or by replacing the extract function with the following one:

```
fn extract(v: &mut Vec<i32>) -> i32 {
    v.sort();
    v.pop().unwrap()
}
```

In both cases, the program will print: `48 35 20 39 42 33 50 29 27 18 17 16 13 12`.

In the first case, each time a value is added to the `v` vector, that vector is sorted again so that the values are always in ascending order. In the second case, the vector is sorted just before a value is extracted from the `v` vector. Both techniques guarantee that the extracted value is always the largest among those contained in the collection.

Both correct versions have the drawback of quite often invoking the `sort` function, which has a significant cost.

An equivalent but much faster version is obtained if you replace the declarations of the v vector and of the add and extract functions, with the following code:

```
use std::collections::BinaryHeap;
let mut v = BinaryHeap::<i32>::new();
fn add(v: &mut BinaryHeap<i32>, item: i32) {
    v.push(item);
}
fn extract(v: &mut BinaryHeap<i32>) -> i32 {
    v.pop().unwrap()
}
```

As you can see, binary heaps are used by invoking the push and pop functions, similarly to vectors. Though, while in these last collections the pop function extracts the last inserted item among those still contained in the collection, in binary heaps the pop function extracts the item having the largest value among those still contained in the collection.

Regarding the implementation, here we can say that both when an item is added and when an item is removed, some items are moved, so that the last item is always the largest; however, the other items are not necessarily in ascending order.

Ordered Sets and Unordered Sets

Another way to use a collection is to insert an item only if it is not already contained in the collection. That realizes the concept of mathematical set. Indeed, in mathematics it makes no sense to say that an item is contained several times in a set.

A way to implement this kind of insertion using a vector would be to scan the whole vector at every insertion, and insert the item only if it is not found. Of course, such an algorithm would be inefficient.

There are several techniques to create a collection that efficiently inserts an item only if it is not already contained, which is a collection that implements the concept of a set without duplicates.

The most efficient technique to search for arbitrary objects uses a kind of data structure named *hashtable*, so such a type of collection is named HashSet.

However, such a collection has the drawback that its items are not ordered. If you need ordered items, you can use a collection using a data structure named B-tree, and therefore it is named BTreeSet. To search this data structure is definitely faster than to search a large vector, but it is usually less efficient than to search a hashtable. Here is an example of both set implementations:

```
let arr = [6, 8, 2, 8, 4, 9, 6, 1, 8, 0];
let mut v = Vec::<_>::new();
let mut hs = std::collections::HashSet::<_>::new();
let mut bs = std::collections::BTreeSet::<_>::new();
for i in arr.iter() {
    v.push(i);
    hs.insert(i);
    bs.insert(i);
}
print!("Vec:");
for i in v.iter() { print!(" {}", i); }
println!(". {:?}", v);
print!("HashSet :");
for i in hs.iter() { print!(" {}", i); }
println!(". {:?}", hs);
print!("BTreeSet:");
for i in bs.iter() { print!(" {}", i); }
println!(". {:?}", bs);
```

It could print:

```
Vec: 6 8 2 8 4 9 6 1 8 0. [6, 8, 2, 8, 4, 9, 6, 1, 8, 0]
HashSet : 2 4 9 8 0 1 6. {2, 4, 9, 8, 0, 1, 6}
BTreeSet: 0 1 2 4 6 8 9. {0, 1, 2, 4, 6, 8, 9}
```

As you can see, the Vec collection contains all the ten inserted items, in insertion order; instead, the HashSet collection and the BTreeSet collection contains only seven items, as there is only one of the two 6 numbers, and only one of the three 8 numbers. Moreover, the BTreeSet collection is sorted, while the HashSet collection is in random order. A different run can generate a different order.

Here is some code to measure the performance of such collections:

```
const SIZE: u32 = 40_000;
// Creating empty collections.
let mut v = Vec::<_>::new();
let mut hs = std::collections::HashSet::<_>::new();
let mut bs = std::collections::BTreeSet::<_>::new();
// Adding elements to the collections,
// measuring the elapsed time.
let start_time = std::time::Instant::now();
for i in 0..SIZE { v.push(i); }
let t1 = start_time.elapsed();
for i in 0..SIZE { hs.insert(i); }
let t2 = start_time.elapsed();
for i in 0..SIZE { bs.insert(i); }
let t3 = start_time.elapsed();
for i in 0..SIZE { if ! v.contains(&i) { return; } }
let t4 = start_time.elapsed();
// Performing binary searches on a sorted vector,
// measuring the elapsed time.
v.swap(10_000, 20_000);
v.sort();
let t5 = start_time.elapsed();
for i in 0..SIZE {
    if v.binary_search(&i).is_err() { return; }
}
// Searching the hashtable, measuring the elapsed time.
let t6 = start_time.elapsed();
for i in 0..SIZE { if ! hs.contains(&i) { return; } }
// Searching the BTree, measuring the elapsed time.
let t7 = start_time.elapsed();
for i in 0..SIZE { if ! bs.contains(&i) { return; } }
let t8 = start_time.elapsed();
// Printing the measured times.
println!("Pushes into Vec: {:?} per item", t1 / SIZE);
println!("Insertions into HashSet: {:?} per item", (t2 - t1) / SIZE);
```

```
println!("Insertions into BTreeSet: {:?} per item", (t3 - t2) / SIZE);
println!("Linear search in Vec: {:?} per item", (t4 - t3) / SIZE);
println!("Sorting of Vec: {:?}", t5 - t4);
println!("Binary search in Vec: {:?} per item", (t6 - t5) / SIZE);
println!("Search in HashSet: {:?} per item", (t7 - t6) / SIZE);
println!("Search in BTreeSet: {:?} per item", (t8 - t7) / SIZE);
```

It could print:

```
Pushes into Vec: 8ns per item
Insertions into HashSet: 121ns per item
Insertions into BTreeSet: 148ns per item
Linear search in Vec: 9.217µs per item
Sorting of Vec: 116.76µs
Binary search in Vec: 37ns per item
Search in HashSet: 24ns per item
Search in BTreeSet: 40ns per item
```

To insert a four-byte number at the end of a Vec, 8 nanoseconds are taken, while inserting it into a HashSet or BTreeSet takes around 15 times as long.

To sequentially search that forty-thousand-items vector for an existing number, around 9,000 nanoseconds are taken. Then, the vector is sorted (actually it was already sorted, so two items are swapped beforehand, to make timing more realistic), in 116 microseconds. To search that sorted vector using the binary search algorithm, an item is found in less than 40 nanoseconds on average. It turns out that, if searches are at least 13 times as frequent as insertions, it is more efficient to sort the array after every insertion and then use binary search.

To search the HashSet for a number, about 24 nanoseconds are taken; and to search the BTreeSet for a number, about 40 nanoseconds are taken. So they are orders of magnitude faster than a vector; the only case in which a sorted Vec with binary search is competitive with a BTreeSet is when first there are all the insertions into the vector, then the vector is sorted once, and then there are only searches.

All this happens in a particular platform, with a particular type of item, with a particular number of items, and with a particular sequence of operations. If you change something of these, the algorithm that used to be slower can become the fastest one.

The best way to optimize a data structure whose performance is critical is as follows. First declare a trait having all the operations that your data structure will offer to the rest of the application. Then create the simplest possible implementation of such trait and use that trait and its methods in the rest of the program. Then you measure if the performance of such methods is good enough. If it is good enough, there is no need to optimize it. Otherwise, you keep changing the implementation of the trait, and you measure the performance of the application until you find a satisfying implementation.

Ordered Dictionaries and Unordered Dictionaries

Another commonly used kind of collection is the *dictionary*, which is a collection accessible by a search key.

Dictionaries can be considered sets of key-value pairs, with the peculiarity that the look-up is performed using only the key. As a consequence, a dictionary cannot contain two pairs having the same key, even if their values are different.

In this case also, there are several possible algorithms, and the two main ones are provided by the Rust standard library with the names HashMap and BTreeMap. The first one, similar to HashSet, is somewhat faster but does not keep the items ordered; the second one is slower, but it keeps the items ordered by their key:

```
let arr = [(640, 'T'), (917, 'C'), (412, 'S'),
    (670, 'T'), (917, 'L')];
let mut v = Vec::<_>::new();
let mut hs = std::collections::HashMap::<_, _>::new();
let mut bs = std::collections::BTreeMap::<_, _>::new();
for &(key, value) in arr.iter() {
    v.push((key, value));
    hs.insert(key, value);
    bs.insert(key, value);
}
print!("Vec:");
for &(key, value) in v.iter() {
    print!(" {}: {},", key, value);
}
println!("\n    {:?}", v);
print!("HashMap:");
```

```
for (key, value) in hs.iter() {
    print!(" {}: {},", key, value);
}
println!("\n     {:?}", hs);
print!("BTreeMap:");
for (key, value) in bs.iter() {
    print!(" {}: {},", key, value);
}
println!("\n     {:?}", bs);
```

It could print:

```
Vec: 640: T, 917: C, 412: S, 670: T, 917: L,
    [(640, 'T'), (917, 'C'), (412, 'S'), (670, 'T'), (917, 'L')]
HashMap: 917: L, 412: S, 640: T, 670: T,
    {917: 'L', 412: 'S', 640: 'T', 670: 'T'}
BTreeMap: 412: S, 640: T, 670: T, 917: L,
    {412: 'S', 640: 'T', 670: 'T', 917: 'L'}
```

An array containing five pairs is used as a source of data. Three other containers are declared and initialized as empty: a Vec, a HashMap, and a BtreeMap. Then, each pair of the array is inserted into such containers.

In fact, all of them will be inserted into the Vec, but only four of them will be inserted into the HashMap and into the BtreeMap, because they do not admit duplicate keys. When the pair (917, 'L') is inserted, it replaces the pair (917, 'C') already contained in the dictionary. Instead, duplicate values are allowed.

Notice that in the vector the items are in insertion order, in the BTreeMap collection they are in key order, and in the HashMap collection they are in random order.

Their performance is similar to that of the corresponding HashSet and BTreeSet collections.

Collections in C++ and in Rust

Those who know the C++ standard library will find useful the following table that corresponds C++ collections with Rust collections.

For some C++ collections there is no corresponding Rust collection. In such cases, the most similar collection is indicated, preceded by a tilde (~), to indicate an approximate correspondence. Such an indication should be particularly useful to those who have some C++ code to convert into Rust code.

C++	Rust
array<T>	[T]
vector<T>	Vec<T>
deque<T>	VecDeque<T>
forward_list<T>	~ LinkedList<T>
list<T>	LinkedList<T>
stack<T>	~ Vec<T>
queue<T>	~ VecDeque<T>
priority_queue<T>	BinaryHeap<T>
set<T>	BTreeSet<T>
multiset<T>	~ BTreeMap<T,u32>
map<K,V>	BTreeMap<K,V>
multimap<K,V>	~ BTreeMap<K,(V,u32)>
unordered_set<T>	HashSet<T>
unordered_multiset<T>	~ HashMap<T,u32>
unordered_map<K,V>	HashMap<K,V>
unordered_multimap<K,V>	~ HashMap<K,(V,u32)>

CHAPTER 22

Ownership, Moves, and Copies

In this chapter, you will learn:

- Why deterministic and implicit destruction of objects is a big plus of Rust

- The concept of ownership of objects

- The three kinds of assignment semantics: share semantics, copy semantics, and move semantics

- Why implicit share semantics is bad for software correctness

- Why move semantics may have better performance than copy semantics

- Why some types need copy semantics and others do not

- Why some types need to be noncloneable

- How to specify that a type must use copy semantics

- How to specify that a type is cloneable

Deterministic Destruction

So far, we saw several ways to allocate objects, both in the stack and in the heap:

- Each variable whose type is a primitive type or an array, and each argument of a function or a closure allocates an object in the stack.

© Carlo Milanesi 2022
C. Milanesi, *Beginning Rust*, https://doi.org/10.1007/978-1-4842-7208-4_22

- Each temporary object is allocated in the stack. A *temporary object* means a space of stack memory used only during the execution of a single statement.

- Each Box variable allocates a pointer in the stack and the referenced object in the heap.

- Each dynamic string and each collection (including vectors) allocates a header in the stack and a data object in the heap.

The *actual* instant when such objects are allocated is hard to predict, because it depends on compiler optimizations. So, let's consider the *conceptual* instant of such allocations.

Conceptually, every stack allocation happens when the corresponding expression first appears in code.

Every heap allocation happens when there is a need for such data. So:

- Box-ed objects are allocated when the Box::new function is called.

- Dynamic strings chars are allocated when some chars are added to a string.

- Collections contents are allocated when some data is added to a collection.

All this is not different from most programming languages.

And when does deallocation of a data item happen?

Conceptually, in Rust, it happens *automatically* when the data item is no more accessible. So:

- The objects allocated by variables whose type is a primitive type or an array are deallocated when the block containing the declaration of such variable ends.

- The objects allocated by arguments of functions or of closures are deallocated when their function/closure block ends.

- Temporary objects are deallocated when the statement that allocated them ends (that is, at the next semicolon or when the current block ends).

- Box-ed objects are deallocated when the block containing their declaration ends.

- Chars contained in dynamic strings are deallocated when they are removed from the string, or anyway when the block containing the string declaration ends.

- Items contained in collections are deallocated when they are removed from the collection, or anyway when the block containing the collection declaration ends.

These deallocation rules differentiate Rust from most programming languages. In any language that has temporary objects or stack-allocated objects, the objects of such kinds are deallocated automatically. But heap-allocated object deallocation differs for different languages.

In some languages, like Pascal, C, and C++, heap objects are usually deallocated only explicitly, by invoking functions like "`free`" or "`delete`." In other languages, like Java and C#, heap objects are not immediately deallocated when they are not reachable anymore, but there is a routine, run periodically, which finds unreachable heap objects and deallocates them. This mechanism is named "garbage collection" because it resembles the urban cleaning system: it periodically cleans the town when some garbage has piled up.

So, in C++ and similar languages, heap deallocation is both *deterministic and explicit*. It is deterministic, because it happens in well-defined positions of source code; and it is explicit, because it requires that the programmer writes a specific deallocation statement. To be deterministic is good, because it has better performance and it allows the programmer to better control what is going on in the computer. But to be explicit is bad, because if deallocations are performed wrongly, nasty bugs result.

In Java and similar languages, heap deallocation is both *nondeterministic and implicit*. It is nondeterministic because it happens in unknown instants of execution; and it is implicit because it does not require specific deallocation statements. To be nondeterministic is bad, but to be implicit is good.

Differing from both techniques, in Rust, usually, heap deallocation is both *deterministic and implicit*, and this is a great advantage of Rust over other languages.

This is possible because of the following mechanism, based on the concept of *ownership*.

Ownership

Let's introduce the term ***to own***. In computer programming, for an object A *to own* an object B means that *A is responsible for deallocating B*. That means two things:

- *Only* A can deallocate B.

- After A has become unreachable, A *must* deallocate B.

In Rust, there is no explicit deallocation mechanism, so the first of the two things is pointless, and this definition can be reworded in the following way. For object A to own object B means that *the Rust language deallocates B after and only after A has become unreachable.* Let's see an example:

```
let _num = Box::new(3);
```

In this tiny program, the Box::new call allocates a heap object that is an integer whose value is 3, and the declaration of the _num variable allocates a stack object that is a pointer whose value is the address of that integer object. We say that such pointer owns that integer, because when _num gets out of its block, and so becomes unreachable, the referenced integer object, containing the value 3, is deallocated. Here we have that a reference owns an object.

Not every reference owns an object, though, as this code shows:

```
let a = 3;
{
    let _a_ref = &a;
}
print!("{}", a);
```

Here, the _a_ref variable declaration allocates a reference, but that reference owns nothing. Indeed, at the end of the nested block, the _a_ref variable gets out of its block, so the reference is deallocated; however, the referenced object, which is the number having value 3, shouldn't be immediately deallocated, because it must be printed at the last statement.

To ensure that every object is automatically deallocated when it is referenced no more, Rust has this simple rule: *in every instant of execution, every heap object must have exactly one owner*: no more, no less. When that owner is deallocated, the object itself is deallocated. If there were several owners, the object could be deallocated several times, and this is a bug usually named *double free*. If there were no owners, the object could never be deallocated, and this is a bug named *memory leak*.

Assignment Semantics

It is quite easy to understand the assignment operation, when it concerns primitive types, which involve only stack allocation. Though, with objects involving heap allocation, assignment is not so simple to understand. For example, what does the following program do?

```
let v1 = vec![11, 22, 33];
#[allow(unused_variables)]
let v2 = v1;
```

The operations performed are these:

- A buffer for the contents of the vector is allocated in the heap.

- The three integers are copied onto that buffer.

- The header of v1 is allocated in the stack.

- The header of v1 is initialized, so that it references the newly allocated heap buffer.

- The header of v2 is allocated in the stack.

- The header of v2 is initialized, using v1. But, how is that initialization implemented?

In general, there are at least three ways to implement such operation:

- *Share semantics*: The header of v1 is copied onto the header of v2, and nothing else happens. Subsequently, both v1 and v2 can be used, and they both refer to the same heap buffer; therefore, they refer to the same object, not to two distinct objects having the same value. This semantics is implemented by garbage-collecting languages, like Java.

- *Copy semantics*: Another heap buffer is allocated. It is as large as the heap buffer used by v1, and the contents of the preexisting buffer are copied onto the new buffer. Then the header of v2 is initialized so that it references the newly allocated buffer. Therefore, the two variables refer to two distinct objects, which initially have the same value. This is implemented, by default, by C++.

- *Move semantics*: The header of v1 is copied onto the header of v2, and nothing else happens. Subsequently, v2 can be used, and it refers to the heap buffer that was allocated for v1, but v1 *cannot be used anymore*. This is implemented, by default, by Rust.

This code shows the move semantics used by Rust:

```
let v1 = vec![11, 22, 33];
#[allow(unused_variables)]
let v2 = v1;
print!("{}", v1.len());
```

The compilation of this code will generate, at the last line, the error: `borrow of moved value: `v1``. When the value of v1 is assigned to v2, the variable v1 *ceases to exist*. Trying to use it, even only to get its length, is disallowed by the compiler.

Let's see why Rust does not implement share semantics. First, if variables are mutable, such semantics would be somewhat confusing. With share semantics, after an item is changed through a variable, that item appears to be changed also when it is accessed through the other variable. It wouldn't be intuitive, and possibly it is a source of bugs. Therefore, share semantics would be acceptable only for read-only data.

But there is a bigger problem, regarding deallocation. If share semantics was used, both the header of v1 and the header of v2 would own the single data buffer, so when they are deallocated, the same heap buffer would be deallocated twice, causing memory corruption.

To solve this problem, the languages that use share semantics do not deallocate memory at the end of the block in which such memory is allocated. They resort to garbage collection.

Instead, both copy semantics and move semantics are correct. Indeed, the Rust rule regarding deallocation is that any object must have exactly one owner. When copy semantics is used, the original vector buffer keeps its single owner, which is the vector header referenced by v1; and the newly created vector buffer gets its single owner, which is the vector header referenced by v2. On the other hand, when move semantics is used, the single vector buffer changes owner: before the assignment, its owner is the vector header referenced by v1, and after the assignment, its owner is the vector header referenced by v2. Before the assignment, the v2 header does not exist yet, and after the assignment the v1 header does not exist anymore.

And why does Rust not implement copy semantics?

Actually, in some cases copy semantics is more appropriate, but in other cases move semantics is more appropriate. Even C++, since 2011, allows both copy semantics and move semantics. Here is a C++ program using both semantics:

```cpp
#include <iostream>
#include <vector>
int main() {
    auto v1 = std::vector<int> { 11, 22, 33 };
    const auto v2 = v1;
    const auto v3 = move(v1);
    std::cout << v1.size() << " "
        << v2.size() << " " << v3.size();
}
```

It will print: 0 3 3.

The first statement of the main function initializes the v1 vector. The second one copies that vector to the v2 vector. The third statement moves the contents of v1 to the v3 vector. The last statement prints the current length of the vectors.

The move C++ standard function copies the value of a vector header to another vector header, like Rust assignments do.

In addition, in C++, the move function empties the source vector (v1). This happens because, in C++, a statement cannot make a variable undefined, so the moved object (v1) must have a valid value.

Therefore, at the end of the program, v2 has a copy of the three items, v3 has just the original three items that were created for v1, and v1 is empty.

In Rust, the way to perform both copy semantics and move semantics is this:

```rust
let v1 = vec![11, 22, 33];
let v2 = v1.clone();
let v3 = v1;
// ILLEGAL: print!("{} ", v1.len());
print!("{} {}", v2.len(), v3.len());
```

This will print 3 3.

This Rust program is similar to the previously shown C++ program.

While in C++ the default semantics is a copy, and it is needed to invoke the move standard function to make a move, in Rust the default semantics is a move, and it is needed to invoke the clone standard function to make a copy. So, the second statement copies the buffer of v1 to v2, and the third statement moves the buffer of v1 to v3.

In addition, while the v1 moved vector in C++ is still accessible, but emptied, in Rust such a variable is not accessible at all anymore. So, the last-but-one statement is not allowed. If it is compiled, it would generate the error: borrow of moved value: `v1`.

Copying vs. Moving Performance

The choice of Rust to favor move semantics is about performance. For an object that owns a heap buffer, like a vector, it is faster to *move* it than to *copy* it, because a move of the vector is just a copy of the header; while a copy of the vector requires allocating and initializing a potentially large heap buffer, which eventually will be deallocated. In general, the design choices of Rust are to allow any operation, but to use a more compact notation for the safest and more efficient operations.

In addition, in C++, moved objects are not meant to be used anymore, but, to keep the language backward-compatible with the legacy code base, moved objects are still accessible, and there is the chance that a programmer erroneously uses such objects. In addition, to empty a moved vector has a (small) cost, and when a vector is destructed it should be checked if it is empty, and that also has a (small) cost. Rust has been designed to avoid using moved objects, so there is no chance of erroneously using a moved vector; and the compiler can produce better code because it knows when a vector is moved.

Moving and Destroying Objects

All these concepts apply not only to vectors but also to any object that has a reference to a heap object, like a String or a Box.

This is a Rust program:

```
let s1 = "abcd".to_string();
let s2 = s1.clone();
let s3 = s1;
```

```
// ILLEGAL: print!("{} ", s1.len());
print!("{} {}", s2.len(), s3.len());
```

It will print: 4 4. Any attempt to access s1 at the end of the program will cause a compilation error.

This is a similar C++ program:

```
#include <iostream>
#include <string>
int main() {
    auto s1 = std::string { "abcd" };
    const auto s2 = s1;
    const auto s3 = move(s1);
    std::cout << s1.size() << " "
        << s2.size() << " " << s3.size();
}
```

It will print: 0 4 4, because the moved string s1 has become empty, but it is still accessible.

And this Rust program:

```
let i1 = Box::new(12345i16);
let i2 = i1.clone();
let i3 = i1;
// ILLEGAL: print!("{} ", i1);
print!("{} {}", i2, i3);
```

will print: 12345 12345. Any attempt to access i1 at the end of the program will cause a compilation error.

It is similar to this C++ program:

```
#include <iostream>
#include <memory>
int main() {
    auto i1 = std::unique_ptr<short> {
        new short(12345)
    };
```

```
    const auto i2 = std::unique_ptr<short> {
        new short(*i1)
    };
    const auto i3 = move(i1);
    std::cout << (bool)i1 << " " << (bool)i2 << " "
        << (bool)i3 << " " << *i2 << " " << *i3;
}
```

It will print: 0 1 1 12345 12345. The last statement first checks which unique pointers are null, by casting them to the bool type; only i1 is null, because it was moved to i3. Then, the values referenced by i2 and i3 are printed.

In Rust, objects are not moved only when they are used to initialize a variable, but also when assigning a variable already having a value, like in this code:

```
let v1 = vec![false; 3];
let mut _v2 = vec![false; 2];
_v2 = v1;
v1;
```

and also when passing a value to a function argument, like in this code:

```
fn f(_v2: Vec<bool>) {}
let v1 = vec![false; 3];
f(v1);
v1;
```

and also when the assigned object at the moment does not refer to an actual heap, like in this code:

```
let v1 = vec![false; 0];
let mut _v2 = vec![false; 0];
_v2 = v1;
v1;
```

Compiling any of the previous three programs, the last statement causes the compilation error: use of moved value: `v1`.

In particular, in the last program, the compiler complains that v1 is *moved* to _v2, even if they are both empty, and so no heap is used. Why? Because the rule of moves is applied by the compiler, so it must be independent of the actual content of an object at runtime. It is because the most important principle of Rust is that it is better to know of possible errors at compile time rather than at runtime. At compile time, in general, the compiler cannot know whether a vector will be empty or not empty when it is involved in an assignment.

But also, compiling the following program causes an error at the last line. How come?

```
struct S {}
let s1 = S {};
let _s2 = s1;
s1;
```

Here, the compiler can be sure that such objects won't contain references to the heap, but still it complains about moves. Why does Rust not use copy semantics for this type that will never have references to the heap?

Here is the rationale for this. The user-defined type S now has no references to memory, but after future maintenance of the software, one reference to the heap may easily be added, as a field of S or as a field of a field of S, and so on. So, if we now implement copy semantics for S, when the program source is changed so that a String or Box or a collection is added to S, directly or indirectly, a lot of errors would be caused by this semantic change. So, as a rule, it's better to keep move semantics by default.

Need for Copy Semantics

So, we have seen that for many types of objects, including vectors, dynamic strings, boxes, and structs, move semantics is used by default. Yet, the following program is valid:

```
let i1 = 123;
let _i2 = i1;
let s1 = "abc";
let _s2 = s1;
let r1 = &i1;
let _r2 = r1;
print!("{} {} {}", i1, s1, r1);
```

It will print: 123 abc 123. How come there is no moved variable?

Well, the fact is that for primitive numbers, static strings, and references, Rust does not use move semantics. For these data types, Rust uses copy semantics.

Why? We saw previously that if an object can own one or more heap objects, its type should implement move semantics; but if it cannot own any heap memory, it can implement copy semantics just as well. Move semantics is a nuisance for primitive types, and it is improbable that they will ever be changed to own some heap objects. So, for them, copy semantics is safe, efficient, and more convenient.

So, some Rust types implement copy semantics, and others implement move semantics. In particular, copy semantics is used by numbers, Booleans, static strings, arrays, tuples, and references. Instead, move semantics is used, by default, by dynamic strings, boxes, any collection (including vectors), enums, structs, and tuple-structs.

Cloning Objects

With regard to the copying of objects, there is another important distinction to apply, regarding which objects it makes sense to copy.

All the types that implement copy semantics can be copied quite easily, with an assignment; but objects that implement move semantics also can be copied, using the `clone` standard function. We already saw that a `clone` function can be applied to dynamic strings, boxes, and vectors. However, for some kinds of types, a `clone` function shouldn't be applicable, because no kind of copying is appropriate. Think about a file handle, a GUI window handle, or a mutex handle. If you make some copies of one such handle and then you destroy one of the copies, the underlying resource gets released, and the other copies of the handle will be referencing an inexistent resource.

So, regarding the ability to be copied, there are three kinds of objects:

- Objects that cannot own anything, and are easy and cheap to copy, and that will remain always so.

- Objects that may own some heap objects but do not own external resources, so they can be copied, but with a significant runtime cost.

- Objects that own an external resource, like a file handle or a GUI window handle, so they should never be copied.

The types of the first kind of objects can implement copy semantics, and they should, because it is more convenient. Let's call them *copyable objects*.

The types of the second kind of objects can implement copy semantics, but they should implement move semantics instead, to avoid the runtime cost of unneeded duplications. Moreover, they should provide a method to explicitly duplicate them. Let's call them *cloneable but noncopyable objects*.

The types of the third kind of objects should implement move semantics, too. But they shouldn't provide a method to explicitly duplicate them, because they own a resource that cannot be duplicated by Rust code, and such resource should have just one owner. Let's call them *noncloneable objects*.

Of course, any object that can be automatically copied can also be explicitly copied, so any copyable object is also a cloneable object.

To summarize, some objects are noncloneable (like file handles), and other are cloneables (explicitly). Some cloneable objects are also (implicitly) copyable (like numbers), while others are noncopyable (like collections).

To distinguish among these three categories, the Rust standard library contains two specific traits: `Copy` and `Clone`. Any type implementing the `Copy` trait is copyable; any type implementing the `Clone` trait is cloneable.

So, the three kinds described are characterized in this way:

- The objects, like primitive numbers, that implement both `Copy` and `Clone`, are *copyable* (and also *cloneable*). They implement copy semantics, and they can also be cloned explicitly.

- The objects, like collections, that implement `Clone`, but don't implement `Copy`, are *cloneable but noncopyable*. They implement move semantics, but they can be cloned explicitly.

- The objects, like file handles, that implement neither `Copy` nor `Clone`, are *noncloneable* (and also *noncopyable*). They implement move semantics, and they cannot be cloned.

- No object can implement `Copy` but not `Clone`. This means that no object is *copyable but not cloneable*. This is because such object would be copied implicitly but not explicitly, and this is pointless.

Here is an example of all these cases:

```
let a1 = 123;
let b1 = a1.clone();
let c1 = b1;
print!("{} {} {}", a1, b1, c1);
let a2 = Vec::<bool>::new();
let b2 = a2.clone();
let c2 = b2;
print!(" {:?}", a2);
// ILLEGAL: print!("{:?}", b2);
print!(" {:?}", c2);
let a3 = std::fs::File::open(".").unwrap();
// ILLEGAL: let b3 = a3.clone();
let c3 = a3;
// ILLEGAL: print!("{:?}", a3);
print!(" {:?}", c3);
```

This program will print: `123 123 123 [] []` `File`, and then some information regarding your current directory, like: `{ fd: 3, path: "/home/yourname/yourdir", read: true, write: false }`. It can be compiled only because the three illegal statements have been commented out.

First, `a1` is declared as a primitive number. Such type is copyable, and so it can be both explicitly cloned to `b1` and implicitly copied to `c1`. So, there are three distinct objects having the same value, and we can print them all.

Then, `a2` is declared as a collection, and specifically a vector of Booleans. Such type is cloneable but not copyable, so it can be explicitly cloned to `b2`, but the assignment of `b2` to `c2` is a move, which leaves `b2` as undefined. So, after that assignment, we can print `a2` and `c2`, but trying to compile the statement that prints `b2` would generate an error with the message: `borrow of moved value: `b2``.

At last, `a3` is declared as a resource handle, specifically a file handle. Such type is not cloneable, so trying to compile the statement that clones `a3` would generate an error with the message: `no method named `clone` found for struct `File` in the current scope`. It is allowed to assign `a3` to `c3`, but it is a move; so we can print some debug information about `c3`, but trying to compile the statement that prints `a3` would generate an error with the message: `borrow of moved value: `a3``.

Making Types Cloneable or Copyable

As said before, enums, structs, and tuple structs, by default, do not implement either the Copy trait or the Clone trait, so they are noncloneable. Though, you may implement the single Clone trait for each of them, of both the Clone trait and the Copy trait.

Let's start from this illegal program:

```
struct S {}
let s = S {};
let _ = s.clone();
```

It is enough to implement the Clone trait for our user-defined type, to make it valid:

```
struct S {}
impl Clone for S {
    fn clone(&self) -> Self { Self {} }
}
let s = S {};
let _ = s.clone();
```

Notice that to implement the Clone trait requires defining the clone method, which must return a value whose type must be equal to the type of its argument. The returned value should be equal to the value of its argument, but that is not checked by the compiler.

Implementing Clone does not automatically implement Copy, so the following program is illegal:

```
struct S {}
impl Clone for S {
    fn clone(&self) -> Self { Self {} }
}
let s = S {};
let _ = s.clone();
let _s2 = s;
let _s3 = s;
```

The last-but-one statement moves away the value from the s variable, and the last statement tries to access the value of such variable. But is it enough to also implement the Copy trait, to make it valid:

```
struct S {}
impl Clone for S {
    fn clone(&self) -> Self { Self {} }
}
impl Copy for S {}
let s = S {};
let _ = s.clone();
let _s2 = s;
let _s3 = s;
```

Notice that an implementation of Copy can be empty; it is enough to declare that Copy is implemented, to activate the copy semantics.

The following program is illegal, though:

```
struct S {}
impl Copy for S {}
```

The error message explains why: the trait bound `S: Clone` is not satisfied. The Copy trait can be implemented only if the Clone trait is also implemented.

But the following program also is illegal:

```
struct S { x: Vec<i32> }
impl Copy for S {}
impl Clone for S {
    fn clone(&self) -> Self { *self }
}
```

The error message says: the trait `Copy` may not be implemented for this type, indicating the type Vec<i32>.

The program tries to implement the Copy trait for a struct containing a vector. Rust allows you to implement the Copy trait only for types that contain only copyable objects, because copying an object means to copy all its members. Here, Vec does not implement the Copy trait, so S cannot implement it.

Instead, the following program is valid:

```
struct S { x: Vec<i32> }
impl Clone for S {
    fn clone(&self) -> Self {
        S { x: self.x.clone() }
    }
}
let mut s1 = S { x: vec![12] };
let s2 = s1.clone();
s1.x[0] += 1;
print!("{} {}", s1.x[0], s2.x[0]);
```

It will print: 13 12.

Here, the S struct is not copyable, but it is cloneable because it implements the Clone trait. Therefore, a duplicate of s1 can be assigned to s2. After that assignment, only s1 is modified, and the print statement shows that they are actually different.

CHAPTER 23

Borrowing and Lifetimes

In this chapter, you will learn:

- The typical programming errors concerning references, which Rust helps to avoid: *use after move*, *use after drop*, and *use after change by an alias*

- The concept of *borrowing* of Rust references

- The concept of *lifetime* of Rust objects and references

- How Rust helps to avoid *use after drop* errors

- How Rust, with its borrow checker, helps to avoid *use after change by an alias* errors

- Why functions returning references need lifetime specifiers

- How to use lifetime specifiers for functions, and what they mean

- Why it may be better to use several lifetime specifiers in a function

Programming Errors when Using References

We already saw that when you assign a variable to another variable, there are two cases: either their type is copyable, that is, it implements the Copy trait (and necessarily it implements the Clone trait too); or their type is not copyable, that is it does not implement the Copy trait (and it may implement the Clone trait or it may not).

In the first case, *copy semantics* is used. That means that a new object is created by that assignment; the original object remains represented by the source variable, and the new object is represented by the destination variable. Initially that new object has the same value of the original object. When each of these two variables gets out of their scope, the objects they represent are destroyed (a.k.a. *dropped*).

© Carlo Milanesi 2022
C. Milanesi, *Beginning Rust*, https://doi.org/10.1007/978-1-4842-7208-4_23

In the second case, *move semantics* is used. That means that, in an assignment, the source variable hands over its represented object to the destination variable. No object is created, and the source variable becomes no longer accessible. When the destination variable gets out of its scope, its represented object is destroyed. When the source variable gets out of its scope, nothing happens.

These behaviors guarantee the proper management of memory, *as long as no references are used*.

Programs written in C and C++ are plagued by errors concerning lifetime of objects, which Rust avoids by design. One such error is the *use after move* error, seen in Chapter 22 whenever the compiler emitted the error message borrow of moved value. Another one is exemplified by the following program:

```
let ref_to_n;
{
    let n = 12;
    ref_to_n = &n;
}
print!("{}", *ref_to_n);
```

First, the ref_to_n variable is declared, but not initialized. Then, in an inner block, the n immutable variable is declared and initialized, and so it allocates a number in the stack, whose value is 12.

Then, the former variable is initialized with a reference to the n variable.

Then, the inner block ends, so the inner variable n ends its scope and its associated object is destroyed.

Then, the object referred to by the ref_to_n variable is printed. But that object has already been destroyed, and now it doesn't exist anymore! Fortunately, the Rust compiler rejects this code, emitting the error message: `n` does not live long enough.

That message means that the n variable is dying at the end of the block in which it is declared, but there are still some references to the object it represents. In particular, the ref_to_n variable still references the object represented by the n variable. In addition, such reference is used later, at the last line of the program.

So, the n variable should definitely live longer; it should live at least as long as all the uses of the references to the objects it represents.

By the way, the corresponding C and C++ program is this:

```c
#include <stdio.h>
int main() {
    int* ref_to_n;
    {
        int n = 12;
        ref_to_n = &n;
    }
    printf("%d", *ref_to_n);
    return 0;
}
```

This program is accepted by all C and C++ compilers. The resulting program behaves in an unpredictable way (although usually it prints another number).

Let's name this kind of programming error *use after drop*, in which an object is used (read or written) after it has already been destroyed, and so, in a way, it does not exist anymore.

But there is another kind of error avoided by Rust, exemplified by the following program:

```rust
let mut v = vec![12]; // A vector is allocated and initialized
let ref_to_first = &v[0]; // A reference to it is taken
v.push(13); // The vector is mutated
print!("{}", *ref_to_first); // The reference accesses the vector
// The vector is implicitly deallocated
```

The corresponding program in C language is this:

```c
#include <stdio.h>
#include <stdlib.h>
int main() {
    // A vector is allocated and initialized
    int* v = malloc(1 * sizeof (int));
    v[0] = 12;
    // A reference to it is taken
    const int* ref_to_first = &v[0];
```

```
    // The vector is mutated
    v = realloc(v, 2 * sizeof (int));
    v[1] = 13;
    // The reference accesses the vector
    printf("%d", *ref_to_first);
    // The vector is explicitly deallocated
    free(v);
}
```

and in C++ it is this:

```
#include <iostream>
#include <vector>
int main() {
    // A vector is allocated and initialized
    std::vector<int> v { 12 };
    const int& ref_to_first = v[0]; // A reference to it is taken
    v.push_back(13); // The vector is mutated
    std::cout << ref_to_first; // The reference accesses the vector
    // The vector is implicitly deallocated
}
```

Needless to say, the latter two programs are accepted by the respective compilers, even if their behavior is undefined. Instead, the Rust compiler rejects the first program, emitting the error message: cannot borrow `v` as mutable because it is also borrowed as immutable. Let's see what's wrong with this Rust program.

First, the v mutable variable is declared and initialized with a vector object containing only the number 12.

Then, the ref_to_first variable is declared and initialized with a reference to the first item of v. So, it is a reference to the object whose value is 12.

Then, another number is added to the vector, whose value is 13. But such an insertion could cause a reallocation in another place of the buffer containing the items of the vector. Even in such a case, the ref_to_first variable would continue to refer to the old, no longer valid, memory location.

At last, the old, possibly wrong, memory location is read and its value is printed, with unpredictable results.

This error has been caused by the fact that inserting items to or removing items from a vector *invalidates* all the references to that vector. In general, this error belongs to a broader category of errors, in which a data structure is accessible through several paths, or aliases; and when that data structure is changed using one alias, it cannot be properly used by another alias.

Let's name this kind of programming error *use after change by an alias*.

To understand how you, with the help of the Rust compiler, can avoid such bugs, the concept of borrowing must be introduced.

Borrowing

Look at this code:

```
let n = 12;
let _ref_to_n = &n;
```

After the second statement, the _ref_to_n variable represents a reference, and it references the same number represented by the n variable. Can we say that the object represented by the _ref_to_n variable owns the object whose value is 12? Is this relation an ownership or not?

It cannot be an ownership, because that number is already represented by the n variable, so it will be deallocated when the control flow exits the block in which that variable is declared. If it was owned by this reference, then it would be deallocated twice. So, normal references (excluding Box objects and inner references in vectors, strings, and other collections) never own an object.

The concept of a reference that does not own the referenced object is named **borrowing**. In the Rust documentation, this word is usually shortened to **borrow**, as a noun. We already saw this word in some compiler error messages.

We say that the _ref_to_n variable *borrows* the number represented by n. The borrow begins when the reference begins to refer to that object, and ends the last time that variable is used with that value. In this case, there is only one use, so that borrow begins and ends in the same statement. But let's consider a more complex example:

```
let a = 12;
let mut b = &a; // start of first borrow of a to b
let c = &a; // start of borrow of a to c
```

```
print!("{} {} ", b, c); // end of borrows of a to b and c
b = &23; // start of second borrow of a to b
print!("{}", b); // end of second borrow of a to b
```

It will print: 12 12 23. The first statement declares a variable that represents a stack-allocated number, whose value is 12. In the second statement, the b variable borrows that number.

The b variable receives another value in the fifth statement, so the previous borrow terminates before this statement. The last use of b before this assignment is in the fourth statement. Therefore, the first borrow terminates there.

The third statement begins a borrow in which the c variable borrows the same object borrowed also by b. Such borrow terminates at the last use of c, in the fourth statement.

The fifth statement begins a borrow in which the b variable borrows a stack-allocated object, whose value is 23, and that is not represented by any variable. Such borrow terminates at the last use of b, in the sixth statement.

Regarding mutability, there are two kinds of borrow, mutable and immutable, like this code shows:

```
let mut n = 12;
let ref1_to_n = &mut n;
let ref2_to_n = &n;
```

In this program, the second statement begins and ends a *mutable borrow*, while the third statement begins and ends an *immutable borrow*. As known, you can take a mutable borrow only from a mutable variable.

Object Lifetimes

We have seen several times the concept of *scope*, which is the block in which an identifier is defined. That concept is related to syntax, and so to compile time, not to run time.

The relative concept related to runtime objects is named **lifetime**. The lifetime of an object is the sequence of instruction executions that starts when a value is assigned to that object, and that ends when that object is destroyed, that is, when it becomes invalid.

The start of the lifetime of an object can be an initialization or any successive assignment to a mutable variable.

Actually, we can talk about lifetimes even regarding references. The lifetime of a reference is defined to be just what has been already named *borrow*.

To determine when a lifetime ends, it is required to make a distinction between references and the other kinds of objects.

For an object that is not a reference, the lifetime ends when that object ceases to have a value, and so it is dropped. This happens when the object receives another value, or when the scope of the variable representing it ends.

Instead, the lifetime of a reference ends just after the last statement that uses that object. References do not own objects, and they do not implement the Drop trait, so nothing happens when their lifetime ends.

A lifetime that corresponds to the scope of a variable is named *lexical lifetime*. So, references have a *nonlexical lifetime*, and the other kinds of object have a lexical lifetime.

During its lifetime, an object is said *to live* or *to be alive*.

How to Prevent *Use After Drop* Errors

The technique used by Rust to prevent *use after drop* errors is simple.

Any such error is caused by a reference that accesses its referenced object in a statement in which that object is no longer defined. So in that statement, the borrow is still alive but the referenced object is no longer alive.

To avoid that a borrow references an invalid object in any statement, it is required that the borrow begins when the object has already been created, and that the borrow ends when the object has not yet been destroyed.

Put in other words, the borrow must be fully contained in the lifetime of the referenced object.

There are two possible violations of this rule. One is to begin the borrow before the object lifetime has begun, like in this code:

```
let _n;
let _r = &_n;
_n = 12;
```

Here the borrow begins and ends in the second statement, but the lifetime of the object whose value is 12 begins in the third statement, and so the borrow is not contained in it. The compiler emits the message: borrow of possibly-uninitialized variable: `_n`. The compiler output also contains the indication that, at the second line, there is a use of possibly-uninitialized `_n`. It means that a borrow of an object, that is a kind of use of an object, cannot be performed if the compiler is not sure that such object has been initialized already.

The other error case is to end the borrow after the object lifetime has ended, like in this code:

```
let _r;
{
    let _n = 12;
    _r = &_n;
}
print!("{}", _r);
```

Here, the borrow begins at the fourth line and ends at the sixth, but the lifetime of the object whose value is 12 begins at the third line and ends at the fifth line, so the borrow is not contained in it. The compiler emits the message: `_n` does not live long enough. This message means that the lifetime of the object represented by _n should be extended to include the last line. Though, this situation could also be interpreted as that the borrow should be shortened to end before the closed brace.

How to Prevent *Use After Change by an Alias* Errors

The rules to avoid using an object that is changed through another variable are somewhat more complex.

First of all, the concept of temporary borrow must be introduced. It is shown by the following example:

```
let mut _n = 12;
{
    let _ref_n = &_n; // starts an immutable borrow of _n
    let _m = _n; // temporary immutable borrow of _n
    let _k = *_ref_n; // ends the first immutable borrow of _n
}
_n = 13; // temporary mutable borrow of _n
_n += 1; // temporary mutable borrow of _n
```

We already know that getting a reference starts a borrow. The third line starts an immutable borrow of _n. Such borrow ends two lines later, at the last use of that reference.

But also the fourth line accesses _n, so we must say that even it starts a borrow, though such access lasts only for the duration of the statement. After that assignment, the object represented by _n and the object represented by _m are not dependent on each other. A borrow that lasts no more than a single statement is named *temporary borrow*. So, at the fourth line we have a temporary borrow of the object represented by _n.

At the seventh line, the _n variable is the destination of an assignment. So, it is accessed, and therefore we must say that also this statement starts a borrow of _n. This statement does not involve other objects, so even this borrow ends in the statements itself. Therefore also in this statement there is a temporary borrow.

This last borrow is different from the previous one, though. In the fourth line, the borrowed object was accessed just for reading it, so it was an *immutable borrow* even if the _n variable itself was mutable. Instead, this last borrow, at the seventh line, accessed the borrowed object for writing it, so it was a *mutable borrow.*

The last line of the example increments _n. This requires both reading and writing the object. When both reading and writing can happen, the writing capability prevails, so we say that even this one is a mutable borrow.

Summarizing, any statement that reads an object, and does not write to it, must be considered as a *temporary immutable borrow* of that object; and any statement that changes an object must be considered as a *temporary mutable borrow* of that object. Such borrows start and end within that statement.

Given that, consider that we have this kind of error when an object is simultaneously referenced by several variables, and its value is changed. To be possible to change the value, at least one variable must have mutable access to such object.

So, the rule to avoid *use after change by an alias* errors is simply this: *any object, in any point of the code, cannot have at the same time a mutable borrow and some other borrows (mutable or immutable).*

Put in other words, any object can have, at any time:

- No borrows

- A single mutable borrow

- A single immutable borrow

- Several immutable borrows

But it cannot have:

- Several mutable borrows
- A single mutable borrow and one or more immutable borrows

So, for each object, Rust computes the lifetime of each borrow of that object, that is the time from a reference initialization or assignment to the last use of that reference value, and computes the intersection of these lifetimes. If a mutable borrow lifetime intersects another borrow lifetime, mutable or immutable, that's a programming error.

To put it clearly, let's repeat the same rules in another way. The only operations allowed on a not-currently-borrowed object are the following ones:

1. It can be borrowed several times only immutably, and then it can be read only by the variable that represents it, or by its single owner, and by any borrower.

2. It can be mutably borrowed only once at a time, and then it can be read or changed only through such borrower.

These rules were adopted by Rust to ensure automatic deterministic memory deallocation, and to avoid invalid references; though, curiously, these rules were already well known in computer science for other reasons. *Allow only one writer or several readers* is the rule to avoid the so-called *data races* in concurrent programming. So, this rule allows also Rust to have data-race-free concurrent programs.

In addition, avoiding data races also has a good impact on the performance of single-threaded programs, because it eases CPU cache coherence.

The Need for Lifetime Specifiers in Returned References

So far, we have seen how to handle references defined and used inside a sequence of statements, without using function calls. Now look at this valid code:

```
let n1 = 11;
let result;
{
    let n2 = 12;
```

```
    result = {
        let _m1 = &n1;
        let _m2 = &n2;
        _m1
    }
}
print!("{}", *result);
```

It will print: 11.

There are the declarations of the variables n1 and n2 representing two objects, whose values are numbers. Then, each of these objects is borrowed by a reference; such references are represented by the variables _m1 and _m2. So, after the seventh line, _m1 is borrowing the object represented by n1, and _m2 is borrowing the object represented by n2. This is allowed, because _m1 is declared after n1, and _m2 is declared after n2, so these references begin to live after the objects they borrow. Such references die at the first closed brace, while the object represented by n1 dies at the end of the program, and the object represented by n2 dies at the second closed brace. So the references die before the points where the referenced objects die.

At the eighth line, there is the simple expression _m1. As it is the last expression of a block, the value of that expression becomes the value of the block itself, so the value is used to initialize the result variable. That value is a reference to the number represented by n1, so the result variable also borrows that number. This is Also allowed, because result is declared in the same block of n1, but after it, so it can borrow the object represented by n1.

Now, let's make a tiny change: in the eighth line, let's replace the character 1 with the character 2, obtaining this code:

```
let n1 = 11;
let result;
{
    let n2 = 12;
    result = {
        let _m1 = &n1;
        let _m2 = &n2;
        _m2
    }
}
print!("{}", *result);
```

This code will generate the compilation error: `` `n2` does not live long enough. ``
This happens because now `result` gets its value from the `_m2` expression, and as `_m2`
borrows the object represented by `n2`, `result` also borrows that object. But `n2` is declared
inside the outer block, so it will die at the last-but-one statement, before `result` dies, and
therefore `result` cannot borrow its object.

All this reasoning is just a review of what we have already seen about borrowing, but
it shows how borrowing can get complicated in just few lines. By the way, the portion of
the Rust compiler dedicated to such reasoning is named ***borrow checker***. We just saw
that the borrow checker has a rather hard job to do.

Now, let's try to transform the two previous programs, by encapsulating in a function
the code in the innermost block. The first program becomes:

```
let n1 = 11;
let result;
{
    let n2 = 12;
    fn func(_m1: &i32, _m2: &i32) -> &i32 {
        _m1
    }
    result = func(&n1, &n2);
}
print!("{}", *result);
```

Declaring and initializing variables is like passing arguments to a function. Assigning
the value of a block to a variable is like assigning the return value of a function to a variable.

The second program becomes:

```
let n1 = 11;
let result;
{
    let n2 = 12;
    fn func(_m1: &i32, _m2: &i32) -> &i32 {
        _m2
    }
    result = func(&n1, &n2);
}
print!("{}", *result);
```

384

The only difference between them is the body of the func function.

According to our rules so far, the first program should be valid, and the second one should be illegal. Instead, the compiler refuses to compile both programs. Actually, both versions of the func function are valid *per se*. It's just the borrow checker that would find them incompatible with their specific usage.

As we already saw about generic function parameter bounds using traits, it is a bad thing to consider valid or invalid a function invocation according to the contents of the body of such function; or, put in other words, to consider valid or invalid a function declaration according to the context in which such function is invoked.

The main reason for this is that an error message for a bad use of a function would be understandable only by those who know the code inside the body of the function.

One other reason is that, if the body of any invoked function can make valid or invalid the code where the function is invoked, to be sure that the main function is valid, the borrow checker should analyze all the functions of the program. Such a whole-program analysis would be overwhelmingly complex.

So, similarly to generic functions, functions returning a reference also must isolate the borrow checking at the function signature threshold. There is the need to borrow check any function considering only its signature, its body, and the signatures of any invoked functions, without considering the bodies of the invoked functions. Of course, such bodies will be checked when these functions are separately borrow checked.

For both the previous programs, the compiler emits the message: `missing lifetime specifier`. *Lifetime specifiers* will be explained in the next section. They are decorations of function signatures that allow the borrow checker to separately check any function.

Usage and Meaning of Lifetime Specifiers

To talk about function invocations and lifetimes, here is a simple example function:

```
fn func(n: u32, b: &bool) {
    let s = "Hello".to_string();
}
```

Consider that, inside any Rust function, you can refer only to:

1. Objects represented by function arguments (like the number n), or objects owned by them

2. Objects represented by local variables (like the dynamic string s), or objects owned by them

3. Temporary objects (like the dynamic string expression "Hello". to_string()), or objects owned by them

4. Static objects (like the string literal "Hello"), or objects owned by them

5. Objects that are borrowed by function arguments, and that preexist the current function invocation (like the Boolean borrowed by b), or objects owned by them

When a function returns a reference, the reference cannot refer to an object represented by an argument of that function or owned by it (case 1), or represented by a local variable of that function or owned by it (case 2), or to a temporary object or an object owned by it (case 3), because, before that function returns, every one of such objects is destroyed. So, the reference would be dangling, that is, referencing an already destroyed object.

Instead, a reference returned by a function can fall in these other two cases:

- To refer to a static object or to an object owned by that object (case 4). Let's name this case: *borrowing a static object*.

- To refer to an object borrowed by a function argument or to an object owned by that object (case 5). Let's name this case: *borrowing an argument*.

Here is an example of borrowing a static object (although this code is not really allowed by Rust):

```
fn func() -> &str {
    "Hello"
}
```

And here is an example of borrowing an argument:

```
fn func(v: &Vec<u8>) -> &u8 {
    &v[3]
}
```

The borrow checker is interested only in the references contained in the return value, and such references can only be of two kinds: those that borrow a static object and those that borrow a function argument. To accomplish its job of analyzing a function without analyzing the body of the functions invoked by it, the borrow checker needs to know which returned references borrow static objects and which borrow a function argument. And for every returned reference that borrows a function argument, the borrow checker needs to know which function argument it borrows, in case that function receives several references as arguments.

Let's see a function signature without lifetime specifiers, and therefore illegal:

```
trait Tr {
    fn f(flag: bool, b: &i32, c: (char, &i32))
    -> (&i32, f64, &i32);
}
```

This function signature has two references among its arguments, and also two references inside its return value type. Each of the last two references could borrow a static object, or the object already borrowed by the b argument, or the object already borrowed by the second field of the c argument.

Here is the syntax to specify a possible case:

```
trait Tr {
    fn f<'a>(flag: bool, b: &'a i32, c: (char, &'a i32))
        -> (&'a i32, f64, &'static i32);
}
```

Just after the name of the function, a parameter list has been added, like the one used for generic functions. But instead of a type parameter, there is a lifetime specifier.

The <'a> clause is just a declaration. It means: *In this function signature, a lifetime specifier is used; its name is "a"*. The name a is arbitrary. It simply means that in all the occurrences it appears, such occurrences *match*. It is similar to the type parameters of generic functions. To distinguish lifetime specifiers from type parameters, the former ones are prefixed by a single quote. In addition, while by convention type parameters begin with an uppercase letter, lifetime specifiers are single lowercase letters, like a, b, or c.

Then, this signature contains three other occurrences of the 'a lifetime specifier: in the type of the b argument, in the second field of the type of the c argument, and in the first field of the return value type. But the third field of the return value type is annotated by the 'static lifetime specifier.

The use of the a lifetime specifier means: *the first field of the return value borrows the same object already borrowed by the b argument and by the second field of the c argument, so it must live for less time than such objects.*

The use of the static lifetime specifier means: *the third field of the return value refers to a static object, so it can live for any time, even as long as the whole process.*

Of course this was just one possible lifetime annotation. Here is another one:

```
trait Tr {
    fn f<'a>(flag: bool, b: &'a i32, c: (char, &i32))
        -> (&'static i32, f64, &'a i32);
}
```

In this case, the first field of the return value has a static lifetime, meaning that it is not constrained to live less than some other object. Instead, the third field has the same lifetime specifier as the b argument, meaning that it should live less than it, as it borrows the same object. The reference in the type of the c argument is not annotated, as the object it refers is not borrowed by any reference in the return value.

Here is still another possible lifetime annotation:

```
trait Tr {
    fn f<'a, 'b, T1, T2>(flag: bool, b: &'a T1,
    c: (char, &'b i32)) -> (&'b i32, f64, &'a T2);
}
```

This generic function has two lifetime parameters, and also two type parameters. The lifetime parameter a specifies that the third field of the return value borrows the object already borrowed by the b argument, while the lifetime parameter b specifies that the first field of the return value borrows the object already borrowed by the second field of the c argument. Moreover, the function has two type parameters, T1 and T2, used as usual.

Checking the Validity of Lifetime Specifiers

We said that the borrow checker, when compiling any function, has two jobs:

- Check that the signature of that function is valid, by itself and with respect to its body. This validates the internal consistency of that function.

- Check that the body of that function is valid, taking into account the signatures of any function invoked in the body. This validates the relationship between this function and all the functions it calls.

In this section, we'll see the first one of such jobs.

If in the function return value there are no references, the borrow checker has nothing to check.

Otherwise, for every reference contained in the return value type, it must check that it has a proper lifetime specifier.

Such a specifier can be `'static`. In such case, such reference must refer to a static object, like in this example:

```
static FOUR: u8 = 4;
fn f() -> (bool, &'static u8, &'static str, &'static f64) {
    (true, &FOUR, "Hello", &3.14)
}
print!("{} {} {} {}", f().0, *f().1, f().2, *f().3);
```

It will print: `true 4 Hello 3.14`. This is valid because all the three returned references are actually static objects.

Instead, this program:

```
fn f(n: &u8) -> &'static u8 { n }
fn g<'a>(m: &'a u8) -> &'static u8 { m }
```

will generate two compilation errors. The error for the body of the f function is: `explicit lifetime required in the type of `n``. And the error for the body of the g function is: `lifetime of reference outlives lifetime of borrowed content....`

Both functions are illegal, because those signatures require that the bodies return a static reference. Instead, in the f function the n reference returned has no lifetime specified; and in the g function the m reference returned has a nonstatic lifetime specified. Actually, both function bodies return the same value received as argument, so such return value borrows the same object as the one referenced by the function argument, which is not necessarily static.

In addition to 'static, the other lifetime specifier allowed is one defined in the parameter list, just after the name of the function, like in this code:

```
fn f<'a, 'b>(x: &'a i32, y: &'b i32) -> (&'b i32, bool, &'a i32) {
    (y, true, x)
}
let i = 12;
let j = 13;
let r = f(&i, &j);
print!("{} {} {}", *r.0, r.1, *r.2);
```

It will print: 13 true 12. This code is valid because the reference returned as the first field of the tuple is the value of the y expression, and the y argument has the same lifetime specifier as the first field of the return value; it is b for both of them. The same correspondence holds for the third field of the return value and the x argument; they both have the a lifetime specifier.

Instead, this program:

```
fn f<'a, 'b>(x: &'a i32, y: &'b i32) -> (&'b i32, bool, &'a i32) {
    (x, true, y)
}
let i = 12;
let j = 13;
let r = f(&i, &j);
print!("{} {} {}", *r.0, r.1, *r.2);
```

will generate two compilation errors, both with the error message: lifetime mismatch. Actually, both the first and the third fields of the return value have a lifetime specified in the argument list that is different from the one specified in the return value type.

Notice that it is possible to use one lifetime specifier for several return values fields. If in the previous code we remove the 'b lifetime specifier, and we replace its occurrences with 'a, we obtain this program, which is valid:

```
fn f<'a>(x: &'a i32, y: &'a i32) -> (&'a i32, bool, &'a i32) {
    (x, true, y)
}
```

```
let i = 12;
let j = 13;
let r = f(&i, &j);
print!("{} {} {}", *r.0, r.1, *r.2);
```

It will print: 12 true 13. However, this solution has a different meaning than the previous one. In the previous valid solution, the two references contained in the argument list had independent lifetimes; instead, in this last solution, they share the same lifetime. In this example, it means that both the references in the tuple returned must live longer than both the function arguments.

Functions are not always so simple as the ones just discussed. Let's consider a more complex function body:

```
fn f<'a>(n: i32, x: &'a Vec<u8>, y: &Vec<u8>) -> &'a u8 {
    if n == 0 { return &x[0]; }
    if n < 0 { &x[1] } else { &x[2] }
}
```

This function is valid. In its body, the value of the function may be returned in three possible points. In all of them, the returned value borrows the same object borrowed by the x argument. Such argument has the same lifetime of the return value, so the borrow checker is satisfied.

Instead, in this function:

```
fn f<'a>(n: i32, x: &'a Vec<u8>, y: &Vec<u8>) -> &'a u8 {
    if n == 0 { return &x[0]; }
    if n < 0 { &x[1] } else { &y[2] }
}
```

one of the possible return values, the value of the expression &y[2], borrows the object borrowed by y; that argument has no lifetime specifier, so this code is illegal.

Even this code is illegal:

```
fn f<'a>(x: &'a Vec<u8>, y: &Vec<u8>) -> &'a u8 {
    if true { &x[0] } else { &y[0] }
}
```

When performing data-flow analysis on this function, the compiler could detect that y is never borrowed by the return value of this function; but the borrow checker insists that &y[0] is a possible return value, so it spots this code as invalid.

Using the Lifetime Specifiers of Invoked Functions

As we said at the beginning of the previous section, one of the two jobs of the borrow checker is to check, when compiling a function, that the body of that function is valid, taking into account the signatures of any function invoked in the body.

As an example of this, get back to the last two programs of the section "The Need for Lifetime Specifiers in Returned References." We said that, according to our rules of borrowing, the first program should be valid and the second one illegal; though, we got the missing lifetime specifier error for both programs. The following ones are those two programs, with the addition of the appropriate lifetime specifiers.

This is the first one:

```
let n1 = 11;
let result;
{
    let n2 = 12;
    fn func<'a>(_m1: &'a i32, _m2: &i32) -> &'a i32 {
        _m1
    }
    result = func(&n1, &n2);
}
print!("{}", *result);
```

And this is the second one:

```
let n1 = 11;
let result;
{
    let n2 = 12;
    fn func<'a>(_m1: &i32, _m2: &'a i32) -> &'a i32 {
        _m2
    }
```

```
    result = func(&n1, &n2);
}
print!("{}", *result);
```

The first program is valid, and it will print 11, while for the second program the compiler will print the message: `n2` does not live long enough. Both have exactly the same semantics of the original programs, which didn't use functions.

The check of the lifetime specification inside the two func functions has been explained in the previous section. Now let's see how the main function in the first of the two programs works, regarding lifetimes.

When func is invoked, the alive variables are n1, result, and n2, declared in that order, with n1 and n2 already initialized. The signature of func says that the result value has the same lifetime specifier as the first argument, and that means that the value assigned to result must live no longer than n1. This actually holds, because result has been declared after n1, so it will be destroyed before it.

Now, let's see why the main function in the second program is illegal. Here, the signature of func says that the result value has the same lifetime specifier of the second argument, and that means that the value assigned to result must live no longer than n2. But this doesn't hold, actually, because result has been declared before n2, so it will be destroyed after it.

Advantage of Using Several Lifetime Specifiers for a Function

We said before that a function that returns a value containing several references can specify a single lifetime specifier for all of them, or a distinct lifetime specifier for each of them. Now let's explain why using only one lifetime specifier may be not as good as using several lifetime specifiers.

This program, which declares a function using two lifetime specifiers, is valid:

```
fn f<'a, 'b>(x: &'a i32, y: &'b i32)
-> (&'a i32, bool, &'b i32) {
    (x, true, y)
}
```

```
let i1 = 12;
let i2;
{
    let j1 = 13;
    let j2;
    let r = f(&i1, &j1);
    i2 = r.0;
    j2 = r.2;
    print!("{} ", *j2);
}
print!("{}", *i2);
```

It will print: 13 12.

Instead, if, in the function signature, we replace all the occurrences of the 'b lifetime parameter with 'a, to obtain the following signature:

```
fn f<'a>(x: &'a i32, y: &'a i32)
-> (&'a i32, bool, &'a i32) {
```

the resulting program is illegal, and its compilation generates the error: `j1` does not live long enough.

In both versions, the f function receives references to the numbers i1 and j1. The returned tuple is stored first in the r variable and then its first and third values are used to initialize the i2 and j2 variables, respectively.

In the first version of the program, the first argument and the first field of return value have the same lifetime specifier, and that means that i1 must live longer than i2. Similarly, j1 must live longer than j2. Actually, the order of the declaration of such variables satisfies such requirements.

Instead, in the second version of the program, there is just one lifetime specifier. In accordance with that specifier, both i1 and j1 must live longer than i2 and j2. Yet, j1 lives less than i2, because j1 is declared in the inner block, so it does not live outside of it, while i2 is used in the last line of the program, and so it must live up to there. This does not satisfy the lifetime requirements.

So, it is better to use a distinct lifetime specifier for any logically independent lifetime.

CHAPTER 24

More About Lifetimes

In this chapter, you will learn:

- How to avoid having to write lifetime specifiers for some kinds of free functions and methods, because such specifiers can be inferred

- Why lifetime specifiers are also needed for structs, tuple-structs, and enums containing references

- How to write lifetime specifiers for structs, tuple-structs, and enums

Lifetime Elision

In the previous chapter we saw that every function signature must specify, for each returned reference, whether that reference has a static lifetime or otherwise to which function arguments its lifetime is associated.

This required annotation may be a nuisance, and sometimes it can be avoided. Let's see an example that can be simplified:

```
trait Tr {
    fn f<'a>(x: &'a u8, b: bool) -> &'a u8;
}
```

In this code there is only one reference among the types in the function argument list, so there were only two possible lifetime annotations: let the return value type have a `'static` lifetime specifier; or do as in the preceding code (i.e.. let the return value type have the same lifetime specifier as the only reference in the argument list). For such a case of only one possible nonstatic lifetime specifier, the Rust language has introduced

© Carlo Milanesi 2022
C. Milanesi, *Beginning Rust*, https://doi.org/10.1007/978-1-4842-7208-4_24

the simplification that, if the signature contains no lifetime specifier, the only possible one is assumed by default. Therefore, the preceding code is equivalent to the following valid code:

```
trait Tr {
    fn f(x: &u8, b: bool) -> &u8;
}
```

Even the following declaration is valid:

```
trait Tr {
    fn f(b: bool, x: (u32, &u8)) -> &u8;
}
```

This is because in the arguments there is just one reference, so it must be the one whose referred object is borrowed by the return value.

The following code is also valid:

```
trait Tr {
    fn f(x: &u8) -> (&u8, &f64, bool, &Vec<String>);
}
```

In this case there are several references in the return value, but still only one reference in the arguments.

You can also omit the lifetime specifier for some returned references only, and specify it for others:

```
trait Tr {
    fn f<'a>(x: &'a u8) -> (&u8, &'a f64, bool, &'static Vec<String>);
}
```

Here, the return value contains three references: the first one has unspecified lifetime, the second one has the 'a lifetime, and the third one (that is the fourth field of the tuple), has the 'static lifetime. However, there is still only one reference in the arguments, so the first returned reference has an implied 'a lifetime.

Such allowed omission of the lifetime specifier is named *lifetime elision*. To simplify the syntax, the lifetime specifier can be *elided* when there is only one possible nonstatic value, and that happens when there is exactly one reference among the function arguments.

Lifetime Elision with Object-Oriented Programming

There are other cases where a lifetime elision can be applied. Consider this code:

```
trait Tr {
    fn f(&self, y: &u8)
    -> (&u8, &f64, bool, &Vec<String>);
}
```

Here, the f function has two references in its arguments, so the previous rule does not apply. However, when a method returns some references, in most cases such references borrow the current object, which is referred to by &self. So, to simplify the syntax, the previous code is considered equivalent to the following one:

```
trait Tr {
    fn f<'a>(&'a self, y: &u8)
    -> (&'a u8, &'a f64, bool, &'a Vec<String>);
}
```

Here is a table of dependencies between the references that appear in this signature.

Reference Contained in the Return Value	Borrowed Argument
First field, having type &u8	&self
Second field, having type &f64	&self
Fourth field, having type &Vec<String>	&self

Yet, you can override such behavior for selected references. In case, say, you meant that the second returned reference had a lifetime associated to the y argument, you had to write:

```
trait Tr {
    fn f<'a>(&self, y: &'a u8)
    -> (&u8, &'a f64, bool, &Vec<String>);
}
```

Here, the object referred to by the second field of the returned tuple must live no longer than the object referred to by y, while the objects referred to by the first and fourth fields must live no longer than the object referred to by &self.

Here is a table of dependencies between the references that appear in the last signature.

Reference Contained in the Return Value	Borrowed Argument
First field, having type &u8	&self
Second field, having type &f64	y: &u8
Fourth field, having type &Vec<String>	&self

Of course, the same rule also applies also for a &mut self argument.

The Need for Lifetime Specifiers in Structs Declarations

In the previous chapter, we saw that this is valid:

```
let x: i32 = 12;
let y: &i32 = &x;
print!("{}", *y);
```

because, although y holds a reference to x, it lives less than x.

Instead, this is illegal:

```
let y: &i32;
{
    let x: i32 = 12;
    y = &x;
}
print!("{}", *y);
```

because y holds a reference to x, but it lives longer than x.

We also saw that function signatures have to be suitably annotated to perform the lifetime check of borrowings, considering only one function body at a time.

A similar issue occurs when a struct contains some references.

This code appears to be legal (but it isn't; it emits the error message: missing lifetime specifier):

```
struct S {
    b: bool,
    ri: & i32,
}
let x: i32 = 12;
let y: S = S { b: true, ri: &x };
print!("{} {}", y.b, *y.ri);
```

while this one is clearly illegal:

```
struct S {
    b: bool,
    ri: & i32,
}
let y: S;
{
    let x: i32 = 12;
    y = S { b: true, ri: &x };
}
print!("{} {}", y.b, *y.ri);
```

The latter code is illegal because y, through its ri field, borrows x, but it lives longer than x.

This case was quite simple, but a more realistic program (explicitly containing the main function) could be:

```
// In some library code:
struct S {
    b: bool,
    ri: & i32,
}
fn create_s(ri: &i32) -> S {
    S { b: true, ri: ri }
}
```

```
// In application code:
fn main() {
    let y: S;
    {
        let x: i32 = 12;
        y = create_s(&x);
    }
    print!("{} {}", y.b, *y.ri);
}
```

This application code is invalid, because, by invoking `create_s`, a reference to x gets stored inside the y object, and so y borrows x, but y lives longer than x.

But how can the application programmer know that the `create_s` function stores into the returned object the reference it gets as an argument, if not by watching the function body? With this code, it is not possible, as shown by the following valid program, which has the same application code of the previous program but does not make y borrow x:

```
// In some library code:
struct S { b: bool, ri: &'static i32 }
fn create_s(ri: &i32) -> S {
    static ZERO: i32 = 0;
    static ONE: i32 = 1;
    S {
        b: true,
        ri: if *ri > 0 { &ONE } else { &ZERO },
    }
}
// In application code:
fn main() {
    let y: S;
    {
        let x: i32 = 12;
        y = create_s(&x);
    }
    print!("{} {}", y.b, *y.ri);
}
```

This program can be compiled, and it will print: `true 1`.

Notice that, in the declaration of the S struct, the `ri` field is annotated by the `'static` lifetime. In this code, the `create_s` function uses the `ri` argument just to decide how to initialize the `ri` field of the structure to create and return. The value of such argument is not stored in the structure. In any case, the `ri` field will surely contain a reference to a static value, which can be `ZERO` or `ONE`, and such value will never be destroyed.

This `create_s` function has the same signature as that of the previous example; but the previous example was invalid, as the argument was stored in a field of the struct, while this example is valid, as the argument is discarded after having been used.

So, without lifetime specifiers, the application programmer would be forced to read the body of the `create_s` library function to know if that function stores the reference it gets as an argument into the returned object or not. And this is bad.

Therefore, there is a need for further lifetime annotations, to allow both the application programmer and the compiler to focus on one function at a time, avoiding having to analyze the body of the `create_s` function to discover if the lifetimes of the objects used in the `main` function are correct.

So, even structs, similarly to functions, must explicitly specify the lifetimes of every reference contained in their fields.

This explains why even the former, apparently valid snippet, in fact generates the `missing lifetime specifier` compilation error.

Possible Lifetime Specifiers for Structs

Actually, for the lifetime of a reference field of a struct, the Rust compiler allows only two possibilities:

- Such field is allowed to refer only to static objects.

- Such field is allowed to refer to static objects or to objects that, albeit nonstatic, preexist the whole struct object and live longer than it.

The first case is just the one considered by the last example program. In it there was the line:

```
struct S { b: bool, ri: &'static i32 }
```

Such a struct actually contains a reference, but it is a static reference that cannot be assigned the value of any borrowed reference. So, there is never a lifetime issue in such a case, provided only static references are assigned to the ri field.

Instead, applying the second case of lifetime specification, the following valid program can be obtained:

```
// In some library code:
struct S<'a> { b: bool, ri: &'a i32 }
fn create_s<'b>(ri: &'b i32) -> S<'b> {
    S { b: true, ri: ri }
}
// In application code:
fn main() {
    let x: i32 = 12;
    let y: S;
    y = create_s(&x);
    print!("{} {}", y.b, *y.ri);
}
```

It will print: true 12. Here, the x variable is borrowed in a more persistent way by the create_s function. Indeed, it is stored in the ri field of the returned struct-object; and such object is used to initialize the y variable in the main function. Therefore, the y variable must live less than the x variable; and it does so. If the body of the main function is replaced by the following code:

```
let y: S;
{
    let x: i32 = 12;
    y = create_s(&x);
}
print!("{} {}", y.b, *y.ri);
```

the usual `x` does not live long enough error would appear.

To see that x could be stored inside the struct, it is not required to examine the body of the create_s function or the field list of the S struct; it is enough to examine the signature of the create_s function, and the signature of S, which is the portion of its declaration before the open brace.

By examining the signature of the `create_s` function, it appears that it gets a reference as argument; a value of S type is returned; and that argument and return value have the same lifetime specifier, `'b`. That means that the returned struct must live less than the borrowed `i32` object.

By examining the signature of the S struct, it appears that it is parameterized by a lifetime specifier, and that means that some of its fields are nonstatic references.

So, we found that the `create_s` function gets a reference as an argument and returns an object parameterized by the same lifetime specifier. This implies that such object could borrow the object referenced by the argument, by storing into itself that object.

The compiler must separately check the consistency of the struct declaration and the consistency of the functions using that struct type. The clause `struct S<'a>` means that S borrows some objects, and the clause `ri: &'a i32` inside the struct body means that the `ri` field is a reference that borrows an object.

Therefore, each reference field in a struct can have only two legal syntaxes: `field: &'static type` or `field: &'lifetime type`, where `lifetime` is also a parameter of the struct itself. If there are no reference fields or only static reference fields, the struct can have no lifetime parameters.

So, there are several possible syntax errors caught by the compiler.

```
struct _S1 { _f: &i32 }
struct _S2<'a> { _f: &i32 }
struct _S3 { _f: &'a i32 }
struct _S4<'a> { _f: &'static i32 }
struct _S5 { _f: &'static i32 }
struct _S6<'a> { _f: &'a i32 }
```

The first four statements are illegal. The declarations of _S1 and _S2 are illegal because the _f field is a reference field with no lifetime specifier. The declaration of _S3 is illegal because the `'a` lifetime specifier is not declared as a parameter of the struct; and the declaration of _S4 is illegal because the parameter `'a` is never used inside the body of the struct.

However, the last two struct declarations are valid. _S5 contains a reference to static objects, while _S6 contains a reference to an object that anyway must live longer than the struct itself.

Lifetime Specifiers for Tuple-Structs and Enums

We saw that when defining a struct type containing references, lifetime specifiers are required. But tuple-structs and enums also are types that may contain references, so also for them, lifetime specifiers are required for any contained reference. Here are examples of them:

```
struct TS<'a>(&'a u8);
enum E<'a, 'b> {
    _A(&'a u8),
    _B,
    _C(bool, &'b f64, char),
    _D(&'static str),
}
let byte = 34;
let _ts = TS(&byte);
let _e = E::_A(&byte);
```

This code is valid, but if any lifetime specifier is removed, the usual `missing lifetime specifier` error is generated.

By the way, notice the definition of the `E::_D` field. That is a reference to a static string slice. But we've seen such things since the beginning of this book; they are the *string literals*.

Lifetime Specifiers for Mutable References

To make things simpler, we never mixed lifetime specifiers with mutable references. Actually, it is allowed, albeit it is quite unusual:

```
fn f<'a>(b: &'a mut u8) -> &'a u8 {
    *b += 1;
    b
}
let mut byte = 12u8;
let byte_ref = f(&mut byte);
print!("{}", *byte_ref);
```

It will print: 13. A reference to the byte is passed to f, which increments it and then returns back a reference to it. It is unusual, because when a mutable argument is passed to a function, usually there is no need to return a reference that borrows it. It is enough to reuse the passed reference.

Index

A

abs method, 283, 286, 287

abs_quartic_root function, 290

Add trait, 315, 316

age method, 268

args standard library function, 244

Arithmetic operation

  adding integer number, 9–10

  breaking literal strings, 14–15

  example, 10

  floating-point, 11–13

  statements, 13–14

as_bytes function, 222, 239

Assignment semantics, 359–362

B

Bare-metal systems, 152

bool type, 364

Borrow checker, 384

Borrowing/lifetimes

  checking validity, 388–392

  C language, 375

  Copy trait, 373

  example, 377

  function, 393–394

  invoked functions, 392–393

  mutable borrow, 378

  object lifetimes, 374, 378–379

  program, 374, 375

  references, 382–385

  rust compiler, 376

  specifiers, 385–388

  use after change,
      alias errors, 380–382

  use after drop errors, 379

Box, 151, 166–167

Boxing/unboxing, 168–169

BtreeSet, 349

bytes function, 222–223

C

Capturing the environment, 184, 185

C *vs.* C++, 167

chars function, 223

clone standard function, 362, 366–368

clone trait, 367, 369, 371, 373

Closures

  cmp function, 187

  definition, 186

  descending order sorting, 186, 187

  Rust, 188

  sort_by function, 188

  statements, 187

  syntax, 188–190

  use directive, 187

Communication channel, 311

Composite data types, 177, 178

const keyword, 21, 86

contains variable, 233

continue keyword, 40

© Carlo Milanesi 2022
C. Milanesi, *Beginning Rust*, https://doi.org/10.1007/978-1-4842-7208-4

Printed in the United States
by Baker & Taylor Publisher Services